This book is dedicated to the memory of three people who shaped my early years:

To my mother, who was one of the most courageous, beautiful people I've ever known, and who gave me the love and courage to be who I am. You were my best friend. I miss you so much, Mama.

To Virgie Chapman, who helped raise me and taught me the meaning of faith, simplicity, and unconditional love.

And to my father, who was a complicated man to the core, but who loved me. I love you, Daddy, and I always will.

Southern Discomfort

– A Memoir –

Tena Clark

ATRIA PAPERBACK

New York London Toronto Sydney New Delhi

ATRIA
PAPERBACK

An Imprint of Simon & Schuster, Inc.
1230 Avenue of the Americas
New York, NY 10020

Certain names and identifying characteristics have been changed whether or not so noted in the text.

First Atria Paperback edition September 2019

ATRIA PAPERBACK and colophon are registered trademarks of Simon & Schuster, Inc.

For information about special discounts for bulk purchases, please contact Simon & Schuster Special Sales at 1-866-506-1949 or business@simonandschuster.com.

The Simon & Schuster Speakers Bureau can bring authors to your live event. For more information or to book an event, contact the Simon & Schuster Speakers Bureau at 1-866-248-3049 or visit our website at www.simonspeakers.com.

Interior design by Jill Putorti

Manufactured in the United States of America

10 9 8 7 6 5 4 3 2 1

The Library of Congress has cataloged the Touchstone edition as follows:

Names: Clark, Tena, author.
Title: Southern discomfort : a memoir / Tena Clark.
Description: New York : Touchstone, [2018] |
Identifiers: LCCN 2018001572 (print) | LCCN 2018036432 (ebook) |
  ISBN 9781501167966 (eBook) | ISBN 9781501167942 (hardcover) |
  ISBN 9781501167959 (pbk.)
Subjects: LCSH: Clark, Tena. | African Americans—Mississippi—Biography. |
  Mississippi—Race relations—History. | Mississippi—Biography. | LCGFT:
  Autobiographies.
Classification: LCC E185.93.M6 (ebook) | LCC E185.93.M6 C55 2018 (print) |
  DDC 305.8009762—dc23
LC record available at https://lccn.loc.gov/2018001572

ISBN 978-1-5011-6794-2
ISBN 978-1-5011-6795-9 (pbk)
ISBN 978-1-5011-6796-6 (ebook)

Praise for Southern Discomfort

"Powerful, upsetting, and deeply hopeful, Tena Clark's *Southern Discomfort* is the brutal and true story of a family coming apart in a fracturing South told from the point of a view of a girl who makes peace with what she survived, fled, and eventually came home to. A brave, wildly engrossing memoir."

—Bill Clegg, author of *Did You Ever Have a Family*

"Here is a slice of the late-twentieth-century South that goes all the way to the bone, and that hurts a bit!—but it feels like it just got to be done. *Southern Discomfort* is a dysfunctional family romance with all the trimmings, and it will also tell you a thing or two about that time and that place that you didn't already know."

—Madison Smartt Bell

"Raw and deeply honest . . . What Clark shows so beautifully is that the people she discusses, as unredeemable as they may at first seem, are much more complex. . . . Clark's narrative draws the reader in to a wonderful story of the South going from old to new."

—*Publishers Weekly* (starred review)

"The Mississippi blues take on new meaning in this tragic yet uplifting memoir. With its Southern setting and themes of racial conflict and civil rights, it's easy to see how this book has been compared to *The Help*. But Clark's debut is an entirely original—and true—story. . . . The overarching theme is love. A highly satisfying look at a flawed family, a conflicted South, and a fraught future."

—*Kirkus Reviews*

"Tena Clark weaves her deeply personal, private struggles together with the painful, shameful struggles she witnessed in Mississippi during the civil rights era in her beautiful, bravely shared memoir."

—Jill Conner Browne, author of the national bestseller *The Sweet Potato Queens' Book of Love*

"Tena Clark is a pioneering force of nature, and her story is as powerful, riveting, and inspiring as she is. Do yourself a favor. Get comfortable and start reading."

—Maria Shriver

"Tena Clark's memoir *Southern Discomfort*, a true coming-of-age story, reads like a Tennessee Williams play. Set in the Deep South where magnolias, catfish, the Bible, guns, alcohol, racism, and carnal knowledge collide, Tena's story confronts the heartbeat of America's identity crisis—a crisis of faith, family, freedom, and truth. This story will make you laugh out loud, cry, and hope that one day you can stand as tall as Tena."

—Debbie Allen

"Tena Clark's astounding memoir engaged me so deeply that I felt the pain of a lonely child in a chaotic home, and, happily at the end, the exhilaration of her hard-won freedom. A wonderful read."

—Norman Lear

"Tena Clark's riveting memoir shows us that even in the midst of fear, anger, and hate . . . tolerance, forgiveness, and love will rise. A triumphant journey and an inspiring read!"

—Sela Ward

Prologue

Where I grew up, girls like me knew our place. We were expected to smile politely and keep our white-gloved hands folded neatly in our laps when we sat in church. We spoke only when spoken to. We said: "Yes, sir," and "No, thank you, ma'am," and "Why yes, some sweet tea would be just fine." Back talk was not an option. We did not ask: "Why?" We did not say: "That doesn't seem fair." We were expected to wear stiff, pressed dresses even under the blazing Mississippi sun, and to have perfectly curled hair and lightly powdered faces in the drenching humidity. As we grew up, we understood that stepping off the prescribed path in any way meant risking it all, and probably losing.

Where I'm from, men like my father—rich, Cadillac-driving, Klan-sympathizing men—made the money. Women like my mother—beautiful, charming, educated only in how to entertain—ran the houses. If these women had any dreams beyond tending to their husbands, babies, and barbeques, they kept those thoughts to themselves.

Black maids, like the two women who tended to me— first, Viola; then Virgie—raised the white children they cared for but were not allowed to sit at the family table, drink from the family's cups, or ride in the front seat of their cars.

Black men and children were still called "boy," as in "What are you starin' at, boy?" And "nigger," as in, "I'm gonna need a few more niggers to pick my pecans this year." If you recoiled from the word, if it made your stomach clench and your insides boil, you were considered a "nigger lover," a dangerous insult. And if word of your sympathies spread, your family feared waking in the middle of the night to a burning cross on the lawn, or a brick thrown through the dining room window during supper.

If your glamorous, tortured wife became an alcoholic, like my mother did, you sent her away to the state mental hospital in a straitjacket to dry out. If your husband was a notorious skirt-chaser, like my father was, you might pull your .38 Colt out at the dinner table and chase him around the house, threatening to kill him right then and there, but only after your dinner guests had left for the evening.

And if you were a lesbian, before you even knew there was a word for the feelings you had had for as long as you could remember, you suppressed this fundamental part of yourself for as long as you possibly could. You lived a lie. You kissed boys and wore their fraternity pins, curled your hair, entered beauty pageants, joined a sorority. You and your friends talked about wedding cakes, honeymoons, and how many babies you wanted, just like you were supposed to. Because that's what good girls did.

Appearances mattered above all. "That's just the way it is" and "Let it be" were common refrains.

Growing up in Waynesboro, Mississippi, in the heart of the Jim Crow Deep South, I never thought there was any other way than the way it had always been. No one I knew ever ventured farther north than Memphis or maybe Nashville, and that was just fine with them.

My roots ran deep into the red earth; the land felt as much a part of me as my limbs, my heart. I hated it with a fury. I loved it with an all-consuming passion. This is the great paradox of the South. It's a savage place, a complicated place, and yet it still burrows into you, like the fangs of one of the water moccasins I used to hunt as a young girl down on the Chickasawhay River behind our farm. There's venom in the soil. But there's an alluring beauty in it as well.

For a time, I assumed I had no choice but to stay on the straight and narrow path that had been laid out for me since birth. I'd wear the pressed dresses, the curled hair, the pin. I'd hold my tongue. I'd mind my manners. I'd play the clarinet and the piano even though I longed to play the drums. I'd marry a man exactly like my father, even though I was attracted to girls from the time I was four or five, when I first laid eyes upon a majorette in her green sequined leotard and white tassled boots. I'd be a charming and gracious hostess. I'd have the children, the impeccable house. Maybe I'd even have the black maid to raise my children and a staff of

black men to pick the pecans and cut the lawn. I'd pass out
finger sandwiches and pour sweet tea. And the cycle would
continue.

Or maybe I'd find out I was stronger than I thought I was.
And the cycle—at least for me—would end.

Chapter One

The Last Birthday

Mama left for good on December 19, 1963. My tenth birthday. "Aloha, baby," she said to me before driving away.

Even before Mama decided she'd had enough, I'd been heavy with sadness. President Kennedy had been killed in Dallas the month before and like most of the country, I was still in shock. And I was scared. What did it mean that the president of the United States could be gunned down? I didn't know the answer, but I was afraid to be asking it.

At least I had my upcoming birthday to distract me. For weeks, I'd been busy with my birthday plans, carefully choosing the guest list and games for my first-ever pallet party, which is what we called sleepovers back then. We'd start with Pin the Tail on the Donkey, then move on to Hide-and-Seek, and before bed we'd try to scare one another senseless with ghost stories told while huddled under blankets with flashlights held under our chins, turning our faces into ghoulish shadows. In fact, I had a mischievous streak and loved scaring the crap out of my friends, especially my younger cousin Rita Faye.

After adding and crossing off names on the guest list, I had come up with the perfect group of twelve girls, and I spent hours sitting cross-legged on my bedroom floor, handwriting each invitation and addressing the envelopes, drawing little stars and hearts in the corners. When I dropped the invitations in the mailbox at the end of our long dirt driveway, my insides fluttered with nerves. So many things could go wrong. An endless number of things, it seemed, and high on the list was Mama, whose drinking had grown steadily worse in the last year, and most days she was passed out on the couch or in bed before dinner.

When my birthday arrived, I woke before sunrise and tiptoed down the hall in my pajamas, the yellow-and-blue-striped linoleum cold under my bare feet. Virgie was at the house earlier than usual in order to prepare for the party, and she stood at the kitchen sink in her blue work blouse and pants; she would change into a stiff white uniform and white stockings before the girls and their mothers arrived in the afternoon. She was humming one of her favorite gospel hymns, "Just a Closer Walk with Thee," which she and I had seen Mahalia Jackson sing on the television a few months before. Virgie had been grief-stricken by President Kennedy's murder just the month before; one day I saw her silently weeping as she went about her work. I had never seen her cry, and it saddened and unnerved me even more than the faraway events I didn't understand. This morning's hymn was the first time I'd heard her hum in weeks. I hung back in the doorframe and listened. The day was off to a promising start.

She turned when she heard the telltale creak of the floorboards and her face practically broke in half with a rare smile. She had a mouthful of crazy, crooked teeth that went in all directions, and I think they must have embarrassed her because she almost never showed those teeth the light of day. So when she did smile, it felt like she was giving a special gift, and that morning it was for me.

"Well, here be my beautiful baby girl!" Even though I knew she had nine children of her own at home, I felt like I *was* her baby girl.

I ran and flung myself into her open arms. Virgie was tall, almost as tall as Mama, but I was born small and on the short side, just like my daddy, so when I hugged Virgie, my head squashed right into her belly. I wrapped my arms around her thick middle and tried, as I always did, to get my fingers to touch on the other side—but I never could, not quite.

She pulled away gently so that she could look into my eyes, and asked, "Now, you tell me, baby girl, what you be wantin' fo' yo' special birfday breakfast?"

"Oh, Virgie, I'm way too nervous to eat!" I protested, but even so, I reached out and grabbed a biscuit, hot from the oven, and broke off a piece to nibble on. I knew Virgie wouldn't let me go without at least a bite of her biscuits for breakfast, even if I refused the gravy. Besides, I wanted to save room for my birthday cake. Mrs. Williams made the best cakes in town, and mine was always special-ordered—red velvet cake with little Christmas trees and tiny wrapped gifts and Santas fashioned into the thick white frosting.

Virgie sent me off to get dressed for school, and I skipped out of the kitchen and down the long hall to my bedroom, lifting the front of my pajama top so I wouldn't spill any crumbs on her spotless floor.

Later that afternoon, after school, I raced to my room, pulling my dress up and over my head so I could put on my favorite overalls and the new Bobbie Brooks plaid shirt Mama had bought me for the party. Then I started back down the hall to the kitchen, too nervous to wait alone in my room for the party to begin.

As I passed the open door of my mother and father's bedroom, I looked in and saw perhaps the only gift Daddy had ever given Mama that she truly cherished: a light pink jewelry box with a ballerina that spun on a spindle to a delicate piano tune, Chopin's "Polonaise in A-flat Major." I loved that the box and its music always seemed to make Mama happy. Not much else did. No matter her mood, no matter her state, the music always made her smile. Peeking around the door to make sure no one was in the room, I walked over to her bureau and picked it up. As I lifted the lid, the familiar, sweet song filled the room. I listened for a few moments, the music making me smile too, just like Mama, then I carefully closed the lid and put the box on the bureau, where it belonged.

In the kitchen, Virgie and Beulah Mae, who worked across the dirt road for my sister Georgia and had come over to help with the party, were busy at the counter putting up fresh-off-the-cob creamed corn. Virgie immediately put me to work, pulling a footstool over to the stove and handing me a spoon so I could stir the roasting corn in the cast-iron skillet.

I stood on my stool at the stove, stirring and daydreaming as Virgie occasionally reached around me to add a dash of heavy cream or a pinch of salt or a shake of sugar to the skillet. I thought about my list of friends and what each might give me for my birthday. Because it was a sleepover party, the other girls would be dressed, as I was, in their after-school play clothes rather than in stiff dresses with petticoats and matching ribbons in their hair. Everyone knew that I was the class tomboy—I was always playing cops and robbers and cowboys and Indians and climbing trees with Burke, my best friend, and the boys at recess—but at least I wouldn't stick out like a sore thumb at my own party. I hated it when my mother dressed me in taffeta and crinoline and curled my hair into long tendrils so I would look like all the other girls. I'd stare in the mirror and barely recognize my own face. And when she put me in pint-size antebellum ball gowns and little white gloves, I definitely didn't recognize my own body. It was as if she hoped that the crinoline and the curls and the Bo Peep hat and white gloves would somehow make me an adorable little Southern belle from the outside in. So far, it hadn't worked.

I stood between Virgie and Beulah Mae, all of us shoulder to shoulder, me stirring while they cut, seasoned, and then scooped the roasted corn into glass Ball jars. I leaned slightly against Virgie, something I did as often as I could, partly for balance and partly for comfort, reassured by her calm and steady presence. I drank in the stillness, feeling it spread through me like warm milk, my eyes getting heavy with sleep.

Then a scream shattered the air. Virgie grabbed me to keep me from toppling off the stool.

"That's it! That's it! *That's IT!*"

Mama's voice was thick with booze. It shook the house and tumbled down the hall toward us in the kitchen.

I squeezed my eyes shut, wishing I could disappear or go deaf or both. *Oh no*, I thought, *not today. No, no, no. Please, Mama, not today. Not on my birthday.* I had done a fair share of praying that the birthday would go smoothly, but I feared I must not have done enough. I dropped the wooden spoon, opening my eyes to watch it disappear into the milky, yellow kernels.

"I will not, I CANNOT spend one more night in this house," she yelled. "I am LEAVING!" The last word was a scream unlike any I'd ever heard and it echoed against the wood paneling of the narrow hallway.

Virgie and Beulah Mae stared at each other for a moment, then Virgie grabbed me by the waist and in one smooth motion whisked me off the stool and put my feet firmly on the floor. Her strong hands lingered on my shoulders, holding on. I knew she wanted to protect me from what was coming, but it was too late—there was nowhere for me to hide and no way for her to stop the power of Mama's hurricane.

"Nows you stay put, baby girl, hear?" she whispered above me, giving my shoulders a gentle squeeze. I nodded, feeling her thick body against the back of my head.

The house erupted. Mama yelled at Daddy. Daddy yelled back at her. Somewhere, we heard a bottle smash to the floor. A chair screeched across hard wood. A door slammed.

"You're always imagining things, V-V-Vivian," my father yelled. My daddy stuttered, particularly when he was angry or nervous, and this time I could hear he was very, very nervous. "N-n-n-nothing is happening with that woman! I s-s-s-swear!"

"SHUTUPSHUTUPSHUTUP!!!" Mama screamed. "Lamar

Clark, if you tell me one more lie I'll kill you. Right here and right now. I will SHOOT you dead, you lyin', cheatin' sonof-aBITCH."

She rushed into the kitchen with her arms full of clothes and with Daddy on her heels, her face flushed and her cheeks damp. She shifted the clothes in order to open the kitchen door with a free hand and then kicked open the screen door to where her Cadillac sat parked under the carport. Peeking around the corner of the counter, I saw her throw her armload of clothes into the backseat, then come back into the house and hurry past us down the hall to the bedroom. Back and forth, Mama and Daddy stomped through the house screaming at each other. Virgie, Beulah Mae, and I watched the action with our heads pivoting like we were at a tennis match. Nobody dared move.

"V-V-V-Vivian! Stop this right now!" Daddy said, but by this time he might as well have been talking to a skewered bull. There was no calming her down. Even I could see she was way past that point.

"I said SHUT UP, you sonofabitch! NO MORE!" she screamed as she ran through the kitchen and out to her car, throwing another armload into the backseat—fur coats and sweaters, dresses and slips, bras and panties, makeup and hairnets.

I caught a glimpse of my mother's wild eyes and could see that her rage and the bourbon had taken over. She had one thing and one thing only on her mind: escape. She had driven off like this before, usually in a drunken uproar, sometimes with her sister, my aunt Jean, her regular drinking buddy, or as we in the South called them, her runnin' buddy. And boy, did they love to run around town and raise hell and a lot of eyebrows. Daddy would call his friends in the sheriff's office and they would find Mama weaving through town, pull her over, and bring her back to sleep it off. But this time felt different.

Standing between Virgie and Beulah Mae, I suddenly remembered: It was my birthday. My guests would be arriving in less than an hour. With their mothers. Desperate to stop Mama, I ran out to where she and Daddy stood by her car fuming at each other and taking great gasping breaths like stallions facing off in the paddock.

"Mama!" I begged. "It's my *birthday*. You can't go. *Please*, not today!"

She stopped, her mascara cutting thin, black trails through the powder on her cheeks, her hair wild around her face. She blinked, as if trying to remember exactly who I was.

"It's my *birthday*," I said again. "*Please*, Mama. You *can't* leave."

I saw her head start to move and then slowly turn side to side in a drunken, loopy *No*. She wiped at her nose and cheeks with the back of her hand, leaving a thin trail of mucus on her face.

I looked down at my feet and there was the pink music box. It had fallen from one of her piles and the lid was off its hinge and one of the legs was missing. I picked it up and held it out to Mama, but she didn't reach for it.

"See, *see*?" I said, opening the lid and shoving it at her as the notes began to echo through the chill of the late afternoon. "It's your favorite song, Mama."

As the music played, I saw fresh tears fill her eyes. I had watched her sober up fast before, but never this fast. I had a hot, hopeful rush of relief that I had done it. I had stopped her from leaving and saved the day. *My* day.

She looked at me then, finally seeing me, and took the box from my hands, gently shutting the lid. She reached out her hand and brushed my cheek with her fingertips.

"Oh, baby, I'm so sorry. I have to go."

I swallowed the urge to say, *You're not sorry at all! You don't HAVE to go anywhere! You just want to go drinking with Aunt Jean!* But I didn't because I wondered if maybe it was all my fault, if maybe I had done something. *Surely* I must have done something if she was leaving me, leaving me on my *birthday*.

"Why? Where are you going? Can I come with you?"

"No, honey. You stay with your daddy."

"But I want to go with *you!*" By now I was the one screaming and crying, and I flung myself at her and clung to her, my arms around her waist and my face buried in the front of her blouse. I was desperate to hold her and keep her from leaving, leaving *me*. I felt her stiffen against me.

"Virgie, please . . ." she said. "Can you take her? Please . . ."

I felt Virgie's hands pull me away and hold me tight, her fingers softly kneading my shoulders. I looked up at Mama through my tears.

"Why, Mama, why can't I go with you?" I begged, trying one last time.

Mama looked over at Daddy and slowly shook her head.

"I have to go. If I don't go now, I never will."

She looked at me with such utter calm that I knew with an awful surety that she meant it. She was done. This was it. This time she was really and truly going to leave and not come back.

She opened the car door.

"N-n-n-now wait one minute, V-V-V-Vivian," Daddy sputtered. "W-w-w-what the hell are all them girls' mamas gonna say when they git here and you're not here? Gotta have a w-w-woman in the house." He saw her look toward Virgie, and added, "Her *mama*, Vivian. Her *mama* should be here."

Mama turned from where she stood by the open car door. Hope surged through me that he had stopped her from leaving, at least for today, and that it was all going to be okay. My friends would come over and Mama would be there and everything would be all right. Nobody would ever have to know any of this happened.

"Virgie," Mama said, "go call Georgia. She'll come and help you with the party." She looked down at me. "I'm sorry, baby. I love you. You know I love you."

"No! You don't love me if you are leaving me! ON MY BIRTHDAY!" I screamed as she turned away from me and got in the car. "MAMA!" Now it was my scream that sounded like a wild animal's. I reached my arms out toward her in the car, but Virgie held me tight.

Mama put her head down briefly, as if in surrender, but then I saw her take a deep breath and square her shoulders. She reached down to push in the cigarette lighter and then started the car. She looked at me through the window.

"Aloha, baby," she said. My mother never said "goodbye."

Always "aloha." I have no idea when this started or why, it just always was. Lord knows she never stepped foot in Hawaii. Aloha.

She put the car in gear and drove away, her eyes looking straight ahead. Plumes of red dust swirled behind the car, making it disappear from view long before it turned onto the main road.

Then she was gone.

I searched through the dust, praying that I'd see the yellow Cadillac reemerge and make its way back up the road. When the dust finally settled, the road was empty and the air was still and silent.

I waited and prayed, but I knew she wasn't coming back. I reached over to take my daddy's hand but discovered he'd already returned to the house, leaving me standing in the driveway. But I wasn't alone. Virgie took my hand and gently folded it in hers. We stood together in that semicircle driveway holding hands and saying nothing for several minutes, me trying not to cry and willing Mama to come back, and Virgie looking straight ahead down the empty road. Finally, she gave my hand two soft squeezes and turned me back toward the house.

"She be back fo' you, baby girl," she whispered, "sho will." She kissed the top of my head.

I stiffened under her touch, as sad and confused and just plain mad as I'd ever been.

"She doesn't love me at all," I said.

Virgie smoothed my hair with her fingers and bent to kiss my head again. "My po' lil' baby girl," she murmured into my hair. After a few moments, she straightened up and gave my arm a little tug.

"We bes' go inside," she said. "We's got a party to put on."

She began to hum "Amazing Grace," a hymn she knew I loved, and we walked back to the house holding hands as she hummed and I quietly sang the words:

> *Amazing Grace, how sweet the sound*
> *That saved a wretch like me.*
> *I once was lost, but now am found,*
> *Was blind, but now I see.*

As we walked up the porch stairs, I looked over at Virgie and saw her brush a tear from her cheek. It was the second and last time I would ever see Virgie cry.

Chapter Two

As hard as it was for me to believe, given all the lunacy I'd witnessed between my parents for as long as I could remember, they were once very much in love. This was long before I was born, but I like to imagine them back then, two strivers with dreams beyond the world they knew. Unlike almost everybody else around them, they both wanted to be somebody. In many ways, they were meant for each other.

My mother, Vivian Crumble Atkinson, had been one of the prettiest girls in Wayne County, Mississippi. She was the seventh daughter of Roy Clifton Atkinson and Vinidray (pronounced vin-EYE-drah) Crumble Weaver, who all told had eight girls and one boy over the span of twenty years. Folks in Waynesboro would snicker that "those Atkinsons never had a television so they made a lot of babies instead." By the time Vivian turned fourteen in 1935 she had already been crowned the Charleston dance champion of Wayne County and was six feet of a wild kind of beauty.

Mama didn't much resemble the rest of her many sisters. Unlike their fair complexions and blue eyes, she had flawless

olive skin, a thick mane of jet-black hair, and eyes the color of
dark chocolate. She liked to say she was an "Indian Princess"—
she truly believed she was descended from Native American
blood. Her sisters all laughed at that, but she was dead serious,
and perhaps she was right. Mama was headstrong and fiercely
independent; right from the start she seemed to be cut from a
different cloth than her sisters. She also had high cheekbones
and full, pouty lips that were always painted bright red. To top
it all off, she had a voluptuous figure, with long, shapely legs
and dainty ankles.

Her only physical flaw, as far as I could tell, was the mangled
scar of what remained of her left ear, which had been nearly
shorn off in a school bus accident when she was a young girl.
Her older sister Clifford, in one of those Herculean rushes
of adrenaline you read about, had saved her sister's life after
the bus slid out of control on a rain-slicked back road and
overturned into a swampy ditch. Clifford managed to crawl
to safety, but then she saw Mama's legs kicking furiously from
beneath the bus. Seeing that Mama was trapped and drown-
ing facedown in the mud, Clifford ran over and, with her
adrenaline pumping, lifted up the bus just enough for Mama
to wriggle free, saving her life. In her efforts to breathe while
trapped in the muck, Mama had twisted her head side to side,
and in the process ripped her ear until it hung by a thin piece
of skin. After the doctor cut off the mangled ear and closed up
the wound, her mother, Big Mama Atkinson, put the ear in a
Ball jar and gave it a formal burial in the backyard. Years later,
one of the sisters decided to dig it up. When they brushed the
dirt off the jar, they saw that the ear was in perfect condition,

but when they unscrewed the lid, the ear immediately turned black and shriveled to the size of a walnut.

I suspect every big family has a black sheep or two and for whatever reason, Mama was the black sheep of the Atkinson clan. She dreamed of making something of her life, besides being a wife and mother. Most of all, she had fantasies of becoming a famous songwriter and performing with a big band in New Orleans, ideas that her mother and sisters ridiculed to no end.

Maybe thinking of herself as the black sheep was easier for her than admitting the truth: Her own mother seemed to despise her, treating her viciously when she wasn't ignoring her altogether. Another family rumor had it that Mama, and perhaps her younger sister, Jean, were not actually Big Mama's daughters. Roy Clifton had a reputation for sleeping with a lot of women, including his own maids; it's possible Mama and Jean were products of an affair and Big Mama had agreed, albeit resentfully, to raise them as her own. Whatever the real reasons for her cruelty, Vinidray Atkinson relentlessly taunted and punished my mother, often beating her with a belt after her sisters blamed her for something she didn't do.

Things didn't get much better for Mama when she fell in love with Lamar Clark.

My daddy, James Lamar Clark, had been born a skinny, penniless runt to Mary Annanett "Nettie" Mauldin and Thomas Lee Clark, subsistence farmers who had six children and buried two others, a set of twins, hours after they were born. Theirs was a life of hard labor. As soon as the Clark children could walk, they worked, from sunup to sundown, either in the fields with the black farmhands, or in Lee (as he was always

called) Clark's small sawmill. While they struggled throughout their lives to keep a roof over their heads, Nettie and Lee
were able to keep their family fed and always stretched what
they had to welcome guests at their table. Known throughout
Waynesboro as a kind man, Lee Clark was also known as a
generous and trusting one, perhaps to a fault, often loaning his
last dime. He worked himself half to death his entire life while
never quite gaining a foothold of security. During the Depression, Nettie and Lee lost the family house and were forced to
move in with Nettie's father, but then they lost that house as
well and ended up on a swampy lot of land by the river that
nobody else wanted. As a boy, Lamar watched all of this with
a growing resolve: One day he would be rich. Really rich.

Though barely reaching five feet six inches, my daddy grew
into a strutting rooster of a man with chiseled good looks and
steely blue eyes that reminded his many female admirers of
Gary Cooper. But his face also held a streak of ferocity. I can
picture him as a boy, bent over the cotton or struggling to see
over the steering wheel of the lumber truck he drove as soon
as he could touch the pedals, determined that he would never,
ever again live hand-to-mouth or work that physically hard,
particularly for somebody else, even his own kin. He would
make the kind of money that allowed him to hire his labor,
rather than be the laborer. He would, in short, make "rich
man's" money, not merely enough to put food on the table and
a secure roof over his head. In photograph after photograph,
his icy blue eyes are squinted narrow with an uncompromis-
ing will. As he aged, he held his mouth in an ever-thinning
line, and his brow grew more and more furrowed. Truth of

the matter is, I don't have a single photograph in which he's smiling. Not one.

Daddy was born in 1917, the same year as John F. Kennedy. But he didn't serve in World War II, having been classified 4F because he was nearly crushed to death by a load of lumber that broke free while he was driving the truck. The doctors who treated him told him he'd be a "cripple" his whole life. While the accident didn't leave him bent or crooked, it did fuel his lifelong hatred for hospitals and doctors. Instead, he found a chiropractor who made a few adjustments, enabling him to live a normal life. Daddy went to him every month for the rest of his life.

Even before he made his real money, my father dressed meticulously: dress shirt and cuff links, pressed trousers— never jeans—tailored sports coat, alligator or Italian leather shoes and belt, and a fedora, always—felt in the winter, straw in the summer. He drove around town like he was the mayor, stopping and glad-handing various merchants and other folks richer than he, making deals. He was always making deals.

It was really no surprise that a man like Lamar would fall in love with a woman like my mother. Mama always had an air of mystery about her that most people, particularly men, found irresistible. Her eyes would sparkle with delight, but her face would remain calm, placid even, the corners of her mouth just barely lifting into an impish smile like she was hiding the world's best secret. Daddy fell hard for those eyes and that grin and didn't know what hit him.

*   *   *

When my parents began their courtship, Mama was only fourteen. Daddy was eighteen with barely an eighth-grade education and an old Ford pickup truck with a windshield cracked like a spiderweb. Family rumor has it that he fancied Mama's older sister Helen first, but as Vivian matured and became taller and more beautiful, his eyes soon wandered to the younger Atkinson sister.

After he traded in Helen for Vivian, the Atkinson girls would hover around as Mama waited for him to pick her up for a date, calling him "that stuttering runt." If Vivian tried to counter their attack or offer a defense of her boyfriend, they'd give her a dismissive sniff, a nonverbal "Says you!"—a gesture for which they all became famous. Soon, Mama'd had enough, and when she was just past her fifteenth birthday, barely of legal age, even for Mississippi in 1936, she quit school, ran off with Lamar, and eloped.

The newlyweds didn't make it too far out of town before Mama's parents were in hot pursuit. Neither Big Mama nor Big Papa Atkinson was the type to let Lamar Clark get away with such bold-faced disrespect.

Like his wife's, Big Papa's nickname suited him. He was massive and mean. He'd sit on the front porch in his rocking chair with a loaded shotgun propped against the house, smoking his pipe and wearing nothing but his boxer shorts. Nothing. He'd call out a "Howdy!" to a passing car and Big Mama'd storm onto the porch demanding, "Roy Clifton! Put on some britches right now!" But he never would. He measured almost six feet seven inches tall and must have weighed in at close to 270 pounds. He was the kind of big that could drag the trees out of the woodlot if the oxen were lame or the tractor ran out of gas, the kind of big that could put his shoulder against a stuck truck and with one shove get it out of a foot of mud.

Big Papa didn't like to spend money. He ran Waynesboro's biggest sawmill, but he and Big Mama and their nine children lived in a small shotgun house, a style popularized in working-class Southern towns because it was less expensive to build and allowed for better airflow in the summer's heat. Usually only twelve feet wide and three or four rooms long, shotguns got their name because it was said that if all the doors were open, someone could fire a shot from the front porch and it would pass cleanly through the house and out the back door. As their family grew, they built a second shotgun abutting the original, thus saving the expense of having to build a fourth wall. And while they had money to pay a maid, a black woman named Biss, they paid her in quarters.

Quarters. It's possible that Biss chose to get the solid, sturdier coins rather than bills: Paper money could quickly be turned into trash by rats or another war, like the worthless Confederate money that filled many an attic trunk in homes across the South. Regardless, she put just about every one of those quarters in a Ball jar and as soon as one was full she would take it out into the woods in the dead of night and bury it, and then start filling another. In those days it wasn't possible for a black man or woman to have a bank account, so Biss created her own: *The Bank of Biss*, I called it. She died in the late 1950s and, as far as I know, never told anyone exactly where the jars were.

Before I was born, Biss had a baby boy and family rumor had it that he was Big Papa's son. Immediately after he was born, Biss was forced to send him to Detroit where her family raised him. I don't think she ever saw her son again, but I fantasize that she told him exactly where the jars filled with quarters were buried and that at some point he came to Waynesboro and, under the cover of a moonless night, dug them all up. I sure hope so.

I never knew if Biss was her full name, or whether it was shortened from something else, or maybe not even her name at all. It's possible her name was *Bess* and mispronounced *Biss* by everyone around her. I just never knew. Still don't. But whether or not anyone in Mama's family knew Biss's given name, she was in many ways their emotional center, giving each of the nine children the love and comfort in short supply from Big Mama and Big Papa. And when Biss died, my mama and her sisters raised all sorts of hell in white Waynesboro when they insisted that she be buried in the family plot alongside generations of Atkinsons.

"She was family," Mama explained, and I knew what she meant. I felt the same way about Virgie. Even though I was only five or six when Biss died, I have a clear-as-day vision of her and Big Mama in the shotgun house's little kitchen, both of them with rolled-up sleeves, dropping the chicken into a pot of grease, pulling sheets of corn bread out of the oven, cutting slabs of butter into a pot of peas or turnip greens, wiping the sweat from their brows with their forearms, all the while talking the secret language women seem to have when they're putting Sunday dinner on the table.

When Big Mama and Big Papa pursued Lamar Clark's truck out of town, they were not, as one might suspect, trying to get their fifteen-year-old daughter back. They were chasing the newlyweds to whup both their asses for daring to run off without Big Papa's permission. When they caught up with Mama and Daddy on the outskirts of town, Big Papa dragged his daughter out of the front seat by her hair and threw her in the dirt. Then he looked right at my daddy.

"You little sonofa*bitch*," he roared, spitting the last word like dust from his teeth. "*You've* got her now, boy."

Big Papa towered a good foot over his new son-in-law, his wide nostrils flaring, the hand that had held my mother's hair still pumping. I imagine he would love to have punched the little bastard, but he was probably afraid he might kill him. Then again, maybe he already recognized something of himself in his new son-in-law: that he too was tough as iron and mean as a snake. The two men stood close enough to spit in each other's eye, Big Papa panting while Daddy remained calm, staring coldly at his father-in-law.

Big Mama stood by watching, her arms tightly crossed under her thick, shelf-like bosom, her eyes hard slits behind her gold-framed glasses. She too tipped the scales on the other side of two hundred pounds and was not somebody you ever wanted to cross. She was always sweet to me, baking my favorite sugar cookies whenever she knew I was coming by for a visit, but my other cousins remember her like Big Papa: as grim as she was solid. Watching her daughter get thrown in the dirt by her husband apparently didn't faze her.

"You'd better not come round asking me for a dime as long as you live," Big Papa thundered, his finger in Lamar's face. Then he took his finger and flicked Lamar's hat off his head and into the dirt.

This is the part of the story that Daddy loved to tell because it was here that he knew he'd won. He'd gotten Big Papa to show his weakness. Flicking a man's hat in the dirt was a straw tiger's last resort, not a true hunter's best move. Daddy reached down, picked up his hat, gave it a few swipes to wipe off the dust, and put it back on his head. Without a word, he turned his back on Big Papa and walked back to his truck. He also turned his back on Mama, still lying in the dirt.

When her brand-new husband walked by her without stopping, Mrs. Vivian Clark pulled herself up, smoothed her hair back over her ruined ear, and followed him to the truck. If she cared that Daddy hadn't reached down to help her, she never said so. She climbed up into the truck, closed the passenger door, and scooted across the front seat to sit leg-to-leg against Lamar. She never glanced back at her mother and father, but then and there she said a silent prayer: *Thank you, God, for getting me out of their house.* And she swore a silent oath: *And God, I promise you, no matter what happens, I will never go back.*

Lamar started the engine, and they sped away like Bonnie and Clyde from a bank robbery—in a squeal of tires and dust. They left Big Papa and Big Mama standing in the road, scowling as the truck disappeared around the bend.

It was the Fourth of July, 1936. Like the fireworks in the sky above them on their wedding night, my mother and father's love was combustible, and it too didn't last long. As with most fires that burn hot, theirs burned out fast. In fact, the romance didn't even last through the wedding night. Rumor has it that Daddy snuck out to a whorehouse in nearby Laurel, barely an hour after consummating his marriage to Mama.

Chapter Three

By the time he was in his thirties, Lamar Clark was the richest man in Waynesboro, and one of the richest in all of Mississippi. He had steadily worked his way up from nothing, starting in his father's fields and sawmill, then doing odd jobs and day labor when he could. After he and Mama married, he left his father's modest sawmill and started driving lumber trucks for Big Papa's much larger mill.

Big Papa may have hated my daddy for having the audacity to run off with his daughter without asking permission, but he couldn't help but admire the savvy businessman his son-in-law was proving to be. So Big Papa stepped back, allowing Lamar to efficiently, almost effortlessly, take control of the business.

It was just a matter of time before Lamar owned Big Papa's entire operation. Not bad for a man with barely an eighth-grade education. However, family gossip had it that Daddy didn't exactly play by the rules and that he got his first real break when he sold some of Big Papa's timber on the black market during World War II. Sounds about right. Regardless of how he made his first real money, Daddy was well on his way by the late 1940s. People still talk about how "Lamar Clark could buy a jackass for fifty cents and before he got it to town, somebody would be trying to buy it off him for a buck." He ran an impressive game, constantly buying, selling, and trading, and always getting the better deal.

Other businesses would follow the sawmill—real estate, hotels and motels, oil leases, cattle. In each one, his tireless work ethic and personal—some might say deadly—charm proved a powerful combination. He loved to say that Big Papa's early threats and indignation were the keys to his success. He said he was determined to prove Big Papa wrong. But I don't think it was that simple. Daddy liked to say he could have made money in a coma, and it seemed to be true. Decades later when he was on his deathbed, he carried on about all the deals he was working and how he could make more money lying in bed than most men could make in a year.

His philosophy was simple: Never owe anyone anything, never be owned by anyone, and never, ever, have to answer to anyone. And he never did, especially to anyone in his family, not even Mama.

One Sunday, Daddy went to the curb store to buy his paper. But the owner, his cousin, had just closed up so he could go to church and refused to reopen for Daddy. Within a few weeks, there was a brand-new Clark's curb store right next door with better prices and longer hours, including Sunday. Daddy's cousin was soon out of business. It's no wonder some folks called Daddy the Dictator of Waynesboro.

His parents, it seemed, received most of Daddy's charity, if not compassion. After the war ended, with his pockets already stuffed, Daddy paid back the debt on the house Nettie and Lee had lost several years before and moved them back into it. He'd visit his father and mother and quietly slip a $100 bill into Nettie's apron pocket. Years later, when Nettie died, Daddy moved his father into a nursing home, but not until he had a new room built there just for Lee, filling it with his belongings from the house so that when he woke in the morning he would feel "at home." Then Daddy had their old house bulldozed into the gully. To him, it represented nothing but poverty and strife and he made sure he never had to set eyes on it again.

Years later, Daddy seldom talked to any of us about his business dealings and associates. And while I never saw him in white robes, or heard him talk about Grand Wizards and lynchings, in order to do business in Mississippi, particularly with the growing civil rights movement in the 1950s, many white men joined, condoned, or at least turned a blind eye to the Ku Klux Klan. Others joined the less violent and what was considered the "more gentile" Citizens' Council, feeling the Klan was a bunch of redneck hillbillies bent on crass violence. But after the deadly riot against integration at the University of Mississippi in 1962, the Council lost its base as more and more white Mississippians decided that guns, burning crosses, and lynching ropes were the means by which to stop integration in its tracks. And while I don't believe Daddy was an actual member of the Klan, he sure as hell never condemned them. In fact, he'd sooner put up a NO VACANCY sign on his empty motel than rent one room to a black family.

* * *

While Daddy was busy building his empire, Mama was busy with her babies. By the time she was twenty-one she had three daughters: Penny was born in 1938, Georgia in 1941, and Elizabeth eleven months later in 1942. Daddy was at the hospital for every birth, pacing the hallways, passing out cigars he didn't smoke, and betting anyone who would take the wager that *this time* he was sure to have a boy. But he never did. He had three girls, one after the other, and each of them grew into beauty queens and majorettes. But Daddy didn't want another beauty queen; he wanted an heir, a *son* who could take over his growing Clark enterprises. After all, wasn't it Vivian's duty to give him that boy, James Lamar Clark, Jr.? (Daddy didn't seem to know or care that the father determines the baby's sex.) But Mama kept pushing out girls. After hearing the news of girl after girl's birth, Lamar would throw his remaining cigars in the trash bin and drive away from the hospital, usually to his latest mistress to soothe his disappointment.

Mama, on the other hand, adored each new baby, and vowed to be a different kind of mother than the one she'd endured. She longed to be loving and attentive, not the sort of mother who picked favorites and pitted her children against each other. When her girls were young, she devoted herself to them completely and relished buying them the frilliest, prettiest dresses with satin sashes and lace collars and matching hats and white gloves and shiny Mary Janes, doing their hair up in a mass of curls, and proudly walking behind them into church every Sunday, looking like a page out of *Make Way for Ducklings*.

But as happy as she was with her growing brood, she was increasingly unhappy with her husband. Over the years, as my father accumulated more and more wealth and power, my content and cheerful mother grew lonelier and more isolated. Daddy always had a woman on the side, and Mama often found herself pacing in front of the living room window late into the night, waiting for his car to pull into the driveway. Many nights it never did.

When their third daughter, Elizabeth, was ten, Mama and Daddy decided to try for *one more* baby: the boy my father longed for, finally, the heir to his empire.

"You were supposed to be the 'save the marriage baby' that didn't save the marriage," Mama said years later. I'm not sure she should have told me that, but she did.

On December 19, 1953, Daddy once again paced the maternity ward of Rush Memorial Hospital in Meridian, passing out cigars. This was it: He was 100 percent positive his fourth baby was a boy, and gave all takers 3:1 odds.

For the last time, he lost his bet.

Chapter Four

Other than her four daughters, the one thing that kept Mama going during her unhappy marriage was her passion for music. It almost took her mind off Daddy's affairs. Almost. Mama loved all music, from big band and blues to classical and show tunes. As a young girl, she had walked from one end of her family's long shotgun house to the other in her own dreamy world, humming out new songs in her head, sometimes spinning through the rooms as she added a dance step to the tune. Usually, her sisters would roll their eyes and do their sniff-in-the-air taunting: "Oh, look who's here, a member of *Our Gang*!" But Vivian was undeterred and would curtsy deeply, as if thanking her audience for its ovation, and pirouette her way through the narrow house and onto its wide front porch. Lord knows she had the looks for Hollywood or New York, and some even said she had the talent. What Vivian never had was encouragement, from either her family or her husband.

Lamar Clark was certainly not unusual in expecting his wife to stay home and tend to his house and children, like a proper Southern wife was supposed to do. It was Mama who was unusual: She thought she could be both the mother and wife Lamar wanted her to be, as well as achieve success in the musical world. But Daddy couldn't begin to imagine such a life. She was there to raise his children and tend his house and look pretty on his arm and in his bed. That was it. End of story. And Mama did all that, but she often needed a tumbler of bourbon to get through the day.

By the time I was a little girl, Mama's musical passion didn't just annoy Daddy; it infuriated and embarrassed him. He didn't read music, he didn't listen to music, he didn't even particularly *like* music, with the sole exception of *The Tennessee Waltz*. If Daddy couldn't understand something, it wasn't worth knowing, and he definitely didn't understand music. And he certainly didn't take the time to appreciate Mama's innate musical talent. I suspect, at the core, he was jealous. She had something she cared about as much as, hell, maybe even more than, him. And in Lamar's world, nothing was more important or powerful than Lamar.

"That ain't real m-m-music," he'd taunt when she played one of her 78s she had specially produced in New Orleans. "Sounds like something a t-t-two-year-old would write," or "You're fooling yourself and wasting my m-m-money on these records. You'll never be one of those songwriters."

As much as he belittled her talent, she kept at it with the dogged determination of a passionate artist, relishing every note and polishing every verse on the page until she was satisfied. With no musical prospects in Waynesboro, she would drive four hours on the old Highway 11 to New Orleans to record one of her songs. Never having learned how to read music, she sang the songs into a tape recorder and then had a musician transcribe them onto the page. I still have her old 78s, and whenever I hear Mama's smoky voice coming through the scratchy vinyl, it reduces me to tears. My sweet, sad mama.

For many years, despite Daddy's fierce opposition, she regularly drove to New Orleans to work with songwriters and musicians. But she would put off telling Daddy she was going until the very last minute, when her bags were packed and in the car.

"You're not going!" he'd command.

"Oh, I already have the appointments. Wouldn't look good to cancel now," she'd say, her voice light and casual.

He'd accuse her of being unfaithful to him, because why would she be driving all that way for nothing? They would go at it for a while, and then she'd throw her mink over her shoulder, take a drag off her cigarette, toss an "Aloha!" over her shoulder, and waltz out the door.

Whenever she returned home after a trip, Daddy would accuse her of sleeping with the bandleader, or one of the music producers, or a sound engineer. She'd laugh him off, with the same dismissive Atkinson-girl sniff in the air, reminding him that they were all "fat, bald Jews," and why would she "ever sleep with the likes of that?" This would shut him up some, given that he had had absolutely no interaction with a single Jew his entire life and if he thought of them at all, he considered them "farners" (foreigners). But it wouldn't take him long to start in again on Mama's trips. It would be the same attack every time she returned from New Orleans.

Sometimes Daddy would send Mama's niece, Francis, along to New Orleans to keep an eye on Mama. A tall, beautiful blonde, she was the Jayne Mansfield of the Atkinson clan and everybody loved having her in their entourage. As they got ready to leave for New Orleans, Daddy would hand Francis wads of $100 bills and tell her, "I want you in charge of paying for everything because I don't want your aunt Vivian to drink it all up. You know how she loves the Sazerac Bar at the Roosevelt. Take her shopping. She can buy anything she wants, except a drink. I need you to take care of her for me." On one trip, the wad totaled $2,500—close to $20,000 in today's money. Francis's parents didn't have two nickels to rub together, so it was doubtful that she'd ever seen a $10 bill, never mind a wad of $100s.

This was not the first time Francis had been recruited as a spy. But it turns out she was a bit of a double agent. On any given day, she and Mama would drive downtown and park in front of the bank next to Daddy's Cadillac. Mama would hand her a quarter and say, "Now you go on into the bank and see if your uncle Lamar is talking to any women in there." Francis would pocket the quarter, walk into the bank, and approach Daddy. He, in turn, would hand her a quarter and say, "Now I want you to tell me if your aunt Vivian talks to any men while y'all are out shopping today." And on and on it went.

But, even with Francis's chaperoning the all-expenses-paid trips to New Orleans, Daddy eventually wore Mama down and her trips became less and less frequent. When she did go, she'd return to Waynesboro distant and sad. She'd spend hours at a time alone in her room, dressed in one of her flowing negligees and matching silk robes, listening to Billie Holiday and Ella Fitzgerald and Nat King Cole, or sitting with her Bible, reading and circling passages that moved her. With little solace found anywhere else outside of her bottle, she escaped into the pages of parables and convictions, finding rare acceptance and approval.

Chapter Five

When I was five, we moved from our first house on the corner of Spring and Clark Streets (the latter of which was named by my father, who had by then plastered his name across much of Waynesboro) to a sprawling house he had built for us on a farm just outside of town on the Chickasawhay River. Pronounced chick-ah-sah-HAY, the river, like many places in the South, was named by one of the many Indian tribes that once roamed its rich earth. The farm was over one hundred acres of rolling hills and fields, thick with the sweet, rich smells of honeysuckle and daphne, jasmine and magnolia, hanging wisteria and succulent banana shrub. Our house was a four-bedroom, two-bath rambler built in the style of an antebellum mansion—even though it was only one story. Mama surrounded the house with weeping willows because she loved to watch the wind play through the branches. There was a pasture filled with animals—cows, horses, and goats—and plenty of fences and long-limbed oak trees for me to climb.

When we moved from Clark Street I didn't care about the farm's potential for fun because the move took me miles away from my best friend, Burke. Burke and I had lived directly across the street from one another since the day we were born. His father, James ("Mister James," always), and his mother, Miss Catherine, were my parents' best friends. Miss Catherine was a Southern belle through and through who got up at four every morning just to "put her face on" so Mister James would never have to see her without makeup. Somewhere, I have an old black-and-white picture of Mister James holding me when I was two months old while Daddy holds six-month-old Burke. No one can remember exactly when their friendship started, but it endured throughout their entire lives.

Burke and I played all day, and then at night we'd signal each other from our beds with flashlights and bird calls. He was the truest friend I ever had—and he also somehow understood, without my ever having to explain, that I too wanted to be a cowboy in our pretend games, never a princess or, heaven forbid, the doomed lady on the railroad tracks. We "was like peas and carrots," as Forrest Gump says of his best friend, and in fact, years later Burke would tell me that I was his "Jenny." On the day we moved from Spring Street, I sat on the back of the flatbed truck crying and waving goodbye to Burke, who stood crying and waving from his driveway. We both thought we were never going to see each other again, and we were inconsolable; we thought I was moving not to *the* country, but to *another* country.

There are stories of Daddy and Mister James before I was born, then both new husbands and young fathers, getting drunk and going down by the river to "fish." But what they were really doing was "telephoning," a shady practice that involved using a car battery and an old crank-up phone to electrocute schools of bottom-dwelling catfish, sending them to the surface and scooping them up with a net. This wasn't exactly legal, even back in the 1930s and 1940s. One time, the town's game warden got wind of what Lamar and his buddy were up to and gave the young men a tongue-lashing, then he confiscated the catfish to fry up for supper because he knew that fried catfish were just as good as food can get.

Daddy and Mister James were also business partners, with Mister James taking advantage of Lamar's Midas touch as well as his often questionable inside deals. Once, Burke heard Mister James tell Miss Catherine, "If I was doin' half of what Lamar is, they'd put me *under* the jail, not just in it!"

I thought Burke and his family were perfect, like the television Cleavers. What I wouldn't learn for years was that both of Burke's parents were also serious drinkers. But nobody ever said a word about that. The same way they didn't talk about hearing Daddy scream insults at Mama in the driveway, or having seen him with such-and-such young lady over at the Dew Drop Inn on Highway 84.

Miss Catherine and Mama formed a fast friendship and spent long hours together. I like to imagine that privately, with a bottle on the table between them and no one else privy to their secrets, they shared some of their demons, divulging some of the darkness and sadness they both suffered. But I have no way of knowing if they ever did. Once we moved from Clark Street, and particularly after Mama moved out of the farm, she didn't see much of Miss Catherine anymore. I wonder now if perhaps Daddy saw to that. If he somehow let it be known to Mister James that Miss Catherine was to keep her distance from Mama. And if Mister James ever thought Daddy's treatment of Mama was cruel or his adultery wrong, he knew to keep his mouth shut or risk losing a solid chunk of his business that insured Clark Oil and Clark Construction and Clark Timber.

While our parents went about their private and public affairs, Burke and I happily rode our bikes all over Waynesboro, ran after the DDT truck spraying for mosquitoes until the poison made us dizzy, caught harmless garter and pine woods snakes while avoiding the deadly cottonmouths and water moccasins, raced my go-cart around and around our semicircle driveway, drank an entire case of warm Coca-Colas on a bet to see who could drink more, only to have it all come back up on the lawn, and got sno-cones at Mary's Store.

Mary was a towering black woman who owned and operated her small, cinder block store on Glitter Lane, a curious name given that it was nothing more than a dirt road lined with tin and tar paper shacks. Mary would welcome us, her only white customers as far as I could tell, with an enormous smile. I never saw her enter sales numbers or a customer's debt into a ledger; she somehow kept all the figures sorted in her head. Instead of a cash register, she had an old suitcase into which she'd throw the coins and dollar bills and from which she'd count out people's change. I never heard a sharp word or an unpleasant exchange with anyone in all the years we visited the store.

I always felt comfortable with Mary and her friendly mix of customers, the same way I did when I visited Virgie or Beulah Mae in their houses in Hiwannee, a tiny community north of Waynesboro where many of the "help" lived. In fact, I felt more comfortable there than in any other store in Waynesboro or Meridian or New Orleans. On any given day, there'd be three or four men sitting around a barrel, on which sat a piece of plywood as a tabletop, playing checkers or cards or dominoes, laughing at each other's stories and drinking ice-cold Coca-Colas. Mary kept jars of pigs' feet on the counter, along with vats of giant pickles that she'd wrap in wax paper and hand out to the customers. And her sno-cones were out of this world—succulent, thick, fruity syrup drizzled over shaved ice. One day, Burke and I decided the whole town needed to know just how special they were, so we got a piece of plywood and painted BEST SNO-CONES! MISS MARY'S STORE, 5 CENTS! Bless her heart, she put the sign up in the window and it stayed there for years and years, until the letters had faded to the point where you couldn't read it anymore.

When we moved to the farm, I learned I would lose Viola. She was my first nanny and had been the one steady adult in my world since the day I came home from the hospital. It was Viola who ran my bath and brushed my hair and kissed my scraped knees before putting on Band-Aids. I adored her and considered her a member of our family, even though she kept her own plate and fork and cup on a separate shelf in the kitchen. But Mama and Daddy told me that she lived fifteen minutes from the farm instead of five, and that that was too far for them to have to drive her back and forth every day. Like most black people in our town, Viola didn't have a car and there certainly was no bus service out to the new house. When our moving day came, I buried my face in Viola's skirts and clasped my arms tight around her waist until my parents pulled me away. I never saw Viola again.

In Viola's place, Virgie appeared. When I first saw Virgie in the kitchen ironing my daddy's white shirts, I ran into the corner and cowered like a scared puppy, refusing to look at her. Finally, I came out of the corner and looked her straight in the eye.

"I hate you!" I screamed. "I want Viola!"

I half expected Virgie to turn back to the stove and ignore my tantrum, but no, that was not Virgie's way. She slowly wiped her hands on the apron tied at her waist and knelt down in front of me, her already arthritic knees cracking with the effort. She didn't smile, but her round brown eyes were as kind and understanding as any I'd ever seen.

"I knows yo' do, baby girl. I knows." She reached out her hand, and just like that I took it.

Virgie had been born in the nearby cotton fields in 1919, the child of freed slaves who had to give her up for adoption because they couldn't afford to feed another mouth. Like generations of slaves and laborers before her, her body became the fuel that fed the machines of a young nation, machines that produced cotton, soybeans, steel, and gold, but mostly cotton. She worked those fields from the time she could walk, all day, every day, even through her nine pregnancies, wearing large overalls to accommodate her bulk. When it came her time, she'd quietly go off and deliver the baby and return to the field soon after with the infant strapped to her back. In 1958, she came to us straight from those fields, grateful for the "easier" work and elevated station of maid to a wealthy white family.

Even though Virgie stood about five feet ten inches tall, she could walk down the main street of Waynesboro and barely turn a head. She was as invisible as a flesh-and-bones person could be. She kept her head down and her gaze on the ground. Her posture was hunched after years of working the cotton and when she came to work for us, she bent those same shoulders over our stove and toilets and beds. When she worked for my family, she was paid $1.50 a day, and it was considered good money in 1958 Waynesboro. In fact, she earned 50 percent more than any other black maid in town. I'd like to think it was because Daddy was generous, but I suspect it had more to do with his wanting everyone to know that Lamar Clark paid his "help" more than anyone else in Waynesboro.

So then it was Virgie who ran my bath and brushed my hair and kissed my scraped knees. It was Virgie who hummed her quiet hymns while rocking me when my mother would leave the house in a screech of tires and a cloud of dust on one of her wild rides. Sometimes Mama stayed away for days and it was Virgie who got me dressed and ready for school. Often it was Virgie who tucked me in at night, sometimes after first putting Mama to bed and cleaning up one of her messes in the bathroom. While Mama smelled of her favorite perfume, White Shoulders, it never quite masked the even stronger

smell of cigarettes and bourbon. But Virgie—as Viola had—
smelled of comfort: melted butter on toast and crisp cotton
sheets fresh off the line and skin warmed by the sun. Virgie
was comfort. She was also safety. And in my world there was
very little of that.

Virgie lived in the black section of Hiwannee, just north of
Waynesboro. Every Southern town had one. Some were called
Colored Town, others Africa Town, some Nigger Town or The
Quarter. But most towns had one, many still do, and every
one of them pulsed with hardship. Dirt and stones surrounded
the wood and tar paper shacks. Flies covered the walls and
the stench of the outhouse was overpowering. There was
no running water. Old newspaper was used to help insulate
the walls. Laundry was done by hand in a tub on the front
porch and hung on a line in the back. There were no screens
to keep the tormenting mosquitoes outside. There was no air-
conditioning or indoor heating. Some lucky folks had fans in
the open windows during the worst of the summer, and most
had pot-bellied stoves or used their stovetops to warm at least
the kitchen on the coldest days. But propane tanks went dry
and the electricity came and went without warning, so people learned to live on their front porches in the summer and
bundled up in layers of tattered clothing in the winter. If it
rained, people got wet. If it snowed, their feet got cold as they
walked through the ice and slush, often ruining their one pair
of shoes.

But as poor as their neighborhood looked to me through
the window of Daddy's Cadillac, its residents, and those of a
lot of black towns across the South, felt lucky to have a roof

over their heads, no matter if it had a few holes in it. And while it was poor, anyone could see that it was full of pride. Flower boxes hung from the windows and there were little smokehouses and gardens in most backyards. Dirt front yards were swept with brooms made from tree limbs, leaving a pattern like a comb through wet hair. The curtains that hung in the windows were thin, but clean. Women who spent long days keeping white folks' homes spotless made sure to do the same for their own.

And even from where I sat in the front seat of the car, I could see that Hiwannee had a lot of love on its slanted porches and in its crowded rooms. Love and laughter and comfort and a lot more of what I didn't have. My home, despite its luxury and acres and acres of land, felt terribly lonely by comparison. A big part of me wished I could live in Hiwannee too.

Chapter Six

After the initial shock of moving out of town and away from Burke and losing Viola, things got immediately better when I realized what endless adventure and beauty life on the farm provided. My sisters were all at least eleven years older than I was and were busy with their own lives. Penny, the oldest, was at college, and Georgia and Elizabeth were both finishing up high school and getting ready for their early marriages. So, I spent most days alone wandering through the fields and pastures, escaping into the fictional worlds I created around me, making forts in the trees and barn, battlegrounds in the fields, and playmates of my dogs and the farm's cows, goats, and of course, Frank, my burro.

Many Saturdays, my aunt Clifford and Penny, my oldest sister who really loved fishing like I did, would come out to the farm to go fishing in the pond behind the house with me and Mama. Virgie would pack us a picnic of Vienna sausages with mayo on Sunbeam bread and cold Coca-Colas and I'd sit on the bank as the older ladies sat perched on their minnow buckets, our four cane poles stretched out into the murky water. I couldn't concentrate on the fishing because I was so busy listening to their gossip, trying to figure out who all and what all they were talking about. Decades later, we four would gather at the pond's edge as often as time and schedules would allow.

On the days when no company would come, I'd go down to the pond alone, hoping to shoot an alligator or a water moccasin with my BB gun. Sometimes I would just sit and listen to the red-tailed hawks screeching or the singing whippoorwills as they circled above, feel the warm, moist air as it moved through the fields, its smell heavy and sweet after the hay had been cut or the gardenias and honeysuckle bushes were in bloom, and watch for deer darting in and out of the woods, careful not to rouse the attention of a coyote. I always had something to do between riding Frank and my horses, helping feed the cattle, or training my collies how to herd without getting stomped. Sometimes I would sing to the cows, marveling at how they would make their slow, plodding way to where I stood in the field and then stand and listen like the best of captive audiences. I thought their doleful stares and motionless bodies were because they were awestruck by my voice. I didn't yet understand that cows' stares are always doleful and they do everything in their power to avoid moving. But they sure would circle around me and stay there until I was finished. Sometimes Mama would look out the kitchen window and shriek, "Tena! Get away from those cows before you get yourself trampled to death!" She didn't understand I considered them my friends.

It didn't take me long to love the farm, and I thought Mama did too, until the day the migrant workers came to pick our pecans. That day I realized just how miserable she had become.

Late fall was pecan-picking season in Mississippi. We didn't have a huge orchard, or really much of a crop, but there was enough for Daddy to give a bag here and a bag there to the business owners around town with whom he worked, and probably to a few of their wives as well.

One evening toward the end of September when I was five or six, Daddy said he expected the pickers in the morning, so the next day I got up early, pulled on my overalls, and started toward the front window to wait for them. As I passed by her open bedroom door, Mama yelled, as she always did, for me to put on a shirt.

"It's chilly and you look just like a boy without one!"

"Aw, Mama, it'll just get sweaty and dirty!"

"Well, at least put on some shoes! You look like a field hand, and I won't have the workers talking about some poor little white child runnin' around the Clark farm!"

Being accused of looking poor, or worse, looking like poor white trash, was just about the lowest insult and embarrassment Mama could imagine. She grew up in what was then and remains to this day the poorest part of the poorest state in the country—Wayne County, Mississippi. Many people were so poor that the only thing that changed *after* the Depression was that when a rabbit ran across the road, no one tried to shoot it for dinner. In the 1950s, when I was born, cars were a luxury for many and the still-unpaved streets of Waynesboro were lined with troughs to water the horses because that was how many folks came and went from town. Horse and buggy. By the time I was five, 55 percent of Mississippians—black and white—were living in poverty, and not some "below the safety-net" benchmark of poverty. There was no safety net. This was poverty that killed, starved, and riddled with disease. This was poverty covered in lice and bleeding sores. This was poverty with rickets and distended bellies and tuberculosis and scurvy. This was poverty in tents and hole-in-the-ground toilets. Some of my classmates came to school so dirty that teachers would ask the child's mother if they could take the girl or boy into the janitor's closet to comb the lice out of their hair.

Except for some of the kids in school and the folks in Hi-wannee, I didn't see much of the ruin around me, sitting at my dinner table or eating platefuls of fried chicken and mashed potatoes at Petty's Cafe, and fried shrimp and hush puppies at The Fish Camp Diner. I lived the sheltered, comfortable life of white privilege. Mama made sure of that. For her, having me and my sisters fed and dressed in the best money could provide was insurance against ever being thought "poor" or "trash."

"I left my shoes outside," I told her over my shoulder as I settled myself in the window to wait for the pecan pickers. "I'll put 'em on out there."

The house behind me was quiet. Daddy was out in the orchard with his foreman, a large and stoic black man named Mayfield, awaiting the workers. Mama was in her room, and Virgie was in the kitchen cooking biscuits and bacon by the smell of it. She and Mama would likely serve the field hands and pickers some of those biscuits with a glass of sweet tea out the back door, come about one or two in the afternoon. I rested my chin in my hands and leaned on the windowsill, waiting. They were late but they'd be here. They came every year, right as rain, all I had to do was wait.

Finally, I saw the dust rising above the trees down the road—vehicles were approaching the farm. Not just vehicles but trucks. As soon as I saw them round the last bend, I was out the front door and running toward the barn before they cut their engines.

"Tena Rix, don't you be runnin' like a g-g-g-girl and get hit by them trucks!" Daddy yelled. He was always warning me off doing anything "like a girl"—running, playing, crying, and least of all, thinking and talking like a girl. I guess he hadn't yet noticed I was one.

The pecan pickers' trucks were dirty and covered in rust. They didn't even look like they could make it up the driveway, never mind to the next farm down the road, and then the next after that, as the workers made their rounds, finding the seasonal work where they could.

About ten men and women scrambled down from the flatbed truck and its cab, all of them black and looking like it had been some time since they'd seen a hot bath and a good meal. A little girl I guessed to be about my age was the last one to clamber down from the flatbed and onto the dusty road. She had on a tattered dress, held together at her shoulder with safety pins, and her hair was braided into tight plaits that stuck out all over her head like little, curly antennae. Her feet were also bare, like mine. I guessed she was probably too young and too little to be of much use in the field, so I ran up to her, grabbed her hand, and asked if she wanted to play. She turned to a woman to ask permission and we were waved off with a smile.

Soon, we were running through the fields, laughing. I loved

pecan-picking season because it usually brought kids my age to the farm. Except for occasional visits from Virgie's daughter Cindy, none of our help were allowed to bring their children to the house while they worked. So it was usually just me and the cows, horses, and dogs. But that day, and for the first time in as long as I could remember, there would be another little girl to play with on the farm.

"TENA!"

Mama's scream echoed across the field, and the girl and I skidded to a stop. All the workers' heads turned toward the big house, their eyes huge in their heads.

"TENA RIX! Get in the house, NOW!" Mama yelled from the back door.

I dropped the girl's hand and sprinted toward the house, careful to avoid the thorny thistles and cow pies scattered in the field. Mama met me at the back door and before I could ask if someone had died, she grabbed my right arm, her fingers pinching my skin. I tried to squirm out of her grip, but she held fast, even tighter as I struggled. She bent down so that her face was just about touching mine, her eyes wide with anger. I could smell that she'd already had a nip or two. I'd seen Mama plenty mad, but it was rare to see her this mad at *me*.

"Don't you EVER hold hands with a nigger again."

"Who, Mama? That little girl?" I didn't know who she was talking about, but I knew my playdate was over.

"You don't *ever* touch a nigger. Ever. Do you understand me?"

That's when I made my first mistake.

"No, Mama."

"What do you mean, *No, Mama?* Don't you *No, Mama* me! I don't ever want to see you touching one again."

I looked into her eyes and there was something wild about her anger. I had heard the word "nigger" often, but mostly from Daddy and men like him. They talked about the black men and women workers on our farm and around town as if they were chattel, still owned and ruled and assessed like animals by their white overseers. I didn't know why, but unlike "Negro" or "colored," the word "nigger" was mean and full of hate. Nonetheless, it was used as routinely and casually as someone's name. But I had never before heard Mama use it. Until that day with the little girl in the pecan orchard.

"They are *nasty*," she went on.

I looked into her eyes and thought, *Mama's done lost her mind. How am I not supposed to touch a colored person ever again? What about Virgie and Beulah Mae and Mayfield?* My second mistake was asking her just that.

Without a word, and without loosening her grip, Mama pulled me through the kitchen, my toes skimming the floor as she half dragged, half carried me over to the sink. I saw Virgie standing in the corner, her eyes huge with worry. She'd seen enough of Mama drunk and mad to know it was only going to get worse. Mama grabbed a Brillo Pad from its saucer and, barely pausing to run it under the faucet, began scrubbing my hand, the one that had held the little girl's, all the way from my fingertips to my elbow.

"Niggers have germs," she said, scrubbing so hard I was sure I would see blood start to seep from beneath the Brillo Pad. "They are *nasty*. They'll make you sick."

"Mama, STOP." I sobbed, trying to wiggle away from the burning pain of the steel wool and her body crushing mine into the hard edge of the tile counter. "What about Virgie?"

Mama's hand slowed.

"Virgie's different."

"But how? She takes care of me, she hugs me and kisses me. Why is she different, Mama?"

My mother stopped, stepped back from the counter, and looked at me, as if seeing me for the first time. Her hair was falling into her eyes and she was out of breath. She looked over at Virgie, her eyes resting on the cracked cup in Virgie's hands. It was Virgie's cup and kept very separate from ours, just as Viola's had been, along with her one fork and one plate.

Mama finally dropped the steel wool in the sink and released her grip on my arm, but her fingers lingered on my skin and they trembled as she gently stroked me, soothing the raw redness she'd just put there. She slowly shook her head.

"I don't know why, baby." Her voice was a ragged whisper. She looked over at Virgie again and then lowered her eyes. "It's just the way it is."

Maybe so, but I never heard Mama use the word "nigger" again.

Chapter Seven

Through all her torment on the farm, there were moments—
perhaps not entire days, but moments—when Mama was
happy. Even though she raged against Daddy's adultery and
despaired about her stalled musical career, she still gave me
glimpses of the carefree, pretty young girl Daddy had once
vowed to love, honor, and obey. When she was in one of her
really good moods, she'd put on a record, flash her trademark
impish grin, and pull me across the floor to dance with her.
As we slid back and forth across the linoleum in our large
kitchen-den, we'd beg Virgie to come join us, but she never
would.

"No, ma'am. Y'all go ahead. I's got my work to do," she'd
say, but I could see a little smile lifting the corners of her
mouth as she bent over the mop bucket or sink and resumed
her scrubbing.

Mama would nod in Virgie's direction and continue dancing and then sing along with the record in her rich voice. Mama
was an alto, with a deep, smoky, even masculine tone, so much
so that when she answered the phone, the person on the other
end would often say, "Hello, sir." One of her favorite songs was

"C'est Si Bon," which she sang with a throaty lustiness—think Rosemary Clooney meets Ella Fitzgerald, with a little Tallulah Bankhead thrown in for good measure:

C'est si bon,
Et si nous nous aimons . . .

She knew it would make me and Virgie laugh and it always did. Even though she didn't read or speak French, someone in New Orleans must have translated the lyrics, because she knew them by heart too.

It's so good,
And if we are in love . . .

As I watched her in those moments when music made her come alive, I began to understand the power of every song and its ability to transform the prisoner to the free, the wretched to the joyous, the crippled to the agile. The notes and words and phrases entered my mother's body like an electric current, filling the emptiness in her as nothing and no one else could. Music replaced her tortured loneliness with company, her dead dreams with a child's optimism for the future, and her scoundrel husband with her own passionate lover, a lover who never lied, cheated, disappointed, or abandoned. I watched the magical transformation and I understood, and I remembered, for I too would need its solace in time.

Her other comfort was the Bible, and she read it as faithfully as a pilgrim heading to the Holy Land. Drunk or sober,

every night she read at least one passage, Psalms being her favorite. I think the 25th Psalm had particular resonance, given
her life with Daddy:

*To you, O Lord, I pray. Don't fail me, Lord, for I am trusting
you. Don't let my enemies succeed. Don't give them victory over
me. None who have faith in God will ever be disgraced for trusting him. But all who harm the innocent shall be defeated.*

She had a Bible by her bed and a gun under her pillow her
entire life. I once asked her why she needed both.

"Well, honey, I gotta have the gun in case Jesus is taking the
night off!"

On good days she and I would often sing "King of the Road,"
really belting out "I'm a MAAAAAN of means by no means,
king of the ROOOOOOOAD!" until we were so hoarse we
couldn't speak. When she was having a bad day and moving
slow and sad, we'd sometimes sit on the couch and put on one
of her jazz albums—Billie Holiday was a favorite—and we'd
harmonize to "Good mornin', heartache, what's new?"

There were even some happy family moments, many of
them spent at the Roosevelt hotel in New Orleans, where
we celebrated several Christmases when I was very little. For
us, New Orleans was the big city, and we loved its elaborate
decorations: Christmas trees on every corner, green garlands
on each lamppost, and a canopy of white lights strung above
Bourbon Street that stretched for blocks. Walking beneath the

lights made us feel like we were in a magical kingdom. We all dressed in our holiday best—crinoline skirts and patent leather shoes and white gloves for us girls, Daddy in his white dinner jacket and black flannel pants—and spent our evenings in the Roosevelt's Blue Room for dinner and dancing.

When I close my eyes I can still picture Mama and Daddy on the dance floor, Mama towering over him while his head nestled on her bosom. I thought they were the most glamorous parents on Earth. Daddy would return to the table and with rare exuberance say, "Girls, my favorite activity in the world is to dance with your mama!" as he reached out and gave Mama's fanny a little pat as she sat down. After he danced with Mama, he would take my hand for his next dance. Still less than three feet tall, I would stand on his shoes and hold on to his waist tightly as he glided us around the floor. I was sure every eye was on us.

Sometimes all my sisters would come out to the farm and we'd go hunting for squirrels and rabbits, not for dinner or anything, just for "sport." Daddy adored the spectacle of it all: Lamar Clark and his five lovely girls walking through the woods of Mississippi, each loaded for bear. Daddy would hand Mama and my three sisters a rifle each from his gun rack, and me my BB gun. He'd walk ahead, king cock on the farm, strutting and preening for an invisible audience, and we'd march behind, our eyes peeled to the trees for prey. As much as I hated the thought of killing an animal, I surely didn't want to miss out on any Wild West action. I could have been Calamity Jane's alter ego, right down to my dusty overalls and cowboy boots, always looking for an excuse to shoot my gun. Eventually some poor squirrel would flip its bushy tail or start chattering in a tree, and the shooting would begin.

After five rifles and one BB gun had emptied their chambers into the two-pound rodent, the bloody remnants would filter down from the tree like furry confetti. Daddy would pick up the biggest piece as if it were a lion he had killed on safari and throw it into the underbrush, then we'd head back to the house, triumphant.

One year, a panther attacked our neighbor's chicken coop, killing many of its flock, then prowled the banks of the Chickasawhay every night for weeks, terrorizing us with its howling. A panther's cry is still one of the most frightening sounds I've ever heard. Its high-pitched screams sound like a woman being murdered in a dark alley. Everyone within fifty miles of Waynesboro kept their loaded shotguns a few inches closer than normal, never leaving the house without it, and no one more so than Daddy. Driving home from a church supper one night, we spotted two eyes illuminated by our headlights in a pecan tree near the house.

"That's him! That's the goddamn panther!" Daddy yelled, slamming on the brakes. "Stay in the car! That sonofabitch is gonna g-g-g-git what he's got comin'!" He grabbed his pistol from under the front seat and jumped out of the car before it had come to a stop.

BAM BAM BAM BAM BAM! He peppered the tree with bullets, emptying the gun's chamber. At last we heard the poor creature fall out of the tree with a *ker-plunk*. Daddy walked over to examine the carcass, tilted his hat back, scratched his head, then slowly walked back to the car.

Daddy hadn't killed the panther. He'd killed my sister's beloved cat. He never quite lived that one down. In fact, it was one of the few stories about him in which he was the butt of the joke that he allowed us to tell and retell. Maybe the only one.

But most days, the family wasn't hunting or laughing at Daddy's mistaking a house cat for a killer panther. And most days, Mama wasn't dancing and singing to her music, even the sad songs. Most days, she was in her room with her other lover: booze. And living with an unhappiness that was slowly gnawing away at her.

Chapter Eight

Meanwhile, Daddy was having the time of his life.

Before I was aware of what to call it, I knew my father had a way with women. Or at least his money did. But honestly, it was more than his money. Lamar Clark had the sort of self-assurance that drew others to him like deer to a salt lick, even while it masked his profound insecurities, beginning with his short stature. My father had the ultimate Napoleon complex. Here was a man who owned most of Waynesboro and yet wore two-inch lifts in his shoes. Here was a man who had a handful of governors, senators, and congressmen in his pocket, and yet shaved his armpits smooth, had regular manicures, and was never seen with a hair on his head out of place. I'd stand next to him at the bathroom counter, fascinated by how he combed thick gobs of Brylcreem through his hair—practically placing each strand one by one until he had it perfectly patterned. Hell, perhaps my daddy was just a metrosexual before his time. Who knows? My daddy's life had doors that I will never be able to open. But what I did know, even then, was that making money and chasing women were everything to him. In that order. They defined who he was. I don't even know if he particularly enjoyed the women or the material possessions all that much once he acquired them. The thrill was all in the chase, and in the control and power that his winning represented.

Having been born dirt poor and without the land-owning pedigree of the true Southern gentleman, Daddy nonetheless carried himself like a tycoon or a Hollywood film star, and he dressed like one too—impeccably, even in the wilting summer heat. He was Waynesboro's Jay Gatsby, and he hosted some of the town's most lavish parties, all the women in gowns with pinched waists and yards of thick petticoats, the men in white jackets and ties. And of course, by the time I was born, he was a millionaire—and he made sure everyone in town knew it, from the multiple new cars he bought every six months for himself, his wife, and all of his daughters, to building our flashy "farm" with its long semicircle driveway rimmed in roses and willow trees, to plastering his name on everything he owned: buildings, companies, streets.

On any given day, Daddy would cruise around town, admiring his own image in his Cadillac's rearview mirror, his left arm dangling out the window, a cigarette between his fingers. When he wasn't entertaining some woman in his car, he and I would tool around town, making his daily rounds. We were a team of two: breakfast at Blaine's Cafe, lunch at Petty's, the post office for the mail, a stop by the bank president's office for a chat, then the teller's window to make a deposit—always a deposit, never a withdrawal—the feed and grain store for supplies and to chat up the salesclerks about the latest news about "them commies up North, bringin' their trouble down *heah* where it ain't wanted." I didn't know what trouble they were talking about, but I guessed it had something to do with the "colored" folks. Just by the looks on their faces when they talked about it, I could see they were both disgusted and angry. And that usually meant they were talking about race or politics. And they were, and that summer of 1961 it was about busloads of Freedom Riders driving through the South protesting for civil rights. But I didn't know about that then. All I knew was that the men talking with Daddy were plenty upset that anyone would dare tell them they were wrong about something, wrong about anything actually.

Wherever we went, men patted my head and women pinched my cheek and made a point of complimenting me or my clothes or my hair. Their fussing struck me as rather ridiculous, because I was always dressed in a simple cotton school dress or shorts, with my hair in a long braid down my back and—in the summer—fresh red dirt on my white Keds. But that didn't stop them from admiring me like I was the next Shirley Temple, even as I fidgeted and twisted away from their pats and pinches.

"Why, I swear, Lamar, this little girl of yours looks more and more like you every day. Lord have mercy, but she's your spittin' image—right down to her pretty, little, stubborn chin!"

"Don't be sullin' up like a girl, M-M-M-Monkey Joe. C-C-C-Come on now and smile for the nice lady," he'd say, and I'd oblige, sometimes even throwing in a curtsy just to play the game. I found that, like Daddy, I also loved the attention and felt a strange power under their admiring eyes. I liked being Lamar Clark's little girl, even if I felt more like his "spittin' image" little *boy*.

My father also lit up when he was around a pretty woman; he would flash his rare killer smile, push his fedora back on his head, and offer her a cigarette before lighting one for himself.

By the time I was six or seven, Mama would often take a bottle of whiskey and disappear into her bedroom after supper, unwilling and most likely unable to remain on her feet. But on those rare evenings when she was sober, or maybe only a little sauced, I'd sit with her as she took off her makeup, and then we'd get in bed and watch *The Many Loves of Dobie Gillis* on the black-and-white TV. Well, I'd watch while she did her puzzle or read from the Bible, her free hand reaching over and lightly scratching my back with her long fingernails. It was a simple gesture, but one that always soothed me to the point of putting me to sleep.

Watching Mama remove her makeup was a ritual I cherished. I sat on the edge of the tub, playing a balancing game with myself, seeing how far I could lean back without falling in, and she'd begin. After tucking her hair into a hairnet, she'd scoop up a big dollop of Pond's Cold Cream with two fingers and expertly spread it all over her face and throat. It was a sort of art in motion, as if she were glazing a fine piece of porcelain with an artist's brush. She'd let it sit on her skin while she filed her nails.

One night, as I watched her, I remembered one of Daddy's admirers from our errands around town.

"Why doesn't Daddy ever say nice things to me or compliment my hair, or tell me I have his pretty, little, stubborn chin?"

She looked over at me, her dark eyes even darker in their

sea of white cream. They softened as she took her finger and traced a line of cold cream down my cheek.

"Oh baby, your daddy's a complicated man," she said. She knew that better than most, and even though she often got drunk and waved a threatening gun in his "cheatin', sonofabitch" face, it was plain she still loved him, and somehow still held a fondness deep in her heart.

"But he doesn't kiss or hug on me. He ain't never said, 'I love you,' or nothing."

"Or *anything*, and of course he loves you," she said. Even though she'd quit school at fifteen, she had never stopped reading and her grammar and vocabulary were better than most college grads' in the town. Her lifelong love of crossword puzzles also helped, I think.

"Didn't he buy you that new BB gun you've been eyein' at the store?" she asked, pushing up the sleeves to her dressing gown and reaching for her jar of Jergens lotion.

I told her I didn't want another present. "Why can't he say nice things, or hug me, like he loves me?" *Like you and Virgie and Georgia do*, I wanted to say. In fact, when I did try to hug and kiss him, he stiffened up like a mannequin in the store window, giving me a dismissive pat on the back as he pushed away from the hug.

"Oh, he loves you all right," she said, warming the lotion between her hands, "but men like your daddy sometimes feel as if they have to wrap their love in a hundred-dollar bill."

And looking around Waynesboro, I could see I wasn't the only one getting my love wrapped in hundred-dollar bills. If anyone cared to look close, and much of the town did, they'd notice that the young waitress and then the pretty bank teller and then the buxom cashier at the Lakeview Restaurant were all suddenly wearing new, expensive clothes in the latest style and doing their hair like Jackie Kennedy. My father may have reviled Jackie's husband, but he must have thought Jackie was the most beautiful woman in the world because most of his women made themselves up to look just like her in a carefully coiffed dark helmet of hair. Often, the woman-of-the-month was also driving a shiny new Cadillac. All courtesy of Lamar Clark. At the time, I didn't connect the dots, but the rest of the town sure did, and in typical fashion, they turned their backs on his and often their own husbands' dalliances.

My mother was another story. Even though for too long she believed she could change him and make the marriage something other than endless heartache, she nonetheless faced Daddy head-on with his countless affairs. Granted, she needed a bucket of bourbon to give her the courage, but she continually challenged him and dared him to come clean. He never did. Instead, in his own little version of the 1950s noir film *Gaslight*, in which the husband slowly drives his wife crazy by altering her reality, Daddy accused Mama of imagining things and demanded she stop listening to "idle gossip" and just "let it be."

None of us recognized it at the time, least of all my mother, but his subtle manipulation of her reality slowly began to eat away at her sanity. He played on the fact that drunks can't remember the details of their own lives, never mind what happened the night before. So he turned her suspicions into what he deemed "pure fantasy." The lipstick on his collar became her own from when she greeted him the night before, town gossip about so-and-so with their new Lamar Clark Cadillac became "just the waggin' of old ladies' tongues." So over time and with Daddy's unrelenting dismantling of her own perception of things, Mama came to believe that she was the one who had done something wrong. When she couldn't remember the night before, it was easy for him to fill in the blanks with lies. But try as my father did to have it both ways—to cheat and to have his wife look the other way, to just *let it be*—he was never able to break her. Sure, she cracked, but she never broke.

Sometimes there wasn't enough booze in all of Mississippi to dull Mama's pain and ease her rage, and she boiled over, like a pot of gumbo with too much flame under it—angry and foaming and stinking up the kitchen to high heaven. One of my earliest memories is of Mama in tears pacing the living room floor. I must have been three or four. She was balancing me on one hip, while she held a drink and a cigarette in her other hand, spilling bourbon and ashes as she bounced me back and forth across the room. My cousin Mary Joyce and my aunt Jean were there, trying to calm her down, and years later told me the way the conversation went.

"He's with one of his whores. I can feel it," Mama said, taking a huge gulp of her drink, the ash from her cigarette falling into her hair. I held on for dear life, as her hold on me momentarily loosened and I slipped down her hip. She hoisted me back up and resumed her pacing. "Damn good-for-nuthin' sonofabitch. Why in hell didn't y'all stop me from runnin' off with him?"

"Ha!" Jean snorted. "A team of horses couldn't have stopped you and you know it."

In her sister, Mama not only had a best friend, she had her best runnin' buddy, and bless their hearts, they sure did their fair share of runnin' all over Southern Mississippi in Mama's various Cadillacs, passing a bottle of bourbon between them and cleaning out the bottoms of more ditches than I can count.

Mama didn't respond to Jean as she stopped by the front window, her eyes searching down the street for his car. Jean splashed some bourbon into her sister's glass.

"Well, honey, you have to make a choice with that little weasel," Jean said, her dislike of Daddy and her jealousy of Mama's nicer lifestyle never far from the surface. "You either leave him, or you stay and try to get him to stop his runnin' around. That's it. Either one."

Mama stayed, but she never got him to stop his cheating. One day, when I was about eight or nine and Daddy had begun threatening to send her off so she could "dry out," she started to notice that one of her very own "best friends," Frances Sawyer, was suddenly wearing expensive clothing and shoes. Frances had also changed her hairstyle to the "Lamar bouffant," and yes, she was driving a spanking-new car, none of which her husband could have afforded.

Hurt and betrayed on all sides, it only got worse when some other "friend" called Mama, crowing about how Lamar had just been seen with Frances and that they were headed to their regular meeting place behind the Western Auto Supply. So Mama called Jean, who came right over; their niece, Mary Joyce, also joined the "party" (truth be told, they were all flirting with serious alcohol problems by then and nothing titillated a drunk more than a fool's errand). They dressed my

mother up in a trench coat, sunglasses, and hat, and drove to
the Western Auto. Sure enough, there were Daddy and Frances,
steaming up the windows of Daddy's Cadillac. After confirming
the gossip, the two sisters and their niece drove away.
Rather than confronting him then and there, Mama bided her
time, waiting for her revenge. She got it.

It happened soon after at a Waynesboro Central High
School football game, and as usual at a football game in the
South, the entire town was there, including Frances, who was
sitting a few rows below us. I watched the scene play out as
if it were in slow motion. I saw Mama look at Frances, and
Daddy look at Mama, and Frances look at both Mama and
Daddy. I knew whatever was coming wasn't going to be pretty.
When the game was over, Mama timed her exit so as to meet
Frances at the bottom of the stairs. A second too late, Frances
looked up to see Mama directly above her. She smiled hesitantly,
but Mama's face was stone. Without breaking stride,
Mama took her last step down the stairs, turned, and using
her entire six feet of body momentum, elbowed the five-foot-
two-inch Frances Sawyer clear over the railing and onto the
muddy field below. Mama kept walking, a huge smile now
on her face and her head held high. She never looked back as
shocked observers ran to Frances's assistance, pulling her out
of the mud and dabbing at her ruined dress with white hand-
kerchiefs. It happened so fast I wasn't sure if anybody else
knew what had taken place. But four of us were damn sure:
me, Daddy, Mama, and poor, muddy Mrs. Sawyer.

Daddy ended his dalliance with her soon after. Once exposed,
he later admitted that the affair had lost its "fun."

Chapter Nine

It took Daddy less than a month to move on to the next affair—this one a poor girl who was barely out of her teens and a student at a nearby college. Word of it got back to Mama right away. One afternoon, Virgie was scrubbing the kitchen floor and I was watching *The Huckleberry Hound Show* in the den when we heard Mama on the phone in her bedroom.

"I finally got him this time, Jean!" Mama yelled to her sister over the phone.

She had received an anonymous call. I've long suspected it was one of Daddy's other lovers, hoping to get him thrown out of our house and into hers. The woman told Mama that Lamar had just been seen on Highway 84 driving toward Waynesboro in his Cadillac, his arm draped around a young woman who was all but sitting in his lap.

"I'm on my way over to pick you up," Mama told Jean. "We are finally going to stop that cheatin' sonofabitch once and for all."

Virgie stood up from the floor, wiped her hands off on a dishrag, and walked over to me.

"Come on, baby girl," she said, reaching down to me on the

floor. "Let's you and me go to the barn 'n see what that old mule of yo's be up to."

As I took her hand, Mama rushed into the room with her .38 Colt, which she'd grabbed from under her pillow, snatched a fresh bottle of Jack Daniel's from the cupboard, and ran out the back door. I felt Virgie's fingers close tightly on mine, giving them a couple of quick squeezes, as if to say, *It be all right, baby, you just hold my hand, real tight, and it be all right.*

Virgie and I trailed after Mama and watched her jump into her car, slam the door, and turn the radio up full blast. Without even looking in our direction, she put the car in reverse. Come to think of it, she didn't bother to look in the rearview mirror either, just threw it into reverse and gunned it out of the carport, taking a long pull off the bottle before slamming on the brakes, putting it into drive, and zigzagging down the driveway, gravel and dirt spitting from under the tires. As she roared past us, we could hear a song blaring from the car radio. I recognized it from Mama's stack of records—Little Richard's "Slippin' and Slidin'":

I've been told, Baby, you've been bold
I won't be your fool no more.

The car disappeared around the last curve in the driveway. "Virgie! Mama's gonna kill Daddy this time!" I cried.

Virgie gave my hand another squeeze. "No she won't, chile. Come on over here and let's sit a spell."

On the front porch stairs, Virgie pulled me into her lap, and the two of us sat while she rubbed my back and talked in her low, smooth voice, telling me it was "gon' be ok, baby girl. She ain't gonna kill yo' daddy, cuz yo' daddy too fast."

In the telling and retelling of the story I heard over the years to come, the details of what happened next were eventually filled in. First, Mama picked up Aunt Jean at her house in town and the two of them sped west on Highway 84 headed toward Laurel, where my father had last been seen heading east toward Waynesboro. With the windows open and the radio blasting, they passed Mama's bottle of whiskey between them. When she drove, Mama drank her whiskey as neat as anyone I ever saw: straight out of the bottle. She steered the car with her left hand, passing the bottle and holding her cigarette with her right. She took a minute to pull her pistol out from under her left leg, where she'd stashed it, to check and make sure it was loaded. It was, but it wouldn't be for long.

"There he is!" Jean shouted.

They saw my father's car approaching from the other direction and, sure enough, a young woman was sitting close enough to be in his lap. Daddy's fedora was pushed back on his head, his left hand holding a cigarette and the wheel while his right arm dangled off the girl's shoulders.

"Take the bottle and grab the wheel!" my mother yelled to Aunt Jean, then she all but threw the Jack Daniel's at her sister, who caught it but not before a splash of bourbon splattered across the front seat.

What came next was one clean series of motions, as elegant as they were miraculous: Mama tossed her cigarette out the window, pulled the pistol from under her leg, half stood, half knelt on the seat to hang out of the driver's-side window, and with the car still careening down the highway driven by her sister underneath her, opened fire straight at Daddy's straw fedora through the oncoming windshield.

Lamar Clark had just enough time after spotting his enraged, wild wife pointing a gun at him to shove the terrified girl's head under the dashboard and duck behind the steering wheel. He knew Vivian was aiming to kill. Just as he raised his arms to shield his head and face, the windshield exploded in front of him, and a split second later, the driver's-side window shattered in a thousand pieces, showering the front seat and Daddy.

As the cars finally passed each other, Mama sat down, resumed control of the wheel, and looked over at Aunt Jean.

"You think we killed the sonofabitch?" Mama asked, her voice calm and her breathing even. She might as well have been asking Jean if she felt like stopping at the Humdinger for a Coke.

Jean took a long swig from the bottle before passing it back to her sister. "I don't know but I sure as hell hope so, because if he ain't dead, he's gonna kill us both!"

The sisters laughed until the tears ran down their cheeks, slapping the dashboard and gasping for breath as they reran the scene—Mama's acrobatics, Daddy's eyes "buggin' out like a frog's," and teaching that "lousy sonofabitch a lesson he won't soon forget." Finally recovering, Mama took the bottle and Jean lit them two fresh cigarettes.

"Well, he had it comin'. Sure as hell did," Mama said. "That bastard. Just wish I'd killed him sooner. Hey, what say we go to the White Hat to celebrate?"

And so my mother and aunt, both thinking they had shot and killed my father and possibly the girl in cold blood, hit the gas and kept driving west to their favorite bar to celebrate. Rumor had it the girl ended up in an insane asylum. I could totally understand why.

Daddy called Georgia to clean up the mess.

Of all of us Clark girls, Georgia was the least like our parents. Where Penny, Elizabeth, and I were all big, loud personalities with opinions to match, Georgia was quiet, steady, and practical. And, aside from Virgie, she was my safety and my steady anchor. There's a picture of Georgia holding me when I was only days old, and even then you could see in her embrace a protectiveness, a shelter that she felt she was put on the Earth to provide for me. Mama always said, "She never wanted to leave your side." And she never did. While Penny, who would argue with a fence post just to make sure she won, was picking fights with Daddy, and Elizabeth, the beauty queen, was ironing her gown for the next cotillion, Georgia was making sure I got to my dentist and doctor appointments.

Georgia had chosen one of the few available careers for a woman in the 1950s—bank teller, and steadily worked her way up until she was the bank's de facto president. But the actual job and its handsome salary went to one of the men she had hired and trained years before. If the blatant sexism bothered her, she never showed it, at least not to me. She had married her husband, Bobby, right out of high school, had one son, and lived in a series of houses our father built for them around Waynesboro. Over the years, she filled in the gaps in my life that Mama was incapable of filling because of her drinking. It was Georgia who went over my report cards and made sure all of my assignments were in on time. It was Bobby who taught me how to swim and ride a bike and hook a worm and swing a golf club. It was to their house that I often ran when Mama and Daddy's fights dragged on and night began to fall. And after our mother's windshield-shattering rampage, it was Georgia who spent most of the night pulling the shards of glass out of our father's skin with her eyebrow tweezers. She plucked them one by one while he sat on a stool in her kitchen in his boxer shorts and a white tank top, wincing as every shard dropped with a *plink* into a bowl on the counter. He looked like he had the measles with a hundred tiny nicks in his face, arms, and neck. Watching the scene from the corner of the kitchen, my eight-year-old's instinct was to giggle, but I wisely held my laughter.

Daddy refused to go to the hospital because he knew the whole town would be talking if word got out, and he just plain hated doctors. So he had his daughter spend all night pulling the glass out of his skin.

Rather than explain to Georgia or my other sisters, who hovered nearby in the kitchen, why the college girl was in his lap in the first place, he ranted on about Mama's being "a c-c-c-crazy, drunk lunatic who could have k-k-k-killed me! Hell, she *wanted* t-t-t-to kill me! She needs to be locked up! G-G-G-GODdamn fool drunk." He kept it up until Georgia told him to "hold still."

At some point in the night, Mama somehow found her way back home. She was a damn good driver, even when she was drunk. Miraculously, she managed to avoid getting in a serious wreck, although her cars always looked the worse for wear with the dings and dents and scrapes of her many fender benders. Daddy always knew she'd been on a wild ride when he'd find her car crazy-parked near the back door, grass stuck in its front grille and clumps of mud puddled underneath.

In the morning, Georgia came over to the farm to make sure Mama got herself out of bed and ready for the day. Then she walked into the kitchen where Daddy sat sullin' up over his coffee with his face and arms covered in tiny bloody scratches and scabs.

"Daddy, Tena can't continue dealing with all this crazy stuff," Georgia said, wishing she could say more, *wishing* she could insist that I move in with her and Bobby and once and for all get out of the house and away from the insanity of our parents' dysfunction. But she knew she could never say those words and make those demands because they would never, *ever* fly with Daddy. Instead, she said, "It's too much for a little girl."

He was silent for a few minutes while she stood in front of him, waiting. Then he lit a cigarette, exhaled a puff of smoke toward the ceiling, and looked at my sister with unflinching eyes.

"Let it be, Georgia," he said. "You know your m-m-m-mama's crazy. I didn't do n-n-n-nuthin'."

After Daddy had gone to work, Mama finally got herself into the kitchen.

"Mama! You nearly killed Daddy last night!" Georgia said.

Mama looked at her, her eyes furrowing in consternation.

"You mean to tell me that sonofabitch is still alive?" she

said. Truly angry and disappointed, she reached for a bottle in the cupboard and poured herself her first drink of the day.

Mama did most of her drinking alone. She had to, because except for some wild times Daddy had with Mister James when he was younger, he was never much of a drinker. Maybe it was living with a drunk. Maybe it was because he never wanted to lose control. Maybe it was that he came from a family of teetotalers—not one single drunk in the lot, which is saying something for any family, particularly one in the Deep South. Whatever the reason, he would spend an entire night out at a club in New Orleans or at their friends' dinner parties, nursing just one whiskey sour on the rare evenings when he drank at all.

So when she needed company, my mother found drinking buddies elsewhere. Sometimes when I came home, Mama would be entertaining—not one of her lady friends from church or one of Daddy's business partners' wives, but Beulah Mae, who'd stop in on her way home from Georgia's to sit a spell with Mama. They'd be at the kitchen table, each with a tall glass of what looked like sweet tea or ice water but without the ice, laughing and slapping their thighs, telling stories. Sometimes Beulah Mae would just be listening and Mama would be talking, low and steady. My mother seemed almost happy those afternoons sitting and sipping with Beulah Mae, and seeing Mama happy in the afternoons was a rare thing indeed.

If Virgie was a stand-in mama, Beulah Mae was a raucous

and crazy aunt, the kind of crazy aunt who would never end up in an institution and yet perhaps shouldn't be allowed to run around entirely free-range either. Most days, Virgie would pay Beulah Mae twenty-five cents for a ride from Hiwannee to Waynesboro and back. Beulah Mae had a license and a car, one of the few black folks who did in those days, but that was about where her ability to drive a car ended. More days than not, Virgie would stumble out of Beulah Mae's car, shaking from head to toe in both fear and rage.

"That crazy fool almos' kilt us!" Virgie would exclaim, as Beulah Mae sat behind the wheel laughing. "She done drive right down the ditch and out t' other side with cars comin' straight fo' us," Virgie would cry out. "I done say my prayers this mo'nin, I did!"

Beulah Mae and Virgie were the original *Odd Couple*. Where Virgie was quiet and reserved, Beulah Mae was loud and profane. Where Virgie barely opened her mouth, Beulah Mae would peel back her lips, revealing the gold of her capped teeth, and hiss, "I'm gonna git me some moonshine tonight and go honky tonkin'." Where Virgie quietly hummed gospel hymns as she worked, Beulah Mae could scare the crows out the trees with her rendition of Ray Charles's "Hit the Road Jack." Where I never once saw Virgie take so much as a sip of liquor, Beulah Mae would upend the Ball jar of clear moonshine whiskey to her lips and empty it down to the last drop. And where Virgie's laughter was rare and guarded, Beulah Mae's guffaw could be heard from Georgia's house clear across the road. They were the best of friends.

But most of the time, Virgie didn't approve of Beulah

Mae's behavior. One afternoon, after Beulah Mae and Mama had shared their tall glasses of whiskey, I heard Virgie scold Beulah Mae as the two of them were getting in her car for the ride back to Hiwannee.

"Yo' doin' Miss Vivian no favors, givin' 'er reason t' drink the afternoon away," Virgie said, shaking her head and clucking her tongue.

"She sho don't be needin' no reason t' gettin' liquored up, you knows that!" Beulah Mae shot back.

"You sho ain't helpin' matters any, s'all I sayin'. Gettin' to be so she be drinkin' all day now. Last thing that po' lady need is somebody drinkin' with her! Miss Vivian's a good woman, she just be so sad all the time."

Virgie got in the car and shook her head with her arms crossed tight in front of her, muttering, "M-m-m. No good a'tall."

Chapter Ten

While Mama drank and sang along to her records in her room, I played. The best days were when Miss Catherine would drop Burke off for the day and he and I would ride around the farm on my horses for hours, both of us bareback and topless, wearing only shorts, exploring the rolling fields and hunting field mice and rabbits. I imagined myself another Little Joe from *Bonanza*, looking just as handsome and brave on the open plains. I relegated Burke to playing Hoss, which he accepted with his usual sweet deference. We turned the hay fields and ponds into a magical world of cowboys and Indians, soldiers and invading armies, trappers and wild bears. But what the magical kingdom and old Western forts never had were any damsels in distress or squaws. Burke and I always were a team of two, two *boys* against the world.

To say I was "confused" about my sexuality would be inaccurate. In fact, I was never confused. I simply never thought of myself as a girl. I thought of myself as a boy. Biologically, I *knew* I was a girl, with all the female body parts, but I never *considered* myself one. While the adults around me commented on "how positively *darlin'*" it was that I preferred to wear cowboy boots and overalls instead of dressing like other little girls in their crinoline and pin curls, I never gave it a second thought. I belonged in a dress as much as a grizzly belongs in high heels.

Mama and Daddy didn't know what to make of my rejection of girlish pursuits and the dresses my sisters favored, beyond labeling me the family tomboy, and assuring themselves and everyone else that "she'll grow out of it, 'ventually." Years later, when I watched the film *To Kill a Mockingbird,* I saw Scout and nearly wept with recognition. It was like I was watching a version of myself on screen. "That's me," I whispered.

That said, my parents tried like hell to move me along from my tomboy "phase," always buying me the frilliest dresses and Little Bo Peep hats and propping me up like a mini mannequin for pageants and pictures. They even involved my sister Elizabeth, who tried to teach me how to do the runway model walk and turn in my Easter bonnet and dress for the camera. I tried to mimic her strut, but I kept looking up to her as if to say: *Ya 'bout done with this nonsense so I can get back to the jungle gym?*

Once, and only once, Daddy hired a fancy photographer to come to the house to take my picture. He wanted me to pose with a toy Texaco oil truck for an ad in the company's annual stockholders' report, and Mama had chosen a dress so big and so stiff the skirt stood up on its own. Kicking and screaming, I was finally wrestled into the dress, its collar scratching against my throat and the crinoline slip making my legs itch. Begging to have a quick pee while the photographer got his lights set up, I grabbed one of Daddy's cigarette lighters, buried it in the folds of the skirt, and ran into the bathroom. Behind the closed bathroom door, I ripped off the dress, opened the linen drawers, which were built into the wall, and with one hand holding the dress, climbed up into my favorite hiding place—the deep top-shelf cupboard above the drawers. It always felt like a fort, where I would imagine myself guarding against the invading Indian tribes. Once settled, I flicked the lighter at the dress until a tiny flame took hold of the stiff material. As I watched, the flame slowly began melting the ugly pink sateen, and as it did, the noxious smoke got thicker and thicker.

"Why do I smell G-G-G-GODdamn smoke?" Daddy yelled as I heard his heavy shoes run toward the bathroom. "What in hell's g-g-goin' on in there?"

Suddenly the cupboard door opened, and there I was sitting with the smoldering dress and the cigarette lighter still in my hand. Without a word, Daddy grabbed me with one arm and threw me over his hip and grabbed the dress with his other arm and threw it in the tub, turning on the water to douse the flames.

Another dress soon replaced the ruined one, and while I didn't try to burn it, I ignored it nonetheless. I just wanted to wear what the boys did so I could climb over fences and jump on horses and scramble up trees.

Aunt Clifford, Mama's sister who had freed her from under the bus years before, would watch me come in from playing, my overalls half-undone, my feet and chest bare and dusty, and my hair a tangle of burrs and curls, and exclaim, "Well, my Lord, Tena! You're just a born tomboy! You know, sugar, since you really want to be a boy so much, if you can kiss your elbow, you'll turn into one!" And she'd snap her fingers. "Just like that!" Little did she know she started a years-long struggle I waged against my upper arm bone, pushing my elbow back while craning my neck and lips forward, trying trying *trying* to connect the two. Although I came close a couple of times, I very much remained, to my dismay, a girl.

Then one day it all became very clear to me. My sister Elizabeth came home with one of her girlfriends from a high school football game in which they were both majorettes. Elizabeth's friend was a tall beauty with white-blond hair halfway down her back. She had long, bare legs that disappeared into an emerald-green sequined leotard and wore white tasseled boots. I looked up from where I sat on the floor playing with my Lincoln Logs, dazed and transfixed. She was the most beautiful creature I had ever seen. Not yet aware of sex or sexuality, I nonetheless knew I wanted to spend the rest of my life with this goddess, or one just like her.

Right then and there I knew I didn't want to *be* a majorette, I wanted to *marry* one. I was six years old.

After that first sighting of the majorette, I suddenly became more aware of girls and women around me, particularly those who, like me, didn't quite fit in. Whenever I drove with Mama or Daddy into town, I hoped we might stop at Cotton Drugstore. Two women ran the store and they were like nobody else in town, mostly because they weren't married and they lived, not with their parents or crazy kinfolk, but with each other. Like roommates, I guessed. One day I asked Daddy about them and he told me they were "Spinsters, old maids, because they never got married."

"Why not, Daddy? Why didn't they get married?" *Women*

had to get married. Didn't they? I didn't know any respectable woman who hadn't.

"Don't ask so m-m-many questions," Daddy said.

"Yes sir," I said.

When I asked Mama, she laughed.

"Oh, your daddy just means they're lesbians. That's when two girls like each other and live together," Mama said. Then, quickly: "But it's a sin. Leviticus, chapter twenty, verse thirteen." She quoted by heart, *"If a man has sexual relations with a man, both have done what is detestable and they are to be put to death. Their blood will be on their own heads . . .* So there you have it. Don't you be hangin' around their store."

Too late. I was hooked, and whenever I came up with an excuse, I would go to Cotton's and pretend I was taking my time choosing a comic book or a candy bar while I peeked around the corner to gaze at these exotic creatures who never got married and liked *each other* instead of men: *lezbeins.*

Chapter Eleven

While I daydreamed of these mysterious women and what it could possibly mean that they could live with, maybe even love, other women, life around me at the farm continued to disintegrate. Mama was downright miserable and took to calling the house "Vivian's Folly," because Daddy built it thinking it would make her happy. But really, he built it to give her something to do besides chase him around town with her .38 Colt.

She tried her best to love the house and had put her heart and soul into making it a showplace of ornate wrought iron grillwork, designer chandeliers, custom-made grass wallpaper, French Provincial furniture, and a painted mural of an antebellum plantation, right down to the Greek Revival mansion and oak trees draped in Spanish moss. Mama also loved the color pink and made sure she was surrounded by it: imported pink slate from Italy for the patio, pink wool carpeting and matching pink walls in the bedrooms, and half a mile of baby pink rose bushes lining the length of our long U-shaped driveway. But the big house and the fancy grillwork and the Italian slate patio hadn't worked to lessen Mama's sadness. Often, when I came in from playing in the fields, I'd find her just sitting, listening to Nat King Cole, reading her Bible or staring out the window, at what I didn't know. I'd crawl up into her lap, put my arms around her, and lay my head against her chest, and we'd sit there in silence. I felt as though, if I hugged her hard enough, I could melt away all her hurt. But that hadn't worked either.

It didn't help Mama or the marriage when Big Papa moved in with us for a spell after Big Mama died. Always a mean old cuss, he got downright ugly in old age, peeing in the corner of the guest room like a dog marking his yard, rather than bothering to walk down the hall to the bathroom. But we had it easy. He stayed for a spell with each of his daughters, and in Aunt Mary's home he took to defecating into a sock and twirling it around the room, flinging his shit all over the walls, furniture, and brand-new, purple, wall-to-wall carpet, which she and her husband had saved for years to afford.

But mean, crazy, or both, Big Papa sure did love me and I loved him right back. He generously bestowed his rare hugs and smiles on his youngest grandchild and took me for rides around town. One hot and muggy afternoon, we saw an old black man walking along the side of the road, his shirt soaked to his skin and his face shiny with sweat. Big Papa slowed the car and leaned out the window.

"Hey, boy," Big Papa said, "ya tired of walkin'?"

The old man stopped, took off his hat, and bowed slightly.

"Well, yessir, I am, I rightly am."

"Well then, ya bes' git to runnin', nigger!" Big Papa said, throwing his head back and laughing as he hit the gas pedal, sending dirt and pebbles flying into the old man's face.

I turned in my seat, looking back as the man wiped the

dirt from his face with a clean white handkerchief. I didn't
say a word, and driving away in the car, I felt the shame of Big
Papa's cruelty as if it were my own. And maybe in my silence,
it was, even if I was only eight years old.

Big Papa died in March of 1963, but his leaving the house
didn't improve my parents' marriage. It was a good thing we
lived way out in the country, because they didn't just fight:
they *brawled*. Hands and fists and feet and hair and nails were
all mixed up as they went at each other, Mama screaming
drunk and Daddy playing defense and trying to keep her away
from one of her guns. Eventually she'd find her pistol or a
shotgun, and then he'd have to wrestle her to the floor, where
they'd roll around and around like something out of a bar-
room fight on *Gunsmoke*, while she screamed about how she
was "gonna kill his cheatin' ass!" And he'd scream that she was
"just p-p-plum crazy drunk! Nothing was g-g-goin' on!"

As soon as they started rolling around, I knew I had a job:
dodge their wrestling bodies and grab the gun out of Mama's
hands before she got a shot off. Then I would run, throw it in
the swimming pool, and call Georgia.

"Mama's drunk and the gun's in the pool again!"

Georgia and Bobby always came in minutes, picked Mama
up off the floor, and got her to bed with ice packs on her
bruises. Sometimes the bruises were so bad that the doctor
was called and I knew to tell him that Mama had slipped in
my puppy's pee, once again.

"My, my, Miss Tena. Haven't you housetrained that pup
yet?" was all he'd say.

Sometimes the fights didn't involve guns and my parents

would just scream at each other until they were hoarse. Those times, I would see Virgie's lips tighten to a thin line and her head move back and forth so slowly and so subtly it was easy to miss. Then she would take my hand and say, "Come on, baby girl, let's you and me go out and see if Frank be lonely out there in the barn all by hisself."

Before my sisters married and moved out, Daddy and Penny would get after it. Mama always said they were like oil and water, but I think they were more like gasoline and fire: they just set each other off. They were also very much alike, in all the wrong ways. Like Daddy, Penny was short, probably only about five feet one inch, and she also had his big personality and a mouth to match it. She never minced words, especially when she probably should have.

Daddy would tell her there was "no way in hell" she was going to date some boy or another, and next thing you knew she'd be headed out the door to meet that very boy. One Sunday, when we were having dinner after church, we heard a faint honk from the end of our long driveway. Penny got up and grabbed her purse.

"Where the hell d-d-do you think you're g-g-goin'?" Daddy asked.

"*Mr. Clark*," she said, her voice dangerously mocking, "I have a date with Jack LaRue."

"I t-t-told you I don't want you anywhere near that b-b-boy!" Daddy yelled, his fork pointed up to her face.

For whatever reason, my sister never saw, or perhaps didn't care, that Daddy's anger could become blind rage with the flick of a switch.

"Well, *Mr. Clark*, I can go out with anyone I please."

Daddy was on his feet so fast his chair tipped over behind him and he had her by the hair before it landed on the floor.

The house blew up.

"Girls, grab Tena and your dinner plates!" Mama yelled to Georgia and Elizabeth. "Get in the bathroom and lock the door!" I think it was less for our protection than for keeping us from seeing our father beat our sister to within an inch of her life.

Just before we stumbled down the hall with our dinner plates, I looked back and saw Mama trying to pull Daddy off Penny. While he held Mama off with one arm, he kicked Penny where she lay on the floor, his sharp wingtip dress shoes hitting her stomach with a sickening *thud thud thud*. From behind the bathroom door, Georgia, Elizabeth, and I cried and listened as glass broke and Penny screamed and Mama threatened to kill Daddy if he didn't stop. Later, Mama said she didn't think Penny would ever be able to have a baby, because he'd kicked her that hard.

Even with his vicious beating, Penny wasn't cowed. A few weeks after Daddy kicked the tar out of her, she walked through the kitchen loudly popping her gum. Daddy sat on the couch reading the *Clarion-Ledger*.

"S-s-spit out that gum, right now!" he yelled. "You know I hate it when you p-p-pop gum. Makes you sound like an ignorant hillbilly."

Mama watched nervously from her chair. "Come on now, Penny. Spit out the gum. You know your daddy doesn't like it."

Penny ignored her. She looked at Daddy, blew a large bubble, bent toward him, and popped it right in his face. Still eye-balling him, she grabbed his feet from the coffee table where they rested, and jerked them off the table in a move so swift and strong, he was knocked clear off the sofa onto the floor, his butt hitting the rug with a thump.

He was off the floor and on her so fast Mama didn't have time to get us in the bathroom. Again, he beat and kicked her hard enough to leave bruises from her belly to her shins.

I think my father hated my sister until the day he died. He sure acted as if he did, and really, what was the difference? Cruelty was cruelty and Penny suffered more than her share. Even getting married and moving out of the house didn't spare her his scorn. After she had children, she was never able to lose the baby weight. She would diet and fail, diet and fail, until her weight ballooned to obesity and it began to take a real toll on her health in the form of hypertension and diabetes.

Daddy was far from sympathetic.

"Look at you. You're d-d-d-disgusting," he said after her second baby had left her nearly fifty pounds overweight.

Although it must have hurt her to her core, she didn't ap-pear to give a shit and continued to goad him. We'd all make a date for lunch with Daddy at his restaurant at the motel, and she'd walk in in one of her muumuus, cheap rubber flip-flops, and her hair in pink sponge rollers. Here the rest of us were all dressed in our finest, and Daddy in his sports coat, pressed trousers, and fedora, and she looked like she'd dressed her-self from the Salvation Army. Which, come to think of it, she probably had. Lord, how that woman loved a bargain! She'd smile her devilish smile at us and plunk herself down in the booth, as Daddy cringed with embarrassment.

If there was one thing Lamar Clark couldn't abide, it was people who didn't toe his line. And Penny's fatal error was in never caring he even had one. I secretly admired my big sister for that; she just didn't give a shit.

Chapter Twelve

Throughout the last couple of years of their marriage, between about 1962 and 1963, and as Mama's drinking escalated, my parents' fights got downright dangerous. I would be playing in my room or the den and hear the voices rising behind their closed bedroom door and know it was about to blow. As quick as I could, I would gather my dogs and take off, just to get outside and away from the violence of their anger. I never wanted to come back in. But eventually the argument would die down as Mama tired, like a wild horse being broken. Her rage would ebb and flow until it petered out or she fell asleep. As violent as their fights were, with Mama landing punch after punch on Daddy as he covered his face with one arm and tried to subdue her with the other, I never once saw Daddy hit her back, or even try to. His sense of honor, while it allowed him to screw around on her at every opportunity, did not allow him to strike her. Ever. I don't know why he didn't hold that same sense of honor for Penny. I also think he was afraid of her, and wisely so. When she was drunk, she was six feet of pure, uncontained fury.

One night, Daddy came home from work and saw that

Mama had had a long day of drinking. Even when she was sober, Mama never cooked much, besides macaroni and cheese or onions and eggs. So on the nights when she was too drunk to go out to dinner, Daddy cooked. Well, "cook" might be too strong a word for what he did. He kept a stack of T-bone steaks in the freezer and would take two out, put them frozen solid in a cast-iron skillet turned up high—no butter or seasoning or anything—put a rock on the pan's lid, and let them cook through until they were charred black and tough as rawhide. Eating dinner took some time because every bite had to be chewed until your jaw ached before the meat was soft enough to swallow. His other "specialty" was corn bread with jam and butter. He baked the bread in the same cast-iron skillet in the oven, then cut the loaf in half lengthwise, filled the middle with blackberry jam and butter, put the halves back together, and then sliced it onto the plate. That was dinner.

While he waited for the steaks or corn bread to cook, he'd often pull an apple out of the fridge and a spoon from the drawer.

"Feel like a little snack, Monkey Joe?" he'd ask.

I'd jump up and sit next to him at the counter. He'd cut the apple in half and with the spoon scrape off a thin layer of the pulp and feed it to me, like a baby in a high chair. Spoonful by spoonful, he'd scoop out the apple, creating instant apple-sauce, until it was just the peel in his hand.

On one of the nights Mama was too drunk to go out to dinner and as I ate the last of the apple off Daddy's spoon, she appeared in the kitchen doorway.

She wore a long, flowing pink negligee with matching slippers and a robe with fluffy pink cuffs and collar. In her left hand was a bottle of whiskey. In the right was her long-barreled, pearl-handled Colt .38. Towering over him, she raised it at my father, its barrel shaking precariously as she tried to focus her eyes. Daddy, looking down at the steaks in the pan, hadn't heard her coming.

"I can smell that little whore on you from here, Lamar," she said, her words slurring, the gun swinging.

Daddy slowly turned, saw the gun, saw me sitting on the other side of the counter, and looked at her.

"Vivian, you just c-c-c-calm down and give me that gun. Tena Rix, you g-g-git over here, right now. Everybody j-j-just calm down."

I slowly slid out of my chair and walked around the counter. As soon as he could reach me, Daddy gave me a shove into the cubbyhole under the counter where we stored the garbage can.

"You s-s-stay right there, Monkey, while I c-c-calm your mama down."

I crouched in the crowded space and listened to the furor above me. All I could see of Daddy was his legs as he slowly inched toward Mama.

"Vivian, baby, c-c-come on now—" Daddy began, but Mama would have none of it.

"You sonofabitch, I know where you've been. I can *smell* her."

"You are p-p-plum crazy. I been working late, that's all."

"Shut UP!" Mama yelled.

Daddy lunged for the gun and the two of them began wrestling like they were in a ring, Mama throwing punches with one arm while the other swung the gun at him with a vicious power, occasionally making contact with his arm or chest or head with a terrible thud. Eventually she tired, and Daddy pinned her down on the floor.

"Tena," he yelled, "grab the gun and go throw it in the pool!"

I jumped out from my hiding place, came around the counter, and saw them entangled on the floor, Mama's legs still kicking and her pretty nightie and robe all tangled up high on her thighs, Daddy's suit coat nearly pulled off his arms. Both of them had ahold of Mama's gun, and it waved above them. Ducking from the barrel's direct line, I got a grip on the stock and pulled it from their hands. I held the gun out in front of me like a dead mouse by the tail, hurried out the back door, and threw it into the swimming pool. When I ran back into the house, Mama was on the floor weeping into her hands, and Daddy was standing at the kitchen wall phone calling Georgia to come help get her to bed.

One day, after a particularly wild fight the night before, I came in from riding Frank around the farm to find the house eerily quiet.

"Mama?" I called out. "Virgie?" I walked from room to room, but the house was empty. Down the long, dark hallway at the center of the house, all of the bedroom doors were open, except Mama's. I tried to open the door, but it was locked.

"Mama? You in there?" I jiggled the handle, but it was locked firm.

Suddenly, Elizabeth appeared. Lately she'd started coming by the house on a more regular basis to check in on our mother. Constantly compared to Elizabeth Taylor and Gina Lollobrigida, right down to a trademark mole on her cheek,

Elizabeth was by far the prettiest of us Clark girls, and at five feet ten inches, the tallest. She was the girl every other girl wanted to be and the girl every boy wanted to be with. Having been the baby in the family for eleven years, I think she felt somewhat usurped when I suddenly appeared, and I'm not sure she ever forgave me for it.

"What's going on? Why you hollerin'?" she asked, impatient and bothered by the noise of my yelling.

I didn't even realize that I had started screaming for Mama to open the door.

"The door's locked and I think Mama's in there."

From behind the door, we heard Ray Charles's song "Born to Lose" playing:

> Born to lose, I've lived my life in vain.
> Every dream has only brought me pain.

Elizabeth tried the door, banging on it harder and harder with her fist.

"Mama! Mama! I can hear you in there," Elizabeth said. "You open up this door! Right now, ya hear?! Come on, Mama. Please open the door."

There was no answer. Elizabeth reached up and pulled a bobby pin out of her hair, unfolding it as she knelt down in front of the door. Her hands shook as she poked the pin into the hole on the doorknob. After a few stabs we heard the click of the lock.

Mama lay on her back on the bed, dressed in her favorite pink negligee and matching robe with long ribbons that went from her collarbone to the floor. Her arms were spread wide, like Jesus on the cross, and her eyes were shut. She looked like an angel. A sleeping angel. Then I saw the blood dripping from both her wrists and I knew she wasn't sleeping.

Elizabeth screamed and jumped into action, grabbing towels from the bathroom. I stood stock-still, looking at my beautiful, tragic mama, wondering if she was alive or dead.

Instead of calling the police, or an ambulance, Elizabeth wrapped Mama's wrists and called Daddy and Georgia, who came within minutes. They loaded Mama into Georgia's backseat and drove her to the hospital's private entrance, in order to avoid the town gossip of a visit to the emergency room. I remained at home with Virgie, and waited to learn whether my mother had died.

When Mama returned the next morning, her wrists wrapped in gauze halfway up her forearms, she moved slowly and allowed herself to be led to bed. When she was settled in under the covers, she looked over at me where I stood by the door, wide-eyed and unsure what to do.

"Come here, baby," she said, and I crawled up and nuzzled next to her, careful to avoid the bandages.

"What happened, Mama? You gonna be okay?" I asked.

She scratched my back with her nails, and I allowed myself to relax against her. "I'm fine, baby. I didn't mean to do what I did. I was a little sad, but I'm fine now. Everything's going to be okay, I promise."

I moved in her arms so that I could put my fingers on her back and gently rubbed them around, as she was doing to me, hoping to soothe the hurt away. As I did, I made a silent vow that from that moment on I would take care of Mama forever and keep her safe. It was now my job. She needed me, I could see that now, and I wasn't going to let anything happen to her, ever again.

Soon after Mama's attempted suicide, I started sleepwalking and having terrible nightmares. I would wake up in the middle of the night trembling, my nightgown drenched in sweat. On really bad nights, I'd find myself standing in the swimming pool with Mama and Daddy waist-deep in the water next to me, their pajamas soaked, shaking me awake. Eventually it got so bad that Daddy had to put a lock near the top of the back door so I couldn't reach it and get out. But I still managed to get out, dragging a kitchen chair to the door and unlocking it. Finally, he put a lock on the door that required a key. After that, they'd find me sound asleep and burrowed in the corner of my bedroom, scratching and clawing as I tried to get "out" of whatever cage my dream had locked me in.

In the morning, I'd tell Virgie about my nightmares and she'd push aside the mop she was holding or the bucket she was filling and pull me into her lap, her arms so tight around me I could feel her heart beating.

"My po' baby girl. You's safe now, baby chile. You's safe now. Sho nuf."

Chapter Thirteen

By December of 1963, Mama had finally had enough and left Daddy for good. She at last had realized that she had to get out. If she stayed, she was either going to die by her own hand or wind up in jail for the rest of her life for murdering my father.

At forty-two, she remained strikingly beautiful. I can still see her as she drove away from the farm, the windows open, her black hair whipping out behind her, her long, slender hands firmly on the wheel, her bright red, nail-polished fingers holding an unfiltered Pall Mall, throwing her head back as she exhaled a long plume of smoke into the wind. Commanding and free. I later understood just how miserable my mother was that day, but in her last moments in that house she was also mysterious, magical, and even dangerous, with a power born from having rediscovered her dignity. She squared her shoulders and held her head high as the car disappeared down the driveway.

It would take me years to fully appreciate how incredibly brave she was to walk out on my father. Leaving a husband and a young child in 1963 Mississippi was practically unheard of. And she had no money of her own, no prospects. She knew when she walked out that she was walking out on a pampered life she'd never be able to re-create on her own. Most women who endured difficult marriages—and many of my mother's friends did—simply bore the abuse, suffering in silence behind a mask of smiles. They ran the house and served sweet tea and hosted their bridge clubs and bragged about their husbands' latest triumphs at work or on the golf course. If anyone suspected their torment, they never spoke of it.

But when Mama dared to name her despair and point a finger at her abuser, she did something that was seen as threatening, plain and simple. This was an open act of rebellion against the deeply ingrained mores of the time, and people feared her defiance would expose an entire town's sad secrets by inviting other women to say "no more" to their suffering sad marriages to bad husbands. The last thing Waynesboro wanted was Vivian Clark to become some kind of role model. And if she actually became one, it was only acknowledged behind closed doors.

She moved into a two-room walk-up above the dry cleaners on Waynesboro's main street. As cheap apartments go, it wasn't too bad, although you could hear the dry-cleaning machines working 24/7 and smell their chemicals downstairs.

She could no longer afford to pay Virgie the $7.50 a week that my father paid her. So Mama offered to pay her what she could afford: one dollar, just one day a week. Virgie accepted.

I wish I could tell you that Mama was never happier, finally free of my father's indifference to her pain. But she wasn't. She was still witness to his endless string of female conquests, who paraded through town in their new cars, clothes, and hairdos.

I have to hand it to her: Whenever she did see Daddy around town—at Petty's Cafe or the bank or the post office—Mama always greeted him cordially, by name. But he would turn his head and ignore her, while every patron looked down at their plate as her "Well, hello, Lamar" hung in the air. She'd brought him enormous shame and he was never going to forgive her. No woman in her right mind walked out on a rich, powerful man, and *no one* left Lamar Clark.

One day, a few weeks after she had left, Daddy figured my mother had learned her lesson above the dry cleaners and told me to get in the car. "We're going for a d-d-drive, Monkey Joe. I called your mama and we're going to go g-g-git her and bring her home where she belongs. This has g-g-gone on long enough."

I was delighted. I bounced up and down in the front seat as we drove into town. Mama was coming home.

"I'm only g-g-gonna ask your mama once. If she refuses, th-th-that's it," he said, talking almost to himself, his left arm hanging out the car window, a cigarette between his fingers, his right hand on the wheel. "As far as I'm c-c-concerned, if she doesn't come home *now*, she'll be as g-g-good as dead to me."

I stopped bouncing up and down. Suddenly, I wasn't sure that Daddy wanted her back because he missed her. With a sinking heart I knew he was going to try to *tell* her to come back not because he loved her, but because Lamar Clark always got what he wanted.

We drove up to the dry cleaners and Daddy gave his horn three quick toots. Mama took her time coming down. When I saw her come out of her building, I jumped into the backseat.

Mama opened the car door and got in the front seat. Daddy lit two cigarettes and gave her one, which she accepted, taking a long drag and letting the smoke out slowly. The car filled with their smoke. The concept of secondhand smoke being potentially lethal, especially to children in the car, was still decades away. Sitting in the backseat, I was simply invisible to them. They loved me, but I was invisible.

"N-n-n-now you listen to me, V-V-Vivian," Daddy began. "Enough is enough. It's time for you to come b-b-back home where you b-b-belong." Even with the stutter, Daddy's voice was soft and smooth.

I took a quick glance at Mama to see if she was buying it. She wasn't.

"I'm not coming back unless you stop your screwin' around," Mama said, her own voice strong but sad. "I can't take smelling another woman's perfume on you for one more night, Lamar. And I won't. Never again."

This time Daddy didn't even bother to deny it. He didn't tell her she was crazy, drunk, or that she should stop listening to foolish town gossip.

"Ah, c-c-c-come on, Vivian. I take care of you, give you everything you want. You know m-m-me. It's a habit I can't b-b-b-break, but I've never *loved* anyone but you. Why, I've n-n-n-never had a baby with any of those other women, have I? Only you." He sounded pleased with himself.

I wondered if they remembered I was in the backseat. Even at ten, I knew it was an odd conversation to have with your child within a mile of earshot, never mind inches. I again snuck a peek at my mother. It wasn't going like it was supposed to.

"But I *ain't* gonna s-s-s-stop screwing around, Vivian," he continued. "This is just who I am. C-c-c-come on now, I'm not going to marry any of them! You're the only w-w-w-woman I'll ever love and you just have to get that into your st-st-st-stubborn head!"

Although hardly sweet talk, for Daddy it was a show of his cards and one he would never repeat. He needn't have wasted it on Mama.

"You can go straight to hell, you sonofabitch!" she said as she jumped out of the car and slammed the door with such force the car shook.

"Bye, Mama!" I cried, my fingers spread wide on the window.

She reached out and matched her fingers to mine on the glass. "Aloha, baby," she mouthed to me.

As she stepped back from the door, Daddy put the car in gear.

"GODdamn it!" he spat, and drove away in a squeal of tires, gravel flying in all directions.

I looked out the back window and watched Mama grind out her cigarette beneath the toe of her high heel and slowly walk up the stairs to her apartment.

"Now, you remember this, T-T-T-Tena Rix," Daddy said as we drove back to the farm, his fingers turning white because he was gripping the steering wheel so hard. "You can never, *ever* t-t-trust a woman," he began. "You give 'em everything they c-c-could possibly want, build them the f-f-fanciest house in town, buy them the p-p-p-prettiest clothes and b-b-b-biggest diamonds, and look how they treat you. Like shit, that's how. Don't you *ever* trust a G-G-G-GODdamn woman, and I don't ever want to c-c-catch you thinkin' like one neither!"

By then he was just talking to himself, his words turning into the low mumble of disjointed thoughts he often fell into. In fact, my father did a lot of muttering, a low rumble of incoherent words to an invisible companion. He often sounded like a motorboat idling at the dock before taking off across a lake. And if you interrupted him asking, "What in the world are you saying, Daddy?" he'd jolt out of his "conversation," slap his thigh, and say, "Okay. On to it." So I left Daddy to his ramblings and turned to look out the window at the passing fields, thinking about Mama back in her little apartment above the dry cleaners, lighting a cigarette and pouring a drink.

In a matter of just a few weeks, my mother and father became the first couple I ever knew to divorce in Waynesboro, maybe in all of Wayne County, Mississippi. The judge turned out to be a cousin of Daddy's, so the paperwork was rushed through in record time. I don't know how my wealthy father who bought new cars more often than most people changed their oil, came up with the figure, but somehow he agreed to pay Mama $150 a month in alimony. People in Waynesboro were scandalized. The richest man in town was throwing mere scraps at the mother of his four children. But as bad as it was, it could have been worse. Just months before my parents' divorce, a man in Calhoun County, Mississippi, petitioned the courts to reduce his alimony payment from $10 a week to $10 *a month*, and *won*. Daddy's alimony, while only a pittance of what he could afford, just barely covered Mama's rent over the dry cleaners, food, gas, cigarettes, and of course, whiskey.

As only a child would think, I imagined she left *because* of me, not in spite of me. Otherwise, why wouldn't she take me with her? I wouldn't learn until years after her death that she sold every piece of her jewelry, most of her furs, even two Japanese porcelain lamps she cherished, to pay lawyers in an attempt to gain my custody. But Daddy had more money and more power, and he made sure she lost her case while spending every dime she had. I'm not sure he wanted me, necessarily. He just didn't want her to win.

Chapter Fourteen

With my mother out of the house and my father preoccupied with work and whatever new lady friend he had on
his arm, I spent a lot of time alone and grew up fast. I had to.
But I was still a ten-year-old child at heart looking for adventure, and I found plenty on the farm—from riding poor Frank
right through the newly tarred driveway, where he got stuck
solid up to his fetlocks, to shooting just about anything that
moved with my BB gun, to all but burning down the barn
when Burke and I were playing cowboys and decided to light
a campfire in the hay bales. The days were full of animals and
BB guns and make-believe games.

The nights were another story.

Every evening after Virgie had left for the day and Daddy
and I returned from eating supper in town, I'd begin my
pleading.

"Please, Daddy, don't leave me alone tonight."

"I don't know what you're t-t-talkin' about, Tena," he'd
say. "I was here all night." Or: "I was j-j-just out in the barn."
Or: "I ran a quick errand." Never once did he say: "I'm so
sorry, you're right, I did leave you alone, and I'll never do it

again." He always insisted that "of course" he was with me all night.

But he wasn't. Night after night, I would wake up in the dark and instantly feel the empty house around me. I'd tiptoe to his room and find the bed perfectly made, no sign of Daddy. One night, I went to his room to find him and saw an oddly shaped lump in the bed. Slowly walking over I lifted the covers and found not a sleeping Daddy but two pillows positioned to look like a body.

Spooked by the empty house and the even spookier shape of the pillows under the covers, I ran to the kitchen, grabbed the biggest knife I could find from the drawer, tucked my nightie into my step-ins, and ran barefoot across a football-size field to Elizabeth's house.

Every night I begged him not to do it again.

"Daddy, please. Stay home with me, *all night.*"

"You're just a sc-sc-scaredy cat, Monkey Joe, with some k-k-kind of imagination on ya. But okay, I p-p-promise. I'll be right here."

But again that night, and many nights after, I found myself alone in a house that seemed to go on forever with dark shadows and strange noises.

A few months after Mama left, Daddy took me to Disneyland, just the two of us, on a trip he decided would make everything about Mama leaving, and the empty house, and my escalating fears, somehow "okay." I couldn't wait to go, not only for the rides, but also for Daddy's undivided attention. But mostly I was thrilled about going to Disneyland because I knew, just *knew*, that Daddy wouldn't dare leave me alone in a hotel room like he did at home, so I'd be safe for two, maybe three, whole nights.

Daddy suffered through the Matterhorn and It's a Small World, and even 20,000 Leagues Under the Sea, with his hands clenched on the bar in front of the seats, his lips closed tightly across his face. I actually think he was more frightened than bored, but he soldiered on.

That first night, Daddy tucked me into bed, closed the bedroom door, and went into the living room in our suite to have a cigarette. I snuggled into the sheets, sleepy and sure that Daddy would stay close by all night.

But I was wrong.

I awoke and listened for him in the other room. Silence. I got up, opened the bedroom door, and called, "Daddy?"

I was alone in our huge suite at the Disneyland Hotel. Still in my nightgown, I took the empty elevator down to the front desk.

"Excuse me, sir. I can't find my daddy," I told the night manager.

Shaking his head, he came around the desk and took me by the hand.

"Come on, honey, I'll go help you look for him," he said.

We found Daddy by the pool, lighting a woman's cigarette and drinking a whiskey sour.

"Why, I was just on my way up, Tena Rix!" he said.

"Don't you think, sir, that your little girl is too young to be left alone in the room? She was very frightened," the night manager said, his voice respectful, but he scolded Daddy in a way few did.

"I haven't been gone five minutes!" he said, jumping out of his chair. "I just came down to grab a smoke."

At least my father had the decency to blush. It wasn't until years later that I learned that Daddy shared, if not my terror, at least some of my worry about the evils that lurk in the night: He bought the only kidnap and ransom policy Mister James, Burke's dad and our insurance salesman, ever sold.

Even with Mama out of my day-to-day life, she still tried to do what normal mothers did: She drove me to doctors' appointments, took me shopping, and on Thursdays, picked me up from school. Well, at least that was her intention, but, more times than not, I was left sitting on the curb for what was sometimes hours, waiting.

One hot and muggy afternoon in April, I waited in air thick enough to chew, sitting on a curb that burned my butt through my thin cotton dress. Behind me, everyone left the school—first the other kids, then the teachers, then the principal. Finally, the last person to leave, the janitor, stood behind me, jangling his keys.

"Your mama comin', Miss Tena, or is that boy who works for your daddy fetchin' you today?"

"Yes, sir, Mama's comin', she's just late, s'all."

I put my head down pretending to read, hoping he wouldn't ask me any more questions. "She's always late," I whispered into my collar.

"You sure she's comin', then?" he asked, sounding not at all sure.

"Yes, sir. She told me she might be a little late cuz she's gettin' her hair done."

That seemed to satisfy him, and he locked the big double glass doors and moved toward his car.

"Okay, then, I'll be headin' on home. See y'all tomorrow, Miss Tena."

"Yes, sir." I waved in his general direction, still pretending like my book was the most fascinating read of my life.

As he drove away, I looked down the road, willing Mama's yellow Cadillac to appear around the bend. It didn't. But then again, I knew it probably wouldn't. It was Thursday, and Thursday was Mama's one day to pick me up from school. Daddy knew she had trouble remembering, so the other four days he had Mayfield do it.

I loved when Mayfield picked me up because not only did I not have to worry that he'd forget me on the curb, we liked the same music and we'd play a game of who could name the song on the radio first. The car would fill with the sounds of Billie Holiday and Nat King Cole and Ray Charles and Ella Fitzgerald and Louis Armstrong and B.B. King and Muddy Waters. Mayfield would wait a few lines, allowing me time to name the song and artist, then together we'd yell it out. He never scolded me for tapping my pencil or fingers on the dashboard, and he would turn the radio up as loud as it would go and we would sing along as we drove through the steamy streets on our way back to the farm. He knew a lot about the music, explaining the difference between rhythm and blues and gospel and jazz and how all the best music was "colored" folks music. I decided right then and there that if I ever got the chance, I wanted to make music just like the "colored" folks did. Those rides with Mayfield made me laugh, and the music would linger in my head for days.

But Thursdays were different, they were Mama's day, so Mayfield wouldn't be coming. And neither, it seemed, would Mama. Not only did she get her hair done every Thursday before she was to pick me up, but it was getting on four o'clock so she'd have been drinking for hours by now. She never forgot her hair appointment, but somehow she nearly always forgot me. I guess getting her hair done was about all she could handle for a day. I just prayed I wouldn't be there 'til suppertime, like I had been once too often.

A few times, after having waited for hours and as the last of the afternoon sun disappeared behind the school, I had to go to Bobby's service station on the fringe of the "colored" part of town, about a fifteen-minute walk along a dark dirt path in the ditch by the side of the road. At least when I got there, I knew I would be greeted by a friendly face and a safe ride to the farm.

On the drive home, I'd beg Bobby not to tell Daddy that Mama hadn't shown up because I knew there'd be a fight. But as soon as Daddy saw the car pull up, he'd know anyway and call Mama, screaming about what a "worthless drunk" she was and "cain't you even remember your own daughter waitin' for you on the curb?" Even with her out of the house and living in her own apartment, there was always a fight. Even, once, when I was being wheeled in for surgery.

It happened after Mama had left, and the house was emptier than normal, so most weekends Daddy let my cousin Rita Faye spend the night with me. One morning, Daddy loaded us into his farm pickup to take Rita Faye back home after a sleepover. It was a cold morning and the roads were slick with ice. As we crossed the first bridge over the river, we all felt the truck swerve, then fishtail over the uneven planks. Rita Faye and I exchanged wide-eyed looks. Unfortunately, Daddy's answer to fearsome road conditions was not moderation and care; he floored it, I guess thinking that the faster we got there, the better. As we crossed the next bridge, the truck went into another spin and before any of us could register the shock, we slammed into and over the guardrail, the front end of the truck hanging precariously above the river, fifty feet below.

I must have blacked out because the next thing I registered was screaming—both Rita Faye's and mine. She was looking at what she thought was a caterpillar on the floor of the truck, but on closer examination she saw that it was actually my eyebrow, which had been torn off. Looking over at me, she saw my head lying in Daddy's straw hat, filling it with blood. I sat up and turned to Rita Faye, who was still screaming. Her nose had been cut wide open between the nostrils and blood streamed from it like a hose. But I was unsympathetic.

"Shut up, Rita Faye! It's just your nose that's cut. Look at me!"

With that, Rita Faye passed out cold.

When we eventually made it to the emergency room, it was filled with irate Atkinson women, all still in their housecoats: my sisters; an assortment of aunts, including my aunt Mary, Rita Faye's mother; and of course, my mother. They were all scream- ing at my daddy, but none so loud as my parents at each other.

Lying there before they sewed twenty-eight stitches into my head, my only thought was, *Please, get me into surgery so I don't have to hear any more of this.*

Chapter Fifteen

Virgie still worked five days a week at the farm, as well as the one day a week she cleaned and did laundry and ironing for Mama. With nine children of her own at home, I don't know where Virgie found the time, or the energy. And, it would take me years to even wonder if her own children resented all the time and love she showered on me when I was little. Why wouldn't they? I can't even imagine Virgie's exhaustion when she finally set foot back in her little house, ten hungry bellies awaiting their dinner, a pile of laundry to wash by hand, and a long line of bodies to bathe and tuck into bed.

It was never discussed or negotiated, but in addition to her other jobs and life, she stepped seamlessly into the role of my caretaker, at least to the extent that she could make me feel safe at home. She was a sanctuary, trying to ease the hurt and pain and neglect caused by my dueling parents.

"You knows they love you, baby girl," she'd tell me, rocking me in her arms. "They does. They jus' got problems, tha's all." And then, as if she'd forgotten I was on her lap, she'd murmur, "My po' lil' baby girl. Dunno what's gonna happen to my baby."

Unlike my mother and father, who were often too preoccupied to bother with me, I could always play with Virgie. Sometimes when I found her bent over the tub, scrubbing the white porcelain with Comet and a rag, I'd sneak up behind her and yell "Boo!" in her ear. Predictably, she jumped, the cheap shiny wig she always wore to work went flying off her head, and the two of us ended up on the floor, holding our bellies with laughter.

On lazy afternoons, when the farm was quiet and the laundry needed hanging out back on the line, Virgie included me in the chore as if it were a holy ritual.

"Come on, baby girl, I gots some laundry need hangin', and I be needin' your help," she'd say, and I would run for the pins, stuffing as many of them as would fit in the tail of my shirt, which I held up like a bowl, and followed behind her out to the line, careful that my bare feet avoided the thorny stickers in the grass. She worked her way through the laundry basket, hanging sheets and shirts, pants and panties, towels and washcloths, piece by piece. As she moved down the line, she would reach down, silently requesting a pin, and I would place one in her hand, like a nurse offering a scalpel to a surgeon, truly believing my task was just as important. Whether it was the quiet of the surrounding fields or the sharing of a simple task or the gentle respect she bestowed on me in asking for my help, those moments remain as dear and sweet as any I have.

But my favorite thing was when Ramey's Rolling Store came rumbling down our road. Like many a rolling store throughout the South, Ramey's was an old school bus that had been painted blue and converted into a mobile grocery store, serving rural Wayne County and selling ice cream, candy, Coca-Cola, soap, flour, and an assortment of other foods and household goods. The tradition of rolling stores serving the outlying regions of the South lived on here and there until late into the twentieth century, but had mostly died out by the 1970s when cars became much more accessible, even to the rural poor.

When Ramey's Rolling Store was about a half mile from the house, it would cross the old bridge over the Chickasawhay River, making a loud *RATTA-TAT-TAT-TAT* as the tires drove over the wooden planks.

"Come on, Virgie! It's almost here!" I'd yell, and run to Daddy's closet to dig for money in his pockets, where I was always guaranteed to find a small fortune in nickels, dimes, even the occasional quarter. Virgie, who would never rifle anyone's pockets, let alone her boss's, would stand by the door.

One time, I spied a large hatbox on the shelf and asked her to take it down for me. When I lifted the lid, I sat back on my heels, wide-eyed. Virgie took one look and collapsed in a heap onto the bed.

"OhmyLordhavemercy!" she said in one breath, her right hand going to her bosom, her left covering her mouth.

In the box were rolls of $100 bills gathered by rubber bands and thrown in randomly, not stacked or organized and definitely not counted, by the look of things. Maybe as many as twenty or thirty rolls, and with the typical roll fitting fifty bills, we were looking at about $150,000, maybe more, in that hatbox on the closet shelf. Lord have mercy, indeed.

"I ain't never seen so much money," Virgie said in what was

surely the understatement of her life. "Didn't know there was that much in the whole world," she said, her eyes only getting larger as she mentally counted the rolls.

I didn't want to admit that I not only knew there was that much money in the world, but that seeing rolls of it stashed in a dusty hatbox neither shocked nor surprised me. I had seen Daddy casually handing out $100 bills my whole life, so part of me figured he had a stash somewhere. Maybe others. Actually, definitely others, and probably even larger than this one. Turns out I was right. Over the years, and whenever stuck for birthday or Christmas presents, he'd give us all cash. One birthday I was handed a $500 bill, on another a $1,000 bill, back when they still printed them. Lord only knows what *those* rolls of bills added up to.

I put the lid back on the box and Virgie replaced it on the shelf, exactly as we had found it, without taking a single bill. A $100 bill was not something I could hand Mr. Ramey without raising a lot of eyebrows. Reaching into a pair of Daddy's nearby pants, I came out with a handful of coins.

"Bingo!" I squealed. "Let's go!"

With my pockets jingling, I ran out to the end of the driveway, desperate not to miss Ramey's bus, while Virgie followed as quickly as her old knees would allow. Jumping up and down at the edge of the driveway like a nervous horse before a race, I watched the bend in the road for signs of the faded blue bus. When it finally appeared, we both waved our hands, yelling for it to stop, as if a crazed white girl and her patient black nanny standing by the side of the empty road could somehow be missed.

"Well, howdy do, Miss Tena, Miss Virgie," Mr. Ramey said, opening the school bus door and tipping his hat. As we clamored aboard, he said, "Whatch'all be having today?"

Virgie still seemed a little stunned from our discovery in the hatbox, so I went about the business of choosing among the peanuts and ice cream and moon pies and Popsicles and strawberry taffy and PayDay and Nutty Buddy and Hershey's candy bars. Once we had settled on a bag of Planters peanuts poured into our ice-cold bottles of Coca-Cola for our treat, we paid Mr. Ramey and walked slowly back to the house, feeling the sweet summer air on our faces and wishing every moment of every day could be so easy. Those times, walking back down the road from our looting of Ramey's Rolling Store, were some of the rare moments when Virgie didn't bow her head in subservience. They were also among the few times when I saw her smile. Otherwise, the only times I saw her smile were for Jack.

Jack was tall, lanky, and thin to the point of being bony. I assumed he was her husband, but I actually had no idea, then or now, if they were ever legally married. I had heard my whole life that "colored folks never bothered getting married." People said it in the same way they said that "coloreds just *loved* to pick cotton and ride in the back of the bus." Whether or not Virgie and Jack were married, they had nine children together, had buried one before he reached the age of fifteen, and raised several of their children's children in a tiny three-room Jim Walter house, a cheap prefab sold by Sears Roebuck for $600, assembled.

Jack never looked me in the eye or even spoke out loud when I was in the room. I realized later his reserve was because of fear, nothing more. Jack didn't have an unkind or rude bone in his body. Virgie always said, "He's just shy," when he wouldn't answer my greeting, "Hey there, Jack!" But he had grown up in a time when black men were routinely beaten or even lynched for speaking "out of turn" to a white girl or woman, and no matter Virgie's place in my heart, he feared crossing that invisible line. Jack worked harder than any man I knew to keep a roof over his family, and on the weekends he liked to sip on his jug of moonshine whiskey and listen to the Yankees play baseball.

Theirs was a house of peace and calm, and although I could never admit it out loud, I often wished I could live there too. When I was at Virgie's house, everything felt calmer, more relaxed. I even breathed easier. I could also be myself, rather than Lamar Clark's daughter. With Virgie, and with Beulah Mae and Aunt Mary's maid, Princie Mae, and Mayfield and all the other black folks in my life, I felt more *me* in my own skin.

Virgie's personality had no extremes. I don't think I ever heard her use the words "love" or "hate," as in, "I love sweet potato pie," or "I hate Mississippi summers." Virgie lived in the gentle middle ground between accommodation and acceptance. And all around her the air felt softer, even kinder. Her children flocked around her like baby ducklings out for a walk, staying close for safety as well as direction. So did I.

I began to take any excuse to go out to Hiwannee and sit in Virgie and Jack's crowded kitchen while she cooked for her brood. Her daughter Cindy was just four years younger than me, and even though there weren't any other white girls in her life or black girls in mine, not in school or in town, Cindy and I became close friends. She was funny and sweet and we got along famously, but sadly, I think she always considered herself a white family's black maid's daughter. There was just no getting around it.

Cindy worked in the same fields that her mother had, earning fifty cents for a day's labor, either picking cotton or peas or digging up potatoes. Like most poor children, black or white, they worked from the time they could walk, sunup to sundown, and were grateful for it. The fields were owned by Van Covington, a good ole Mississippi boy and distant relative from Mama's side of the family, who would sit on his wide porch and watch over his workers, occasionally shouting at one of them, "I can see you, you lazy nigger!" and warning them to "get back to work" before he came out to the field "to git you back to work myself!" Cindy worked the Covington fields full-time from about four years old until she went to school, and then on the weekends and during summer vacations all through her childhood and adolescence.

As much time as her mother spent with me and with my sad, out-of-control family, and as jealous as she was of it, Cindy never let me know. And, rather than resent being given my "poor box" of clothes, as we called hand-me-downs, she appreciated it. In fact, she and her sisters loved that they were the only girls in their one-room school in Hiwannee sporting barely worn Bobbie Brooks pedal pushers and blouses, some with the tags still on. Years later, she said she could still remember the smell of that box of crisp, new Bobbie Brookses. I must have had a lot of clothes I barely or never wore, because between Rita Faye and Cindy and her sisters, there were a lot of girls running around in my discarded clothes and shoes.

It didn't happen very often, but Cindy would occasionally come out to the farm with Virgie in the morning and we'd play all day. She told me that I was the only white girl who ever talked to her, much less played with her. And mine was the only swimming pool she was allowed into, even though she was scared to death of getting in the water because she couldn't swim. Taking a page from Daddy's "trial by fire" training, and I have to confess, with more than a touch of *Dennis the Menace* in my blood, I would push her into the pool, hoping she'd somehow just get the hang of it. But all I did was instill a lifelong fear of swimming in her.

As often as I could, I'd go with Virgie to her Hiwannee Baptist Church. Where I grew up in the South, church, like football and barbeque, is not only religion, it's mandatory and I'd been going to church my whole life. All of us Clark girls were stuffed into our Sunday best and packed into a pew, lined up like dolls on a shelf, piety painted on the faces around me while we listened to the exhortations about damnation and salvation from the pulpit. Even as a girl of eight or nine, I'd look around me and recognize people I'd seen with Mama or Daddy at a party the night before, sometimes drunk, often out by the swimming pool smoking cigarettes and talking about "the nigger problem." I'd look up at the choir ladies in their perfectly pressed white robes and think, *How does that work? You drink all night, gossip all day, and come here and sing about taking "A Closer Walk with Thee" and it's all forgiven?* But if I dared utter a word in question to Mama, she'd answer with a stinging pinch on my arm and a sharp "Hush up!"

I had been baptized in the Methodist Church and later

again in the Southern Baptist Church, after Georgia was finally able to convince Daddy that the Baptists had better youth programs. They also had better baptisms. In the Methodist church, I had been sprinkled, but the Baptists, who didn't recognize the Methodist baptism, gave me the full dunking in a big tub by the altar. Once I was a Baptist, I too would be swept up in the preacher's admonition at the end of the service, "The Lord has put it so strong on my heart, that there is someone out there to be saved, you know who you are! So we'll sing one more stanza of 'Just as I Am,' while you make your way up. He knows who you are and *so do you*. This could be your last chance. Come on now. God is waiting."

I probably went up two or three times a year to be saved, not that I felt any particular shame had to be erased from my soul, but it was nonetheless an intoxicating brew of theater, fear, and faith.

Virgie's Baptist church was different. Not only did I not know the troubled lives of the faces around me, but the main event was not the sermon, although the reverend sure could work up a sweat talking about THE GOOD LORD JESUS! A-*MEN*! It was the music. I didn't care what the hymn was, but the minute I heard the first chords from the upright piano near the altar, I would leap out of my seat, eager for the choir to start in. Soon, the walls and rafters in that small little building would all but bend and creak with the power of those voices. None of the folks needed a hymnal to sing along, and soon neither did I.

Along with the music, I loved the sheer spectacle of Sunday service in Virgie's simple church. Here were folks who struggled to put clothes on their children and food in their bellies, but on Sunday, it was different. On Sunday, these same folks walked down the center aisles in stiff dresses and pressed shirts and pants and clean white gloves and fancy hats— Oh, the hats those ladies wore! Feathers and plumes and veils and eight-inch brims in colors I didn't know existed in hats—fire engine red, emerald green, canary yellow, electric blue, and royal purple. Oh yes, Sunday was the day when all their hardship and poverty, oppression and fear, stayed outside while they praised the Good Lord to the rafters, and thanked that Good Lord for everything they *did* have, not bemoaned what they lacked. I watched it all in wonder, and absorbed the lesson of their gratitude as best I could.

While I was welcomed into Virgie's all-black church, and I considered her part of my family, the racial fears and hatreds roiled around us throughout the South, where schools, churches, stores, buses, lunch counters, bathrooms, water fountains, hospitals, and doctors' offices remained stubbornly segregated. I'd see the separate entrance for COLORED around the back of Dr. Dabbs's office, and even at ten years old thought, *Oh Lord, they think that colored people have different germs? Different blood in their veins? Is there different medicine for them?*

I knew not to ask Daddy about it, that he would just dismiss me with a "Now don't you go thinkin' like a girl, Tena Rix. You know it's just the way it is." So I'd ask Mama what they were thinking with the WHITE/COLORED dividing line drawn through the middle of our town, but she would just echo what Daddy said and what I had heard my whole life: *It's just the way it is, Tena. It's nothin' for you to worry about. Just let it be.*

Then one afternoon it *was* something for me to worry about. Mama was driving me and my girlfriends to our dance class at the famous Mary Alpha studios in Meridian, about an hour north on Highway 45. Her pint bottle of bourbon was tucked discreetly, she thought, under her left thigh, out of sight of the girls in the backseat.

My girlfriends all had on their tutus and ballet slippers, but I loved tap dance and sat in Mama's front seat clicking my shoes together, excited to show the teacher what I'd learned while doing my tapping exercises across the linoleum kitchen floor and driving Virgie half nuts in the process. As we left Waynesboro and started crossing over the Chickasawhay River, we were stopped at a police roadblock.

I shot a sideways glance at Mama, who moved her leg so that the bottle was fully hidden underneath it. I could only pray the police officer didn't lean in the window and get a whiff of Mama's breath.

"Well, what's wrong, officer? Has there been some kind of a wreck?" Mama asked.

So far so good. She didn't even slur "officer." By this time in the day, Mama was usually a good two or three hours into her drinking, so I was relieved she was able to come to a smooth stop and put a concerned look on her face.

"Well, ma'am, you gonna have t' take a dee-tour," the policeman said, pushing his hat back off his forehead and wiping his sweaty brow with a dirty handkerchief. His belly hung over his belt, and I could see sweat stains spreading under his arms and around his collar. "We're draggin' the river, looking for that nigger and those two Jew-boys from up North who are stirrin' up trouble, tryin' to git *our* niggers t' vote. Now them boys've gone missin' and they got us lookin' all over for 'em."

I looked at my two girlfriends in the backseat, but they didn't even seem to notice we'd stopped and continued chatting away and comparing their tutu ruffles. I looked at Mama, who gave me a warning glance. Her unspoken words hung between us: *Don't you make a peep.*

"My Lord! How *awful!*" Mama said, putting the car in gear.

"Well, them folks up North juss don't git it. We's fine down heah," said the officer, adjusting his belly with a great hoist of his belt. "Niggers's happy, we's happy. I guess those fellas shoulda stayed home and minded they own business. They had it comin'. Sho did."

"I s'pose you're right," she said, rolling up the car window. She drove away fast, before I could ask why the men had it coming.

Two weeks later, the bodies of twenty-one-year-old James Chaney, twenty-year-old Andrew Goodman, and twenty-four-year-old Michael Schwerner would be found in an earthen dam, ninety miles north, in Philadelphia, Mississippi. Chaney, a black man from Meridian, Mississippi, had been beaten and shot three times. Goodman of New York City and Schwerner of Pelham, New York, both white, had each been shot once through the heart by the KKK. As a boy, Michael Schwerner had defended a schoolmate of unusually small stature from bullies. That boy was Robert Reich, the future U.S. Secretary of Labor.

Chapter Sixteen

Mama mostly drank alone in her dreary apartment as she watched television and did her crossword puzzles. On the days I would visit, I kept a careful eye on her, making sure the area rugs didn't trip her up, that she had at least a little food in her stomach, and that her cigarette was firmly extinguished after she fell asleep. Some days, she would decide she'd had enough of her four walls, and get in her Cadillac and drive around town drinking. In fact, for all of my mother's insane drunk driving, ironically it was my sober-as-a-church-mouse father who tempted death behind the wheel: In the logging truck that nearly crushed him; in the rollover that nearly took his arm; then when he all but slid off a bridge and came within inches of killing himself, me, and Rita Faye. But Mama? Nothing more than a skinned knee falling *out* of the car once she got to where she was going. Miraculously, she drove as drunk as anyone I ever knew without killing herself in the process. More than once we were nearly killed when she flew over the railroad tracks as the train barreled toward the intersection.

"Mama!" I'd scream.

"Lawd have mercy!" Virgie would gasp from the backseat.

She'd accelerate all the more as the train passed by us so close I could see the eyes of the terrified engineer.

"Mama! It nearly hit us!" I'd say.

She'd put the bottle to her lips and smile. "Nearly, but it didn't."

But what about next time? What if I'm not in the car to warn you? I thought, but said nothing as my constant worry about keeping her safe fluttered through my stomach.

Drunk or sober, Mama always drove as if she were escaping something, like a bank robber jumping in the front seat with the loot and yelling to his cohort to "step on it!" And if she wasn't a safe driver, she was at least a well-practiced drunk one.

Some afternoons she and Aunt Jean would decide to visit their favorite bar in Laurel, thirty miles west on Highway 84. Unlike Waynesboro, in the heart of dry Wayne County, in Laurel you could go to a bar, have a few drinks, and buy a bottle for the ride home. Or, you could also just go to the drive-thru and buy a bottle without leaving your car. On most trips to Laurel, "the Mothers" would drop me and my cousin Michael at the city's largest and legendary music store, where we'd spend hours strumming the bass guitars and pushing the trumpets' and clarinets' finger buttons. One day I wandered over to the drum set, my fingers hesitantly reaching out to feel the taut "skin" of the drumhead nearest me. I had been "drumming" on random surfaces my whole life—crib slats, school desks, concrete sidewalks, fences—but didn't connect my obsessive tapping to any real instrument. Seeing my fascination, the store manager handed me a pair of drumsticks and said, "Go for it, honey. You sure cain't hurt 'em any."

At first shyly, and then with growing confidence, I tapped on the drums. From random *ratta-tats* on the drumhead, I quickly progressed to a more rhythmic beat, until I was lost in the sound, the vibrations coursing through my fingers and arms, and my breath in sync with my hands. Although I was only ten, I knew that whatever that sensation was, I wanted more of it. Soon, I was picking up anything that even faintly resembled a drumstick—pens and pencils, forks and spoons, sticks and fence slats, rulers and letter openers—it didn't matter so long as I could hold them between my fingers like the man at the store had shown me and hit some hard surface. The best part was, unlike my awkward strumming on a guitar or my pitiful honks through a trumpet, my drumming felt like music and the music felt like it was coming straight out of me.

Mama loved that I loved music, like she did, and started taking me with her on her now rare trips to New Orleans. Walking into the Blue Room with her, I realized why she had persisted in those trips all those years, even in the face of Daddy's torment. As we crossed the threshold, the bandleader's face lit up when he saw Mama and he waved to his orchestra to stop the music. Mama and I stood in the doorway and waited. I looked up at her and saw a smile on her face that I hadn't seen in a long, long time. It was simple and pure; it was joy.

"Ladies and gentlemen!" the bandleader boomed. "May I present the talented and beautiful woman who wrote this next song, my dear friend, Mrs. Vivian Clark!" And with that, the band started in on her song, "My Sweet Buzzin' Sea Bee," a simple ditty about a handsome sailor in World War II.

She never made any real money selling her songs, but writing them and hearing them played gave her some of the few rare moments in her life of pride and happiness; more than money could have bought.

After about eight months living above the dry cleaners, Mama couldn't take life in the same small town with Lamar Clark any longer, and she moved herself, first to Laurel for a few months, then to Mobile, Alabama. While I felt some relief that I didn't have to keep as close an eye on her, I had a new worry that she was so far away. Every other weekend, I would take the Trailways bus ninety miles south down Highway 45 to visit her. Daddy would drop me at the station and hand me a crisp $100 bill for "spending money." Mama would tuck the bill away, refusing to use any of it in restaurants. We'd spend the weekend eating frozen TV dinners of stringy Salisbury steak and tasteless chicken potpies and mashed potatoes and green peas. After dinner, I waited for her to pass out on the couch or in bed so I could take her lit cigarette and stub it out in the ashtray before she burned us both to kingdom come.

It had been hard to watch her self-destruct before my eyes, but that decline became a veritable swan dive off a cliff after she moved to Mobile. She had always dressed to the nines in the latest fashions and, even after four babies, her figure was beautiful and well maintained. She had her hair and nails done once a week without fail, and her shoes and handbag always matched. But after she left Mississippi, it was as if she no longer had to appear before judgmental eyes, and she gained weight and started wearing nondescript cheap and shapeless sundresses with elastic straps that would get all kind of bunched up over her now enormous breasts. She also had four or five muumuus she rotated through that became faded and pocked with cigarette burns, and she looked sad and destitute in them. I don't know what happened to her pretty clothes, maybe she sold them, maybe she just didn't fit in them anymore, but she started resembling the run-down, out-of-luck hovels where she lived. All she seemed to care about was drinking.

Whenever I could, I persuaded Virgie to come with me to Mobile, even though I knew she hated to leave the comfort of her small town, where she felt safe and knew where the COLORED bathrooms and drinking fountains were. A misstep in Waynesboro in the mid-1960s could get her verbally reprimanded, maybe slapped, but a misstep outside of Waynesboro could get her beaten, or killed. But even in Waynesboro, when she'd start fiddling and twitching around and I'd ask her if she had to go to the bathroom, she'd shake her head and say no, she'd hold it until we got home, not wanting to use the filthy COLORED bathroom at the Texaco station or the even worse outhouse behind the grocery store. But even knowing her discomfort, I dreaded going to Mobile alone, and I begged her until she gave up and agreed to come with me. Besides, I knew that with Virgie along we'd all have at least one good meal and I would feel safe.

On one visit, after Mama's Bible reading, when it came time for bed, Mama headed to the bedroom and pointed Virgie to the couch.

"No!" I said. "I want Virgie to sleep with us, in the bed. I don't want her on the couch."

Both women looked at me in horror—Mama didn't want to share the bed with Virgie, and Virgie really didn't want to share the bed with the two of us. Not only would it be cause for lynching in some parts of Mississippi *and* Alabama, but both she and Mama were tall, ample women and Mama's bed was only a double, barely a foot wider than a twin.

"I's be fine on the couch," Virgie said, her eyes pleading with me to *stop this nonsense, right now!*

"No, Virgie. I want you to sleep in the real bed, with us."

Mama dragged me into the bathroom.

"You listen to me, Tena Rix. Virgie does not *want* to sleep in my little bed with the two of us, and besides, if your daddy ever hears that she did, there will be hell to pay and you know that."

I knew it. I had seen the people in white hoods walking between the cars in the church parking lot with donation buckets. I had seen how Jack and other black men kept their eyes on the ground when I spoke to them. I knew that if there was a fire and Virgie was found in bed with two white women, *she* would be the one to be dragged out and put on the end of a rope. I knew all of that, but by that time I had put my foot down and I refused to budge.

Ever since I had begun having nightmares after Mama's suicide attempt, and particularly after she left the farm, deep, restful sleep had eluded me—except for this one blessed night in Mobile. While probably neither Mama nor Virgie slept a lick, I fell into a deep-coma sleep of pure peace and safety, nestled between two of the women I loved most in the world, and who loved me right back.

Chapter Seventeen

With Mama in Mobile, Daddy was now fully in charge. Well, "in charge" might be a bit of an exaggeration. Except for his signature T-bone steak or corn bread with blackberry jam and butter, he didn't do much in the way of cooking. Occasionally he'd crumble a handful of saltine crackers into a glass and add milk, which I thought was just about as good a snack as the Good Lord could drum up. On really special occasions he'd make my favorite treat, one his mother had taught him how to make. He'd put a few handfuls of peanuts in an old white T-shirt, twist it into a ball, then smash the peanuts with a hammer. Then he'd mix the crushed peanuts with molasses, pour the whole concoction onto a cookie sheet, and bake it into an out-of-this-world, gooey taffy. That was just about the limits of Daddy's kitchen prowess. But I didn't go hungry: We ate out three meals a day, nearly every day.

Daddy also didn't have the first notion of how to tend to the various grooming demands of a pubescent girl, beginning with my thick mane of hair. His solution was to drop me at Bobbie's Beauty Parlor to have it chopped off. While I was actually thrilled to be rid of its cumbersome upkeep and tendency to get caught in my bicycle tires and the bars of the jungle gym or swing set, Mama took one look at my bob cut to just under my ears and started to cry.

During the week, Daddy dropped me off at school. I'd hop out of the car and quickly slam the door shut because he didn't like to linger at the curb. Actually, he didn't even like to bring the car to a complete stop before tearing off again, so it was best to jump out and away from the car door to avoid being dragged off with it.

"Now you do g-g-g-good, Tena Rix, and I'll see ya for dinner," he'd yell out the window, his hand reaching down to push in the cigarette lighter.

I liked school. Well, at least I liked having a roomful of other kids around. I could have taken or left the lessons, if not some of our teachers.

Mrs. Geraldine Gardner, our sixth- and seventh-grade homeroom and math teacher, had an unfortunate resemblance to the witch in *The Wizard of* Oz, with buckteeth; a long, pinched face; and a sour expression. She also was either dirt poor or just cheap as could be, I never knew which. She'd get her hair cut at the barber because it only cost ten cents, and every day she took home leftover cartons of milk and rolls from the school cafeteria. She was also hell-bent on finding reasons to punish us. She never had children of her own, and I don't even think she cared much for kids. She sure didn't care much for us. Every day at least one of us would be hauled to the front of the class and either paddled on our butts, or forced to put our hands over the edge of her desk so she could rap our knuckles hard with a wooden ruler. One of the worst and most painful indignities was when she forced us to stand in the front of the class with our palms faceup and bent back so she could snap them hard with rubber bands. These were the days before corporal punishment was outlawed in public schools.

While Burke will tell you that Mrs. Gardner was a hell of a math teacher, making it as fun as any subject he ever studied, I don't remember anything positive about her. What I remember is that she always seemed to have a beef with me and would routinely call me out for being fidgety. Like every teacher I had before her, she hated my habit of tapping my pencil on the desk. One day I forgot my pencil case entirely and she made the mistake of teasing me about it.

"What's this? The richest girl in Wayne County can't even afford a pencil!" she taunted. "Look, children, the poor little rich girl doesn't have a pencil!"

I didn't tell Daddy what happened, knowing he was likely to explode and embarrass me. But a few days later, I was home playing with my best friend, Ginger, and before I could stop her she told him, "Mister Lamar, did Tena tell you what Mrs. Gardner said to her the other day?"

Daddy turned to me with a fearsome look. "Tell me now, Tena."

So I did.

He turned to Georgia and said, "If Mrs. Gardner ever does another thing to her, you better tell me, Georgia, 'cause Tena won't." Georgia nodded dutifully. "Yes, sir. I will."

Wouldn't you know it, not three days later Mrs. Gardner caught me tapping my pencil during a test and marched me to the front of the classroom. Our school was designed so that each room had a door that opened to the outside. That day, as a thunder and lightning storm tore through town, Mrs. Gardner took me to that outside door, opened it, and made me stand in the open door's crack for the rest of the class while a hard rain pelted my face and clothes. When I got home, soaked, Daddy'd had enough. A few days later, he was standing in the door of our classroom asking Mrs. Gardner to "step outside, ma'am," so he could have a word.

With my whole class watching through the classroom door, he walked her to the large plate glass at the front of the school. In a voice that echoed down the empty linoleum hallway, he said, "If you ever s-s-say or do another G-G-G-GODdamn thing to my daughter that's hurtful or embarrassing, I will p-p-pick you up and throw your ass through that G-G-G-GODdamn window. Do you hear me?" Daddy always emphasized the "GOD" in his "GODdamns" when he was mad. And he was fire-spitting mad that day. No one was going to ridicule Lamar Clark's little girl. Least of all a witchy-looking woman with a cheap barbershop haircut.

She was dabbing at her eyes when she returned to our classroom. After that, she left me alone, and Burke will tell you I got a bit sassy with her. Yes, I suppose I gave her some lip because I knew she'd never bother me again. Lamar Clark wouldn't have stood for it.

With Mama gone, Virgie was tasked with taking me shopping. But as soon as we entered Bedsole's, Waynesboro's only department store, Virgie froze. Staring at her were four sets of scornful eyes from the clerks on the floor, as if all were demanding, *What do you think you're doing? You can't afford to buy a single thing in here.*

So Daddy took me shopping, usually to Marks Rothenberg, a very upscale department store in Meridian. We'd go to the girls' department and he'd tell me to "pick out whatever you want," and he'd hand a wad of cash to the woman behind the counter.

"Whatever she wants," he told the clerk, "we'll take one in every color. I'll be back in an hour."

That was shopping with Daddy. Christmastime was no better. He'd drop me on the corner of Azalea and Mississippi Drives in downtown Waynesboro, hand me his trademark $100 bill, and say, "Go buy presents for your sisters and your mama, and a fruit basket for Virgie. I'll be back in an hour to pick you up." I stood on the curb, looking at that $100 bill, and thinking, *Some merry Christmas.* And there was something particularly insulting and impersonal about a fruit basket for Virgie, given all that she did for me, and for Mama, and for him. To me, she was family, and family shouldn't get a ridiculous fruit basket at Christmas.

While Daddy and I didn't do much shopping together, I did love going with him to run his errands. My girlfriends were playing with Barbie dolls and dressing up in their mothers' old gowns, but I played Daddy's sidekick. Most mornings we were up before the sun, and Daddy would go out and start the car to get it cool on hot days and warm on cold days before I got in, and then we'd ride into town to have breakfast at Blaine's

Cafe. He'd have eggs, sausage, grits and gravy, and coffee, and I'd have a Coca-Cola and doughnuts. From there he'd drop me at school or, on the weekends, we'd walk across the street to the post office, and I would jump up on the long table by the mailboxes while he opened his mail, tipping his hat and shaking hands with folks as they came through to get their mail.

Daddy's mind went at a fever pitch. Driving around town with him was like being in an episode of *Looney Tunes*, as he'd mumble to himself in a low, incessant hum, sounding like one solid word of mush: "that-som-bitch-better-not-think-he-can-git-away-hmhmhmhm-better-call-Joe-down-at-the-mill-hmhmhmhmhm-gotta-git-that-price-down-before-hmhmhmhmhm . . ." And when he wasn't incoherently mumbling, he'd go into some sort of trance and turn the volume on the car radio all the way up and then back down: "Today IN JACKSON, the Texaco station on HIGHWAY EIGHTY-FOUR reported THAT A MAN was found asleep IN THE STOREROOM . . ." Up and down, up and down, until I'd yell at him to stop.

"Daddy! I can't take it!" I'd shout, and only then would he take his hand away, without apology or acknowledgment that he'd been doing anything out of the ordinary.

"On to it," he'd say, and those three words would somehow clear his head and reset his clock. Then he'd tell me about his latest deal, always bragging that he'd gotten the better end of it because "that sorry sonofabitch doesn't know who he's dealin' with."

Some afternoons, after his errands, we'd go to his office in Waynesboro's only strip mall, which he had built. When we drove up, there'd usually be a line of folks, men and women, black and white, all of them poor, waiting. When they saw his car drive into the parking lot, they'd take off their hats and bow slightly in greeting. When I saw their faces, most of them looked scared and nervous, some even desperate.

"Daddy," I asked him once, "why do those men look so afraid?"

"Cuz it's Friday, and Friday is p-p-payday, and they still don't have enough money to pay the rent and feed their family. I'm their last s-s-stop."

I didn't ask if he would help them; I guess I didn't want to hear that he might not.

"You just remember, Tena Rix, everybody has their p-p-price. Ain't a sonofabitch out there that cain't be bought. Not a one."

Along with "Don't you go thinkin' like a girl" and "Never trust a woman," these were his pearls of wisdom.

On Sunday evenings, after the weekend's football games on which Daddy had bet tens of thousands of dollars, our rides took us to his bookie's home outside of town. The house fascinated me, mostly because it was like a castle deep in the woods, with a ten-foot wrought iron fence surrounding it, a massive gate that had to be opened by remote control, bars on all the windows, and security cameras mounted everywhere you looked. Some days, Daddy would bring the man a bag of cash in a brown paper bag, but most days he'd arrive empty-handed and leave the house with a bag stuffed full of $100 bills, some of which poked out the top of the bag. On the drives to and from the house, he'd tell me why he was such a good gambler.

"Your daddy's the luckiest s-s-sonofabitch there is, Tena Rix," as if it were that easy. "Most guys walk out with n-n-nothing. I walk out with bags full of money."

One Saturday afternoon, Burke, Daddy, and I were at home watching a football game, and after any major play on the field, Daddy would pick up the phone and bark a few orders to "put another thousand" on this team or that team. He said it without an ounce of doubt, hesitation, or second thoughts. He knew he'd picked the winner. The world, it seemed, did Lamar Clark's bidding, even the football teams and the horses and the greyhound dogs and the boxers in the ring. And indeed, luck seemed to follow him, given the number of stuffed brown paper bags coming into the house. But his bookie didn't share his luck. I learned that on the same night as one of our trips to the walled-in fortress, the bookie was shot execution-style with his hands tied behind his back and a bullet in his forehead, while his girlfriend was pistol-whipped, tied to a tree, and forced to watch his murder. I'm sure Daddy found another bookie, but I never met the man.

Mama always told me she thought Daddy was part of the Dixie Mafia, and maybe she was right. Mister James loved to tell the story of hearing that somebody tried to screw Lamar Clark out of his share of some earnings, so Lamar got in his Cadillac and drove straight to the seediest part of New Orleans to collect it. That time, at least, he had the sense to leave me at home. He parked in front of a windowless storefront, knocked on the battered steel door, and told someone through a little window in the door that he wanted to see the boss. He was taken into a dark room, lit only by one overhead bulb, where some oily character was sitting behind a desk smoking a cigarette. The man was expecting him. Lamar was handed the money in the standard-issue brown paper bag.

"You got your goddamn money, now git your goddamn ass outta heah," the man growled from behind his desk.

According to my cousin's version of the story, Daddy was so scared he drove the entire 170 miles back to Waynesboro in less than ninety minutes, his loaded pistol on the seat next to him.

And when he wasn't demanding payment from hoodlums, he was doing so with his own relatives. My older cousin Bubba will tell you that all of Wayne County knew never, ever to mess with one of Lamar Clark's daughters, and if you did, to expect to pay a hefty price. Elizabeth's first husband, Hank, evidently forgot the rules one day and gave Elizabeth a shove that sent her falling against the refrigerator in their kitchen. She ran home, crying up a storm, to tell Daddy.

Daddy listened for less than a minute.

"Tena! Get in the car, we're going to have a little t-t-talk with Hank."

Now, at this point in the story, you'd be right to ask why in the world he'd want to have his young daughter along for the ride, a ride he knew damn well was going to involve a righteous father's rage. I didn't question it at the time, but now I realize it was all part of his grooming me, his showing me that "*this* is how powerful people take care of folks who mess with them or their family," and that I should take notes. But at the time I just hopped in the car, happy as always to be his sidekick.

Daddy drove up to Hank's office on two wheels, and honked the horn. Funny how he always honked for others, but when anyone honked at him or one of his daughters, there was hell to pay. I once heard that the term "honky" was coined by black Americans because of the arrogance with which whites summon people to their cars, as if they are just too damn important, or lazy, or both, to walk up to the door and knock. Daddy earned the name, and as always, he sat there honking until Hank came out of the building.

"Hey there, Mister Lamar, Tena, whatch'all up to?" Hank asked, leaning against the open car window, happily ignorant of the answer.

Hank had been a star linebacker and at the top of his journalism class at the University of Southern Mississippi, with offers from some of the best newspapers from New York to Chicago upon graduation. But Lamar had no intention of letting Elizabeth leave Waynesboro with her new husband, and so he bribed Hank with a new house and a good job in an insurance company. Hank took the bait, but in the frustrated years that followed, he found solace in the bottle, a solace that eventually killed him.

But that day, he was still my handsome brother-in-law, and although I knew it wasn't a social call, I loved seeing his smiling, sweet face.

"Tena, git in the backseat," Daddy barked. "Hank, g-g-git in the car. You and me are g-g-gonna take a little ride." Daddy's lips barely opened as he spoke.

I jumped in the backseat and Hank got in the front. I watched his Adam's apple bob in his throat as he swallowed several times. He seemed to finally understand it wasn't a social call.

Daddy drove away from the curb with his trademark squeal of tires. Not a word passed between them, and I kept my mouth shut in the backseat. When we hit the outskirts of town, Daddy turned onto a dirt road, pulled over, and shut the engine off.

"I j-j-j-just got one question," he said, looking straight out the windshield, not at Hank. "Did anything unusual happen this morning b-b-between you and my daughter?"

I looked at Hank and felt real pity for my brother-in-law. I loved him, and hated seeing him so scared. He swallowed again, and I watched one bead of sweat trickle down his face from his temple to his chin and drop onto his shirt.

"No, sir," Hank finally said.

"I'm g-g-gonna ask you again," Daddy said. "Did anything happen that I should know about, like you pushing Elizabeth up against the 'frigerator?"

From the backseat I thought, *Oh my Lord, Hank, just say yes!*

Hank swallowed hard. "Well, you know that Elizabeth can be a handful and that sometimes in a marriage . . . We had a little spat, like all couples, things might have gotten—"

Hank stopped talking because Daddy had pulled a gun out from under his right leg and cocked it. Then, calm as can be, he put the barrel to Hank's left temple.

"I'm gonna ask you one more G-G-G-GODdamn time to tell me what you did to my d-d-d-daughter."

"I'm sorry, Mister Lamar, sir, I'm sorry, I'm sorry," Hank sputtered, the sweat now dripping from him like rain from a roof. "I'd had a little too much to drink last night and things got a little heated and—"

"Okay, then," Daddy said, cutting him off. Then, as easy and smooth as a knife through butter, he uncocked the gun and tucked it back under his leg. "If I ever hear that you've raised so much as a f-f-f-fingernail to my daughter, they'll find you f-f-f-floating facedown in the Chickasawhay. You got that?"

Hank was much bigger than Daddy, but Daddy's gun was the great equalizer. Hank got the message.

His and Elizabeth's marriage lasted seventeen years, but I doubt Hank ever again pushed my sister with any more force than a feather duster.

Chapter Eighteen

Without a wife to curtail his catting around, if in fact that had ever curtailed him, Daddy entertained his lady friends with an even more reckless abandon. One afternoon I was at the home of my friend Lynn, whose parents were hosting a barbeque. As the adults milled around the backyard, sipping their bourbon and Cokes and dirty martinis, they suddenly noticed something going on in a house across the yard and began pointing and snickering, the women holding their hands to their mouths in red-faced shock. I followed their gaze. When the adults noticed I too was looking, they hushed up. In the living room of the house, I could see a woman lying on the sofa, her skirt bunched up around her waist, and my daddy on top of her.

I didn't know exactly what was happening, but I knew enough to be mortified. I burst into tears and ran inside to Lynn's room. Lynn's mother followed me in.

"Honey," she said, reaching out to stroke my hair, "that was wrong of us. We shouldn't have been looking and laughing."

"I hate him! I hate my daddy!"

"Ah, honey, grown-ups often do things they shouldn't," she said.

When Daddy came to pick me up an hour later, she walked me out to the car.

"Next time you entertain, Lamar, I suggest you close the drapes," she said, her voice tight.

"I don't know what you're talking about," he said, his voice even tighter. "Tena, git in the car."

"Yes, sir," I said, my face swollen from crying.

Although he flushed a deep red down to his shirt collar and the veins on his neck looked like they were going to burst, he never admitted to her or me that he had been doing anything that afternoon for which he need apologize.

He would create elaborate ruses to avoid admitting his ways, at least to me. Once, rather than admit that he was taking his latest girlfriend on a trip out of town, he announced he was headed to Switzerland, and would be gone several days, maybe a whole week, and that he would bring me the "biggest, best present ever." As mad as I was that he had left, again, I spent the days dreaming of the fabulous gift I'd get from the magical-sounding *Switzerland*.

When he returned, I ran out to meet his car, eager to see what he'd brought me "from Switzerland."

"Here ya go, Monkey Joe!" he said, and handed me a peach-colored plastic umbrella.

I stood in the driveway stiff as a statue holding the ridiculous umbrella at arm's length. First of all, did he not notice that I had never, ever used or wanted an umbrella, to say nothing of a peach one? I always preferred getting wet rather than carrying a silly umbrella. And second, in what universe did he think that a peach umbrella was proof of a trip to Switzerland?

"You got this in *Switzerland*?" I asked, the offending umbrella still hanging from my hand.

"Sure did!" he crowed. "You cain't buy 'em anywhere else in the world!"

I knew that he was lying, that he probably hadn't gone to Switzerland and had merely picked up the umbrella at some gift shop as an afterthought, but I never challenged him.

His inability to ever admit the truth made me crazy, but it was very, very effective: There was a part of me that for years believed that perhaps Switzerland *was* the only place that made peach umbrellas.

A few months after I turned twelve, Daddy bought me my first car, most likely in order to free himself from having to drive me around town. No matter that the legal driving age in Mississippi at that time was fifteen, he had come home with a navy blue 1966 Camaro when I was tall enough for my feet to touch the pedals. And I was, almost. I still needed a pillow behind my back, the seat pushed all the way forward, and my right toes pointed forward, like a ballerina's on pointe, to reach the gas pedal.

Once in the driver's seat, I looked at him standing by the car door.

"I don't know how to drive a car, Daddy," I said.

He lit a cigarette and threw the match in the dirt.

"You know how t-t-t-to drive a GODdamn tractor, don't you?" he demanded.

"I guess," I admitted.

"Then there you go," he said, getting in his car parked nearby. "Same thing. I gotta get to work." And off he sped.

Turns out he was right, and soon I was outrunning the county sheriff on Highway 84, spinning the Camaro into cornfields to hide and praying the dust would settle before they drove past my hideout in the tall rows. Sometimes when I got home and climbed out of the car, Beulah Mae, there to pick up Virgie, would be standing on the porch, laughing.

"Lawd have mercy! I done 'spect Mister Lamar to be gittin' outta that car. You just like yo' daddy. Y'all drive up, open the door, git one leg out, and that car still be movin'. I ain't never seen nobody drive like y'all."

She was one to talk, given her nearly killing herself and Virgie every day driving out to the farm. Still, I had to smile at her comparing me, a twelve-year-old girl, to the fearsome Lamar Clark.

Chapter Nineteen

After about a year of miserable living in Mobile, Mama came back to Waynesboro even more destitute than when she left, if that was possible, and moved into a run-down, two-bedroom house behind the grocery store. And if that wasn't bad enough, I was soon forced to join her.

Georgia and Daddy, but mostly Daddy, had decided a girl of twelve needed to live with her mother. To her credit, Georgia had begged Daddy for years to let me move in with her and Bobby, but he'd refused, in part because he thought it would look bad and the town would be talking: *What's happening over at that Clark house? First Vivian up and walks out on him, and then he sends that poor little girl to live with her sister?*

But I think his refusal also had to do with his wanting to teach me something. Sure, I wasn't the boy he always wanted, but I had a good head on my shoulders and I wasn't easily intimidated. Poisonous snakes and angry horses and shady bookies didn't faze me. And while I didn't have his ruthlessness, and was already too liberal for his tastes, I spoke my mind and could match his stubbornness toe to toe. He loved and hated my strong will, and he wasn't so crazy about my big mouth when it challenged him. Still, we were a team.

So when he and Georgia came in to tell me I had to live with Mama, I didn't understand why. I loved my mama, but his wanting me to move out felt like rejection, which sat like a cold, hard lump in my chest. And, I was scared. Not only would I be leaving the only home I had known, Virgie—my one rock, my one anchor—would be leaving my everyday life.

"Listen up. Me and your s-s-sister been talkin'," Daddy began, looking over at Georgia who stood wringing her hands. "She agrees with me that you're a young lady now, and a young lady needs to be livin' with her m-m-mama."

"*Who* says that?" I asked, instantly furious. I didn't like that Georgia had been part of this decision. "I love Mama and take care of her when I visit, but why do I have to live with her?"

Georgia moved toward me and put her arm around me. "Honey, Daddy works all the time and you need to be with Mama. But nothing's going to change. You'll be able to visit her with me and Elizabeth and Penny whenever you want."

I pulled away, hurt and enraged.

"You just need a babysitter to make sure Mama doesn't burn the house down, or try to kill herself again," I said, trying my damnedest not to cry.

Georgia looked at me tenderly, but Daddy lit a cigarette and put on his hat to leave.

"That ain't it at all, it's just t-t-time for you to live with your mama," he said. "I work all the t-t-time and you need to be with your mama, that's all." He was done talking about it.

I looked at my sister, the woman who had always been there for me, and saw both sadness and resolve. It was done. There was nothing more to discuss.

On the Saturday of my move, I stormed around my room packing, fuming, and stuffing clothes and shoes and books into boxes and a couple of suitcases. As my mood darkened and my temper rose, I made the decision that I would never let anyone tell me where I lived or what I could do and couldn't do ever again, starting with living in Mama's grim little house. My entire life, I had been forced to accommodate my parents' erratic behavior: Mama's drinking, Daddy's cheating, Mama's leaving, and then Daddy's being in charge. Just when I'd finally found a routine I could tolerate, a new way of life was being forced on me. I felt like I'd been tricked. Betrayed.

Virgie came in to check on me as I angrily slammed drawers and threw clothes I wouldn't take into a pile in the corner.

"What's wrong, baby girl?" she asked, sitting on the edge of the bed.

I looked into her worried eyes and my anger instantly faded. I sat next to her and put my head in my hands.

"I don't fit in anywhere, Virgie. I feel so alone. Nobody wants me."

"Now, don't be talkin' nonsense, you gots plenty of folks who love you," she said. I felt her large hand gently massage circles onto my back, the way it had for nearly my entire life.

I shook my head and wiped my eyes on my sleeve, straight-

ening to look at her. She pulled her hand away from my back
and tucked both of hers into her lap.

"But I just don't *fit in*, anywhere. I don't *belong* anywhere.
Sure, Mama and Daddy and Georgia love me, but . . ."

Virgie looked at me for a long while, then turned to look
out the window of my room and to the great magnolia tree
behind the house. After several quiet moments she spoke.

"Well, you's special. You's my baby girl and you's special
and one day, you's gonna find yo' place. I's promise you that."

I put my arms around her and my head on her shoulder and
we sat on the bed until we heard Daddy's car in the driveway.

Once I had moved my suitcases into Mama's house, they sat
stacked in the small storage room that doubled as a bedroom
at the back of the house. Mama slept on the couch. She'd always been scared of the dark, even with a loaded pistol under
her pillow, but living alone had only made it worse.

I painted yellow daisies on the bedroom wall and got a lava
lamp, and made the most out of my new home, but Mama
wasn't helping with the transition. She was mostly drunk or
sick on the couch with what grew into an astonishing list of
ailments, everything from pancreatitis and diverticulitis to
pneumonia and heart disease and high blood pressure. She
even suffered the loss of half her tongue because of her addiction to Aspergum. (Even more remarkably, it grew back!)
Over the years—and I am not exaggerating—she spent hundreds of nights in the hospital, so many my sisters and I finally
lost count. As the illnesses came and went, she consumed a

staggering amount of pills. Doctors used to say, "If you and I need one pain pill, your mother needs three—her constitution is so strong."

As her drinking had increased, along with a huge list of real ailments, she'd also developed a healthy case of hypochondria. She had always obsessed over every hangnail. Now, granted, she had drunk her pancreas into a constant state of painful inflammation, and her lack of anything resembling real exercise softened her bones and weakened her muscles. Her idea of exercise was to sit in a chair and move her arms up and down, in and out, for about five minutes. My sisters and I would listen to her latest complaints and cry, "Mama! Swear to God, we're gonna put 'I told you I was sick' on your tombstone if you don't stop with all of this!" She'd just smile and say, "You'll see. Just go ahead, make fun of me."

Unfortunately, it didn't matter how sick she felt, she would still sit me down for her nightly Bible reading. It was only a chapter or two, but it was all I could do to sit through it. She'd been reading from the Bible my whole life, but sitting in that depressing little house, feeling trapped at the foot of her chair, and looking up at a cheap, backlit painting of Jesus knocking on some random door above her on the wall made me want to jump out of my skin.

So between her ailments and her oppressive Bible hour, I never quite settled into living at her house. Instead, I lived like a vagabond, moving between Mama's, Georgia's, Elizabeth's, Penny's, and the new house Daddy built closer to town after he sold the farm. He wanted no part of Vivian's Folly after she left it. I bet he even toyed with the idea of bulldozing it into the gully like he had done with his parents' house. Eventually he built a monstrosity I called the Mausoleum because it was made of gray marble and had gray marble pillars topped with gray marble lions lining the long driveway.

Wherever I laid my head at night, I trudged back to my mother's in the morning to change my clothes for school. I'd walk into her small house, where the air was already thick with cigarette smoke, and she'd be on the couch watching television, her crossword puzzle in her lap. Sometimes, too often in fact, one of her boyfriends would be there as well, smoking a cigarette in the easy chair, nursing a cup of coffee and looking as old and tired as the chair he sat in.

On the mornings when it was just Mama in the house, she always, *always* had an errand for me to run.

"Hey, baby, go over to the Tastee Freeze real quick and grab me a malt," she'd say, already slurring her words even though it was barely eight o'clock in the morning. "My stomach is sour and that's just about the only thing I can think of that might taste good."

"I bet your stomach's sour," I'd say under my breath, "a carton of cigarettes and a gallon of whiskey will do that."

"What's that, baby?"

"Nothin', Mama," I'd say, gritting my teeth against my anger and frustration. "I'll be right back. Vanilla or chocolate?"

And so it went. Once back in Waynesboro, nothing really changed for my mother. Never having worked a day in her life, Vivian Clark wasn't about to start. She had returned to Waynesboro as she had left a year before: drunk. She spent her days on the couch, drinking, watching television, doing her crossword puzzles, and underlining passages in her Bible. Although only forty-five years old, alcohol had finally begun to take a toll on her beauty and her skin—her jawline was sagging, she had bags under her eyes, and her cheeks and nose were sprinkled with gin blossoms. Her drinking started up first thing in the morning—a mug of coffee and a tumbler of bourbon on the TV tray by the couch. By the time night fell, she would more often than not pass out, with that same bottomless glass of bourbon in one hand and a cigarette burning between her fingers.

Often she was doubled over with painful pancreatitis, curled up in a fetal position on the couch. On the nights I did stay with her, I'd turn off the light on the end table and take the smoldering cigarette from her fingers, just as I had when she lived above the dry cleaners and in Mobile. And those were the nights she came home. I'd frequently have to call Georgia or Elizabeth at two or three in the morning because Mama still wasn't home from the VFW dance or from having a few drinks with a "male friend."

I was never entirely free of fear, the fear that she would get hurt, or hurt herself, or not wake up after a particularly bad night, or drive her car into an oncoming train, or set herself and her house on fire. My self-imposed job of making sure she was safe was exhausting, and seemingly endless.

Oddly, and against all reason, she could also be a happy drunk, the life of the party, funny and engaging. So much so, that after she left Daddy, I thought, *Well, maybe it's not so bad now that she's not getting drunk and pulling out her gun and threatening to kill Daddy. At least the drinking seems to cheer her up*. She was also a great audience, drunk or sober. When Petula Clark's "Downtown" came out, I learned the words by heart and without too much provocation would get my hairbrush, jump up on the couch, and give Mama a one-woman show while she yelled, "Let me hear it, girl!" from her recliner, legs crossed, drink and cigarette in hand.

But, she was still a drunk. Sometimes I would grab the bottle away from her, and she would rail against me, swinging while she tried to grab the bottle back and screaming, "Leave me the hell alone!" To which I would yell back, "You think I *want* to be here, watching you drink yourself to death? Being your *babysitter*?!"

Those were the ugly days. Like any drunk, she had her share of them. Unlike other suspected drunks in our town, she did nothing to hide what she had become. She didn't give a rat's ass who knew. She wasn't the town's only drunk, but she was one of its most visible. She had left the richest man in Wayne County and ended up penniless and hammered in a run-down shack behind the grocery store, weaving her Cadillac through the streets of Waynesboro with the radio blasting. And yet she still walked into Petty's or Blaine's or the Humdinger like a queen into her castle. Waynesboro didn't know what to do with her. They loved her, but she had, quite simply, become an embarrassment.

Once, and only once, she came to one of my basketball games. For months, I had begged her to come watch me play full-court ball, but she always said she was too busy or tired or just plain "not feelin' well enough" to come. But I knew what she meant: The games were played in the late afternoon or early evening and she was too *drunk* to come. Then one game, there she was. The minute I saw her, I instantly regretted having pushed her into coming. Her purse over her arm, her cigarette in her hand, she was already wobbly drunk, her eyes glazed, her smile loose.

I ran up and down the court, taking shots and passing the ball, and watched as she greeted people too loudly and laughed with a great swoop of her arm, her handbag swinging widely, almost hitting a few folks in the head. When she stumbled and nearly fell on top of Georgia and Bobby as she tried to climb up to a seat in the bleachers, Daddy, who'd been watching nearby, leapt up and stormed over to her. He grabbed her arm and said something, inches from her face. She jerked away, again nearly falling. What I couldn't hear was his telling her to "Git your drunk ass outta here," that she was embarrassing herself, and me, and to "Git on home." And she did.

She never came to another game. And, I was glad she didn't.

There were two things Daddy cared about: making money and his reputation. By this time the entire town was *tsk-tsk*-ing Lamar Clark's inability to control his ex-wife. It was bad enough that Vivian had walked out on him. Now, years later, he still couldn't put her in her place, couldn't force her to stay home and drink behind the curtains, like you were supposed to do. In short, she had become an embarrassment to him.

So Lamar Clark came up with a plan.

Chapter Twenty

Whitfield. The name struck cold fear in the heart of every Mississippian, particularly those old enough to remember its history. Named for the small town in which it was located, about ten miles outside of Jackson, the Mississippi State Hospital had a century-old reputation as a barbaric penal colony even before it became the state's "lunatic asylum." Whitfield was, in short, the last stop for many of the state's criminally insane, drug addicts, alcoholics, and the just plain "nervous," as those who suffered some sort of mental breakdown were called. Inmates, those who survived, would come out thinner, sometimes even shorter, and all around lesser souls than they were when they went in. And those were the ones who made it out alive. Years later, when the hospital built a new service road, more than one thousand bodies were unearthed. There were gruesome stories of ice-water baths, electric shock therapy, unauthorized lobotomies, patients defecating in buckets in the corners of dark, dank isolation cells, and hollow screams that echoed through the stone hallways and staircases, day and night.

Mississippi had its share of rehab and detox centers, but they were all private, and all expensive. Daddy wanted Mama to quit drinking and stop being an embarrassment to him in Waynesboro, but he sure as hell wasn't going to bankroll an expensive rehab. Not while there was Whitfield. Lamar Clark had waited a long time for revenge on the wife who walked out on him, and now was his chance. That man could hold a grudge.

After a weekend in Jackson billed as a shopping spree for the five Clark girls—me, my three sisters, and our mother—we were all headed back to Waynesboro. The car windows were open, letting in the spring air, which was warm and sweet. I was in the backseat between Mama and Penny, and Elizabeth was up front with Georgia, who was driving. My sisters were uncharacteristically quiet. But Mama, who at lunch had had even more to drink than she normally did, which was saying something, was in a good mood and she and I sang along to all our favorite songs on the radio, "King of the Road" being our absolute favorite. After a few songs, she decided she'd waited long enough and, with her little secret smile on her face, without warning or provocation, she began:

"Trailer for sale or rent . . ." she crooned in her smokiest voice.

I knew my cue.

"Rooms to let, fifty cents . . ." I joined in, pushing gently into her body with my shoulder.

We sang through the song, then both took a big deep breath for our finale.

"I'm a man of means by no means, KING OF THE ROOOOOOOAD!"

"Okay, okay," Elizabeth said. "Georgia and I have heard enough."

Mama and I giggled, and Elizabeth turned up the radio to drown out any ideas we might have on singing another round.

Even though I had my own car, Daddy strictly forbade me from leaving the town limits. Even so, I knew the roads heading in and out of Waynesboro well and was proud of my ability to read and follow maps. So I noticed when we turned off Highway 49 and were no longer headed back to Waynesboro. Instead, we were on a rutted dirt road; Spanish moss hung from the trees and the heavy stink of swamp gases filled the car. Mama noticed too.

"What are we doing?" she asked, her eyes darting from window to window. "Georgia, *where* are we going?"

I knew the answer as soon as we pulled into a driveway and saw the redbrick buildings and the sign: MISSISSIPPI STATE HOSPITAL.

"NO!!!" My mother's scream was that of an animal. It sounded like the panther that had prowled the riverbank behind the farm.

I saw what was happening. My sisters, and I, it seemed, were committing our mama to Whitfield. Putting her away. Locking her up. Treating her like a violent criminal, or an insane monster. I was powerless, and full of panic. My mind raced with the surreal horror of it all—*This can't be happening!! What can I do to stop it?* And with the panic, I also felt dread. Even though I knew nothing of their plan to bring her here, I would be part of it. Forever.

"Now, Mama, just calm down," Elizabeth said, turning around in her seat to pat Mama's leg. "Everything's gonna be all right. This is for your own good."

Mama slapped Elizabeth's hand away with a vicious swipe.

"DAMMIT! YOU TURN THIS CAR AROUND, RIGHT NOW, AND TAKE ME HOME! Y'ALL HEAR?" Mama yelled, her hands clutching the back of the front seat so hard I could see the bones of her knuckles and the purple veins under the skin.

Georgia kept driving.

"NO, NO, NO!" The words came out in short little gasps as my mother beat the back of the seat with her fists.

I looked at my sisters to figure out how this had all happened, but none of them would look at me. Then I knew. *Daddy.* He had done this. And my sisters, Georgia and Elizabeth, at least, had no choice but to help. While Whitfield was drastic, they knew Mama needed help. What they hadn't figured was that in getting her to Whitfield, Daddy had finally gotten his revenge. They agreed to having her committed to Whitfield, but only because Daddy had promised she'd get the best care his money could buy.

"Mama, it's for the best," Georgia said. "You're gonna get the help you need in there."

Mama grasped the door handle, pulling ferociously on it, like an animal desperate to claw its way out of a cage, but Elizabeth was able to hold down the lock from where she sat in front. In a terrible duel, they started slapping at each other's hands, trying to gain control of the button. I'm sure if Mama had been able to open the door, she would have leapt out and started running. But she was trapped. She started screaming and then rolled down the window, trying to squeeze her way out of it.

"Tena! Grab ahold of her!" Elizabeth yelled at me.

I didn't budge. More than anything in the world I wanted her to get away. I didn't grab her, but I didn't help her either. I'm not sure I could have, but I didn't even try. I just sat there, sobbing.

Seeing I wasn't going to help, my sister turned around in her seat and pulled Mama back in the car by the waistband of her skirt, like a dog by its collar.

Just then, we rounded the last bend in the long driveway, and I saw two orderlies in white coats trotting toward the car; one of them held a white cotton jacket with leather straps and steel buckles, its arms already spread wide. I'd never seen one before, but I knew that it was a straitjacket.

The car stopped, the doors were unlocked, and the men were on our mother like linebackers, pulling her out of the car and tackling her to the ground. She kicked and screamed, her dress bunching up high on her thighs revealing her garter belt, and her high heels screeched across the paving stones as she twisted and squirmed to free herself.

"Let me GO! NOOOOOO!" She looked up at us in the car as she struggled. "Girls! Don't let your daddy do this to me!"

All four of us sat in the car watching the nightmare and crying, but no one moved. We were set as if in stone. After several horrible, brawling moments, the orderlies wrestled her arms into the jacket's sleeves, crossed them in front and then around her, and buckled the row of straps behind her back. It was a sound I won't soon forget in this lifetime: the leather straps pulled tight and their buckles secured with a series of loud clinks. The men dragged her to her feet. Her stockings were torn and her high heels were left lying on the cold pavement. Mama's thick black hair had come loose and hung over her face. For one of the few times in my life I saw the scarred remains of her ear, her greatest physical shame laid bare for the world to see. Her mascara was smudged down her cheeks, but her eyes were dry. Normally dark brown, they flashed with a fury that turned them black.

"I will *never* forgive you girls. EVER. Do you hear me?" she screamed, looking at Georgia and Elizabeth, knowing they must have gone along with Daddy's plan. Whether cooperative or conned, they were its lynchpin. I was too young and Penny too disliked by our father to have been part of it. But Mama's words stung me as well.

We knew she meant it. Through all of her wild behavior and erratic mothering and miserable life with Daddy, our mother always said exactly what she meant. Georgia and Elizabeth looked away. Penny and I stared from face to face, shocked and helpless, not knowing what to say or do.

The only thing I knew about Whitfield was that people sometimes didn't return from it. And now I watched as my mother was half dragged, half pushed up its stairs. She disappeared through its heavy front doors that closed behind her like a vault.

I looked at Georgia and Elizabeth in the front seat, both of them crying into their hands, and for the first time in my life, I realized how much power Daddy had over all of us. Although they had planned this with him, he had told them it would be "just fine!" That he'd "paid extra, so she'll be treated extra special." But he had sent her to a place that put her in a straitjacket, dragged her through its doors, and locked her away, and it was too late to do anything about it. Mama was headed to a cell, probably a padded cell, until she calmed down. She was utterly powerless. No matter what she was saying to those orderlies, or to the nurses and administrators who'd check on her for the foreseeable future, somebody else would determine her fate. She had no voice. But along with the shock and horror, I also felt a flicker of hope: *Maybe he's right. Maybe this is a good place. Maybe Daddy does care about Mama and only wants what's best for her.* Also, I felt some relief. Knowing for a little while, at least, it wouldn't be my job to keep her from harm. Others were in charge of her safety and for that I felt enormous relief.

There is a moment in every girl's life when she stops being a child and begins to grow up. Despite all I'd seen in my thirteen years, I lost any remaining sense of a child's innocence the day I watched my mama being dragged through Whitfield's doors in a straitjacket, every ounce of dignity being torn away from her. That was the day I realized the difference between those who wielded power and those who had none. And that as much as I loved my mama and wanted to protect her from harm, there was nothing I could do to save her from the men in white coats, or from whatever was waiting for her behind those solid oak doors.

Georgia dried her eyes, collected herself, and turned the ignition.

"Daddy says it's all for the best. She has to stop drinkin' and she will. She'll come home and everything will be all right. It will be all right." Her words faded off, as if she didn't entirely believe them.

As she drove down the hospital's driveway and back onto the highway headed east to Waynesboro, I turned around in my seat and looked out the back window to the front doors of Whitfield.

"Oh, Mama," I whispered, low and quiet so my sisters couldn't hear me, "I'm so sorry. I couldn't save you, Mama." A sob escaped my lips, and I buried my head in my arms against the backseat. "Daddy tricked us, Mama. We didn't know. I promise, we didn't *know.*"

And so it was. Our daddy had once again made sure he triumphed. This time, in doing so he had locked our beautiful mother behind bars, in a straitjacket, like a wild animal caught in a hunter's net. None of us knew when, or possibly if, we'd ever see her again. We'd all been duped and betrayed that day.

On that drive back to Waynesboro, none of us spoke a word. I sat behind Elizabeth with my chin resting on my hands on the window frame, tears streaming down my cheeks.

As I watched the sleepy towns go by, I wondered, *Will I ever see Mama again?*

Chapter Twenty-One

In the time Mama was away at Whitfield, I worried constantly. Were they taking good care of her? Was she getting better? What if she never came back? What if she now blamed me, as well as my sisters, and hated us as a result? I knew she was particularly mad at Georgia and Elizabeth, but what if after a few days at Whitfield, she hated me too?

I tried to imagine what it would be like to have her back, and to have her back sober. I'd forgotten how it was when she was not drunk, just sitting and talking and eating and laughing without a drink in her hand. I could barely remember a single day that hadn't ended with her falling onto the couch or being carried to bed half-conscious. She had been so drunk for so long I'd forgotten what her sober smile looked like and what her sober voice sounded like. I'd forgotten what it felt like to be held in her sober arms.

Six weeks to the day after being hauled away, my mother was released from Whitfield. My sisters and I had not been allowed to visit her, and she hadn't written. She refused to let any of us come to get her. Instead, she arranged for one of her boyfriends, Bernie, from Mobile, to pick her up and bring her back to Waynesboro.

Because we didn't want her to return to her rat-nasty shack behind the grocery store, Georgia was able to convince Daddy to buy her a small cinder block house in a better neighborhood. She wouldn't have to worry about rent ever again. But, she wouldn't own it either. Daddy was adamant that the title remain in his name, never hers. And it never was, until long after he'd been gone.

My sisters and I had furnished the place and put flowers in the window, hoping to make it feel like home. We had a party waiting, but even with the balloons and a WELCOME HOME, MAMA! banner above the door, the house didn't feel festive and my stomach ached with nerves. I had seen her black eyes as they dragged her away, and I knew that kind of anger just doesn't fade like you hope it would, particularly where Mama was concerned. She had been betrayed by her own blood and she wasn't about to forget it.

We all took turns pacing by the front window, waiting for the car to turn into the driveway. It was close to suppertime by the time it did. Even though we'd been waiting all day, when the car finally arrived, we all stayed put, as if we had been nailed to the floor.

Mama came up the front stairs, opened the door, walked into the little living room, and stood there with one hand on her hip, the other holding a cigarette. Bernie lingered in the doorway. She wore a pretty dress and high heels, scuff marks marring the leather. Her mink stole was around her shoulders and her purse was over her arm. They weren't the clothes she had been wearing six weeks earlier when she'd disappeared into Whitfield, and I had no idea how or where she'd gotten them. She looked better, maybe tired and pale but she'd lost weight and her face was less bloated and her eyes less bleary than when she left, although her expression could have been carved in marble for all that it revealed.

Bernie followed her in, took off his hat, and nervously looked around the room at each of us.

"Surprise! Welcome home, Mama! We're so proud of you!" we said, finally finding our voices and hesitantly moving toward her.

She deftly stepped around us and walked into the kitchen. We followed her through the house. She put her purse on the kitchen table with a *plunk*, opened the clasp, and took out a pint of Jack Daniel's. Without a word, she untwisted the cap and threw it across the kitchen where it bounced off the far wall. It was the only sound in the house. She paused, standing there with the bottle in her hand, going from face to face, looking each of us in the eye to make sure she had the full command of the room. It was unimaginable to think she didn't. A hurricane could have taken the roof off the house and none of us would have budged. Then, with her eyes not blinking, not wavering, she raised the bottle to her lips, threw her head back, and drained the entire pint in one long pull. I don't think it took her more than five or six swallows to empty the bottle. As the last amber drop disappeared down her throat, she slammed the bottle on the table, wiped her mouth with the back of her hand, and looked each of us square in the eye.

"I will stop drinking when I am good and DAMN ready and not one minute sooner. Let's go, Bernie."

She turned on her heel, shoulders square and head held

high, and left. Bernie quickly put on his hat and tipped it in our direction before scampering out the door after her.

We ran back into the living room and watched as she walked down the front stairs, got in the car, closed, not slammed, her door, and sat there waiting for Bernie to start the engine.

Unable to just let her leave after not having laid eyes on her in six weeks, I ran out to the car.

"Mama! You just got home! Where are you going?"

She looked at me and I thought—I hoped, at least—that I saw a softening in her eyes. Maybe there was, but she still didn't smile.

"Aloha, baby," she said, just as Bernie put the car in gear and jerked out of the driveway.

"I love you, Mama!" I yelled as the car turned onto the street.

As they drove away, her hand emerged from the car window and with a single flick of her wrist she flung her cigarette into a ditch. Mama never looked back.

Even if her drinking killed her, she was not ever going to let another soul tell her what to do or when to do it. Daddy had been the last.

After Mama had returned from Whitfield and her six weeks of forced—and failed—rehab, she got back to the business of hard drinking. And I moved back in with her to once again make sure she didn't burn the place down. I think the only time she didn't drink from sunup to sundown was when I was sick, and she would sober up and bring me soup and take my temperature and hover over me the way mothers just seem to know how to do. One day, when I was home sick from school, she looked out the front window and saw my father lingering on the sidewalk. She cursed and opened the front door.

"For heaven's sake, Lamar, get in here! I'm not gonna bite you! I'm not even gonna *talk* to you!"

Daddy came in sheepishly and skirted by her like he was avoiding a rattlesnake in the road. He came into my room with a bag of Popsicles and his pocketful of medicine, which we jokingly called his Iffers. He and Mama both had them, their supply of cure-all medicines: "If I git a headache, I got aspirin. If I git a stomach bug, I got a pink Pepto. If I git dizzy, I got another pill." Iffers, they called them. This was parenting, Clark-style.

Most days, Mama held court from her worn, blue velvet recliner with the manual leg lift, cigarette burning in one hand while her other held a glass of whiskey or moonshine, telling us the ways of the world or reading from the Bible. After leaving Daddy, she had become your garden-variety, born-again Southern Christian. She read from the Bible like Daddy read from his morning newspaper—every day and with a fierce commitment to the Word's literal meaning. She then pontificated about being saved and going to heaven or hell and always, *always* tithing your 10 percent to the Lord.

But one thing seemed to confuse her: Jews. She wasn't quite sure if she should keep her distance because they were going straight to hell for not believing that Jesus Christ was the son of God, or if she should kneel down to them because they were, after all, God's Chosen People. So, she struck a balance and every month sent a check to a rabbi in New York City she'd read about who preached about helping Jews make a pilgrimage to their homeland of Israel because that was what God wanted. So, every month after she received her $150 alimony from Daddy, she'd sit at her table with its Naugahyde cover and write out fifteen one-dollar checks to her list of charities. For over thirty years the rabbi in New York received one of those checks. Later he told me Mama was his most faithful and fervent tither, Jewish or Christian, in all his years at the altar.

One thing she was never confused about was sex, or more precisely, what she called nasty sex. Her lectures on that would go something like this:

"Sex is just plain nasty . . . Never have sex, and remember, even if you don't have sex you can still get pregnant just by being in the same room with a boy's penis. And don't EVER let a boy lie on top of you, because even if you both have clothes on, his sperm can still get inside you and make you pregnant. So it's best to just steer clear of boys *and* their penises altogether . . . All boys are after one thing and one thing only . . . Girls who do anything besides holding hands with a boy are whores . . . And don't ever masturbate; you'll go blind."

She always told us one too many things about our daddy.

"Your daddy is disgusting," she'd say, taking a long swallow of her drink. "He's always got a cloth up under his front seat. Now, girls, don't you ever touch that cloth."

"Why, Mama?" we'd ask, playing right into her tale.

Mama accused Daddy of all sorts of evils and sins. To this day I don't know if any or all of it was true.

We also heard a lot about hymens. A lot. My sister had fallen off the high end of the seesaw in second or third grade. Much to my sister's torment, Mama would tell the story often about how she had been called to the school, and when she arrived found my sister, "bless her heart, with blood in her panties and a broken hymen and, oh my Lord, now she'll never find a man because once your hymen is broken no boy is ever going to want to marry you."

Mama didn't quite fill in the blank of *how* the boy wouldn't know you didn't *have* a hymen until *after* he married you because, Lord knows, he would never find out *before* the marriage, unless you were a filthy whore. But then he wouldn't have married you in the first place because no good boy would ever marry a girl without a hymen.

And around and around her "logic" would go, same lecture, same prohibitions, her tone a reflection of how much she'd had to drink before she started. My sisters all commented later that it was amazing any of us ever had sex or got married, given Mama's rants against all forms of carnal knowledge.

Strangely enough, even with all that talk about hymens, she never actually told us where the damn thing was or what it was there for. So, when the day finally came for me to find out, I went running into the living room screaming, "Oh my Lord, Mama! I'm bleeding! Where's it coming from?" Her answer stopped me in my tracks.

"The third hole."

Say again?

"Well, baby, you have three holes down there."

I looked at her as if she had just said, "Oh, and by the way, you were born with two heads but we chopped one of them off."

"I most certainly do *not*! I have two! One for pee and one for poop!" I shouted, as adamant as I was petrified of the possibility she was right.

"Nope, you got three. There's one in the middle of those other two," she said, then went back to her crossword puzzle.

And so ended my mama's anatomy lesson.

Puberty also brought me unwanted breasts that I just wished would go away. I had absolutely no use for them. I particularly detested mine because they were very out of balance: an A cup on my left, a C on my right. No one in my life really made a big deal of it, except Elizabeth, who, in typical older-sister fashion, took every opportunity to make fun of me. She even called me Cyclops more than once. But then again, maybe she was just jealous that I still had my hymen intact. Come to think of it, I guess I still do.

I never explained to Mama the real truth of it: I had no real use for my female body parts. They felt like they belonged on someone else's body. Ever since my days of playing with Burke, just the two of us *boys*, I rarely gave my sexuality a thought, except of course in some detached way when I remembered the majorette or the Cotton Drugstore ladies. But those women were somehow separate beings, not like me at all. I thought of myself as an entirely unique being. No one else was like me, shared my thoughts, or felt disconnected to their physical selves and their sexual bodies. And in fact, I had never really thought of sex in any way but functional, something animals and other people did occasionally and only then to reproduce. It was that simple and nothing I had to worry about.

Chapter Twenty-Two

President Johnson and the U.S. Congress had declared civil rights for all the law of the land in 1964, but Mississippi stubbornly ignored the message. Black and white Mississippians continued to live entirely segregated lives. Any white who dared challenge segregation was declared a communist, or worse: a *nigger-loving communist*. The few white folks—and most of them were ministers—who *did* speak up in favor of integration, faced losing their country club memberships and their pulpits. I attended a segregated school, worshipped in a segregated church, shopped in segregated stores, and ate in segregated restaurants.

At Petty's Cafe, where we had dined several days a week for as long as I could remember, the humiliation of watching Virgie eat outside rankled me to the core. Even as a little girl, I'd tried to take a stand.

"Where do you think you're going?" Daddy asked me when I stood up from the table, my dinner plate of veal cutlets and hush puppies in hand. I was five and Virgie had just started working for us.

"Out to the back step to eat with Virgie. If she can't sit in here, then I don't want to either."

"Now don't you be making trouble for Virgie," Daddy said. "You sit your little butt right down, ya hear? Besides, maybe Virgie doesn't *want* you out there with her."

On that last point, he was right. She in fact *didn't* want me out there with her, making a scene. That was the last thing she wanted.

"Go on back in, Miss Tena," Virgie said as soon as she heard the screen door squeak behind her. "You's sure gonna get me in a heap a trouble."

But I didn't go back in. I squeezed next to her on the porch step, pushing at her bottom with mine until we both fit on the narrow step and had settled our plates in our laps. As we ate our veal cutlets and sipped our sweet tea, I'd steal quick smiles at her and sometimes, just sometimes, she'd smile back.

In the summer of 1967, Daddy and I were watching the *CBS Evening News* when I heard Walter Cronkite announce that President Johnson had nominated the first black American, Thurgood Marshall, to sit on the Supreme Court. *Now, finally*, I thought, *it's time. Waynesboro can't stop civil rights any longer.*

The next day, I decided to introduce Petty's to their first black customer and I drove over to Virgie's house.

"Virgie, come on. We're going to lunch!" I said.

She met me on her front porch.

"Well, where's we goin'?"

"Petty's!"

Her face froze.

"Oh please, Miss Tena, *no no, no ma'am, no way*," Virgie begged. "Mr. Lamar'll kilt me dead, he will, if'n he hear I be eatin' *inside* Petty's. Please, you is gonna get me in real trouble."

I finally convinced her to get in the car, but not until after *another* battle when I insisted she sit in the front seat with me. I actually had to reach back and lock the rear passenger doors to prevent her from slipping into the backseat. When she finally tucked herself into the front seat, she scrunched so far down I don't think she could see over the dashboard. Nonetheless, I was thrilled that I would be introducing her to the *inside* of Petty's and to the first meal served to her by whites. Her entire life, she had been the one serving them. But times had changed. I thought.

When we drove up, I saw that there was a line out front of Petty's. It had only seven tables, so it wasn't rare to wait, but with Virgie by my side, I knew it would be the longest wait for a table I'd ever had. I parked the car and opened my door.

"Please, baby girl, let me wait here. *Please*," Virgie begged. By this time she had scrunched so far down in the seat she was practically under the dashboard.

"Virgie, stop," I said. "It's the law. They can't refuse to serve you!"

I was so excited to share this with her, to give her this gift of progress. But as we got out of the car and took our place at the back of the line, the chatter among the lunch regulars went dead.

"Hey there, Mister Earl, Miss Betty. How y'all today?" I asked two of my parents' friends whom I recognized from church. "Isn't it a pretty day?"

I looked each angry person in the eye, smiling, challenging them to say a word. Challenging them to say something to Lamar Clark's daughter. They didn't, as I knew they wouldn't. They didn't dare. They just glared at me, and all but spit at Virgie. Virgie kept her eyes on the ground, and kept as much of her body hidden behind mine as she could, as if trying to disappear, not an easy thing to do since she had a good seven inches and close to a hundred pounds on me.

When it was finally our turn, we walked in, the little bell above the door ringing as it opened, and every head in the small restaurant turned to stare. Not just stare, but gape— mouths open, forks and coffee cups stopped in midair. You could have heard a mouse fart in the storeroom. I guess they thought my lining up outside with Virgie was a stunt, and that I wouldn't possibly *dare* to bring her inside.

"Come on, Virgie," I said, "here's a table."

Virgie's head was down and her eyes on the floor. All other eyes in the café remained on us.

"Please, Miss Tena, less juss go home," she whispered.

"Hold your head up, Virgie. You belong here just as much as anybody," I whispered back.

I reached for her hand and gently pulled her toward the table. I felt like her feet were stuck in eight inches of mud. Finally, she sat down.

"Whaddya say we git one of Mr. Petty's famous veal cutlets?" I asked, my voice louder than necessary since I was the only one talking in the entire restaurant.

Mr. Petty walked over to our table. He was tall and skinny,

reminiscent of Mr. Green Jeans on *Captain Kangaroo*, and just as sweet a man. He was beloved in Waynesboro. Not only did he attend every single football game at the high school, the town would eventually name the field after him. My bringing Virgie into his restaurant clearly embarrassed him in front of his other customers, but I hoped he would be too worried about losing his *best* customer, Daddy, to make a big scene. And while he didn't yell at me or throw us both out, he did have to let his other customers know this wasn't his idea.

"What'll it be, Miss Tena?" he asked, ignoring Virgie, whom he knew as well as he knew any other citizen of Waynesboro. Behind him, I could see Mrs. Petty as fat as he was thin, and their black broiler cook and black dishwasher—all three staring at us over the kitchen's swinging saloon door. I ordered for the two of us and Mr. Petty walked away without a word. Virgie kept her head down and her eyes on the Formica tabletop.

"Come on, Virgie, it's fine. I promise. It's finally legal for you to be here. No one's gonna kick you out. They can't!" I said, still whispering and hoping I was right.

When our lunch was ready, Mr. Petty approached our table with the two plates. Without a word, he dropped Virgie's plate of veal cutlets and mashed potatoes onto the table from about four inches up, splattering her blouse and face with gravy and bits of potato. I was amazed the plate didn't break in half. He put my plate on the table in front of me and walked away.

The other patrons watched, but said nothing. I thought I heard someone snicker, but I couldn't tell who.

Virgie hadn't moved. The potato and gravy slid slowly down her cheek.

"Virgie," I said, and reached out with my napkin to catch a piece of potato before it fell off her cheek, "you hold your head high. You have every right now to sit here." But Virgie's head remained bowed, and she said nothing as she picked up her fork and began eating, quickly and without pleasure.

Suddenly, the pay phone on the wall rang and Mr. Petty walked over to answer it.

"Yup, she's here all right, Mister Lamar," he said, looking at me. He reached the receiver out. "It's your daddy, Tena," he called out, loud enough for everyone to hear.

"Oh Lordie," Virgie moaned.

My Keds squeaked on the linoleum floor as I stood up and took the phone. There wasn't another sound as every pair of eyes in the room watched me.

"Hey, Daddy," I said, trying to sound relaxed and cheerful, "whatcha want?"

"Tena Rix Clark, you g-g-git out of there NOW," Daddy roared. "You know very g-g-g-good GODdamn well you can't be takin' no n-n-nigger into Petty's, even V-V-Virgie." I could almost feel his spit through the phone.

The other customers stared at me, their forks and sweet tea glasses suspended above their tables, waiting. My stomach churned and I'm sure my face was beet red, but I'd be damned if I was going to let them know I was nervous.

"Why, Daddy! It's pretty much the same as every day. You know Petty's"—I gave Mr. Petty my sweetest smile over the receiver—"it's always good, but I'll read today's specials to you if you want."

"Tena, GODdamn it!" Daddy roared so loud I pushed the receiver hard against my ear, hoping no one else could hear. "You s-s-s-stop this bullshit and g-g-g-get out of there before something bad happens. You're playing with fire. Now g-g-g-git the hell OUT of there!"

"Fried chicken, mashed potatoes, coleslaw, turnip greens, and of course, your favorite, corn bread and peach cobbler. Virgie and I are havin' veal cutlet."

"You get your ass home NOW, young lady!" he yelled and slammed the phone down.

"Okay, Daddy," I said into the dead phone. "Suit yourself."

As I hung up the receiver, I looked over at Mr. Petty and smiled. "Daddy decided he'd just eat his lunch at home."

Hoping my legs would hold me, I walked over to our table and sat down.

Virgie looked at me miserably.

"Mister Lamar's mighty upset, ain't he? I could hear his yellin' from here. Oh Lordie, girl, what you got me into?"

"Oh, don't worry, he's fine," I lied. "He's just hungry."

Virgie shook her head ever so slightly, and we both turned back to the now-cold mess of our lunch. When we finally managed to finish our meals, Virgie rose and started to clear the plates off the table.

I heard a few customers snicker and saw them nod in our direction. I reached out and put my hand on her arm.

"No, Virgie, sit down," I said as quietly as I could so others wouldn't hear me. "You don't have to do that."

"Well, sure I do, Miss Tena. Them plates sho not be clearin' themselves."

"That's what we paid for, food *and* service. They'll come get the plates."

Virgie looked at me, scared and confused, and I finally, *finally* understood. I realized that I had exposed someone I dearly loved to ridicule and scorn and actual danger, all for my own sense of pride. I had brought her here to show her that change had come to the world, even to Waynesboro, and instead, all I did was show her that Mr. Petty and every other white Southerner in the place hadn't changed an iota. If I hadn't held her arm, refusing to let her pick up the plates, she would have cleared every plate in the cafe, powerless against the pull of tradition, of our shared dark history.

With my hand pulling on her arm, she finally sat down, slowly and with great effort, her head still bowed. Not wanting to wait for the check, I pulled out a five-dollar bill, more than twice what we owed, and put it under my plate. Now it was my turn to keep my head down so that the other patrons couldn't see my tears.

"Come on, Virgie, let's go home." She didn't argue.

Virgie climbed in the backseat, and I didn't protest. In silence, I drove her home to Hiwannee.

As she got out of the car, I finally spoke.

"I'm so, so sorry, Virgie," I said. My eyes filled with tears, and I pushed them away with the back of my hand. "I really thought you would like it. I thought it would be a big deal. To make history."

"I knows you did, baby girl, I knows. I sees you tomorrow."

She turned and moved toward her house, her head slowly rising and her shoulders squaring as she walked up the porch stairs and disappeared through the front door.

Chapter Twenty-Three

I grew up in a town where a lot of people lived lives of lies, and rumors surrounded them like mosquitoes around a porch light. Some of those rumors involved whether the husband, but never the wife, was homosexual. It was speculated behind closed doors and gloved hands, with titters and snickers. I listened to those rumors, wondering if any other woman in town, besides the Cotton women, was a lesbian, but no one else ever was suspected. It was always the husbands whose sexuality was gossiped about. Then one night, I got the answer to my own question.

I was fourteen, the perfect age for babysitting, when my sisters and their friends starting having their kids, so I was never without work. And loving kids, I loved the work. One night I was babysitting for a lady I'll call Mrs. Robinson (like the fictional cougar in *The Graduate*), when she came home early from a party without her husband. She seemed flushed and nervous, but I figured she'd had one cocktail too many, something I was all too familiar with. I gathered up my homework and headed for the door.

"Hey, sugar," she said, slightly slurring "sugar" and making me instantly uneasy. "Would you mind waitin' one minute while I go get my checkbook?"

"Sure," I said, and sat back on the couch to wait. She disappeared into the bedroom.

When she hadn't reappeared in five minutes, and then ten, my uneasiness became jittery apprehension. I took a few steps toward the bedroom door, calling out, asking if she was okay and was it all right if I headed on home.

"Tena, come in here for a sec, would you?" she called from inside the bedroom.

Every instinct I had told me to run in the opposite direction, that whatever awaited me on the other side of the door could only mean trouble. Nonetheless, I pushed it open. There sat Mrs. Robinson on the edge of the bed, naked, a sheet covering her lower half.

Of all the violent rush of emotions that instantly flooded through my body, from the hair follicles on the top of my head to my now-cement feet, two were predominant: panic and desire. I had no idea what she was up to, but the sight of her breasts and her offer of them to me was something I had never, ever thought possible, not in my world, not in Waynesboro, and certainly not from a beautiful, sexy, adult woman. The realization that I wanted nothing more than to reach out and explore their beauty struck me dumb, and I stood in the doorway, paralyzed.

She smiled a slow, languorous smile.

"Come over here, sugar, and sit with me for just a bit," she said, lightly patting the bed next to her.

"Ah, ah, ah, I really should be g-g-g-gettin' on home," I said, suddenly developing a nervous stutter as bad as Daddy's.

"Come on now, just for a minute," she repeated, her hand now reaching out for mine.

Ignoring her hand, I nonetheless approached the bed and sat down a few feet away. She scooted over so that her leg pressed up against mine through the sheet.

"Look at me, Tena."

Obediently, I looked at her, keeping my eyes so far from her breasts I was practically staring at the ceiling.

"Do you think my breasts are beautiful?" she asked, her fingers tracing one of her breasts and then lightly cupping it.

"I-I-I think I should go," I said, now more afraid than aroused. *Where in hell was this going? And what in hell would I do if it went any further?*

"I asked you," Mrs. Robinson said, her voice getting hard and a little mean, "if you think my breasts are beautiful."

"Yes, ma'am," I said, hoping beyond hope that would satisfy her and she'd let me go.

Instead, with a great *whoosh* of her arm, she pulled back the sheet, revealing her entire naked body.

"I want you to see a woman's beautiful body."

Finally, I got up, ran out of the bedroom, through the house, and out the front door. I didn't stop running until I made it to Mama's house five long blocks away.

Scared, confused, and terrified of what might come next, I stupidly told Mama what happened. To my horror, she immediately picked up the phone and called Mrs. Robinson and began cussing her out from here to Tuesday, even threatening to call the sheriff. Then Mama got quiet and looked at me as she held the receiver, listening to Mrs. Robinson. After a few more moments, she nodded and hung up without saying goodbye. She turned to me.

"She says you just happened in on her while she was changing. Tena, honey, did she really say those things to you or did you just let your imagination get carried away on you?"

I desperately wanted my mother to protect me from things like what just happened and to always have my back and believe me unconditionally, but I also was glad for the escape hatch. I could just say that yes, it was all a misunderstanding, and maybe convince myself of it too. That way I would never have to confront the fact that I had been aroused by the sight of Mrs. Robinson's breasts, or to wonder why she felt that I, at fourteen, was a ripe target for her frustrated desires. The last thing I wanted was to face all that, so I too, like every other person in my life, just *let it be.*

Habits die hard, and they die particularly hard deaths in the South when it comes to secrets and truth.

Mama and I never discussed it again, but I did run the scene through my head over and over, marveling at what had happened and trying to find an explanation. Sure, I was a tomboy, and I had no interest in dating, to say nothing of having sex with boys, but did this woman think I was a lesbian or was she attracted to me because I was a tomboy? And why, with all of Waynesboro to choose from, would she single me out to touch her breasts? Whatever the reasons, I prayed to God to give me just a chance to figure it out. Just one encounter with a girl. I was sure that was all I needed to get rid of the feelings, the *urges*, once and for all. Maybe one kiss would make them go away.

Looking back years later, I realized that Mrs. Robinson had manipulated my youth and my fear and my nascent homosexuality to her advantage. But back then, all I could do was wonder at my kaleidoscope of emotions and wish that they would go away, while at the same time I was fascinated and somewhat obsessed that I had those feelings at all. And yes, I was proud that she found me attractive. I'd been called cute and adorable and precious my whole life, but this was different. This was sexual and it sent a shiver straight through me.

There was another woman in Waynesboro—my friend Lynn's aunt Wendy—who also became a curiosity to me because she lived with a woman, but not as her roommate.

"Her *girlfriend*, but we don't talk about that," Lynn told me when we were playing at her house and I saw a picture of Aunt Wendy on the shelf.

Before I knew what it meant, I heard Mama and her friends calling Aunt Wendy a "bull dyke." I didn't know what a "dyke" was, but she did in fact resemble a bull: thick, stocky, and totally masculine, so at least that made some sense. And in my confusion about my own sexuality, I joined in the town's snickering and finger-pointing.

One day, Lynn and I were in my room at Mama's house playing records and drinking Coca-Colas. Our talk turned nasty, as young girls' talk about other girls often does, and Virgie suddenly appeared at the door. It was her one day working for Mama and she had been in the living room ironing. She didn't say a word, but the look on her face instantly silenced my cruel chatter.

After Lynn left, I went into the kitchen and sat at the counter. Virgie turned from the sink, where she was washing the lunch dishes.

"You's remember, baby girl, everybody be somebody," Virgie said, and she turned back to the sink and continued washing the dishes.

Chapter Twenty-Four

In 1968 the world was reeling. Martin Luther King Jr., and Robert F. Kennedy had been assassinated within two months of each other. I watched bloody riots at the Democratic Convention in Chicago protesting war halfway around the world in a little-known country called Vietnam. And I saw Olympic athletes in Mexico City raise black-gloved fists against racism back home in America. But in Waynesboro, people quietly went about their business, as they always had, and as they would continue to do for another staggering forty-five years, when Mississippi was finally shamed into officially abolishing slavery. That's right. The paperwork abolishing slavery in the good ole Hospitality State of Mississippi wasn't filed until *2013*, and only then when a reporter doing some research discovered the "oversight" by lawmakers.

"We're just fine down heah. We don't want change, id'n that right?" I would hear Daddy's friends say over and over. "Everybody's happy. The coloreds's happy, we're happy. Just leave it be."

Oh, we had our share of racial unrest, but if you weren't black or in the Klan, you might not have known anything was amiss at all. The most I heard from folks around town in reaction to Dr. King's assassination was that "the uppidy nigger was just askin' for trouble. Had it comin', if you ask me." Like President John F. Kennedy's murder nearly five years earlier, his killing was not mourned by anyone in my white world. And even though I had only been ten years old when Kennedy was assassinated, his loss scared and confused me, and it broke my heart.

During JFK's short presidency, real change had seemed possible, even in Waynesboro. I had watched the president's 1963 landmark speech on civil rights with quiet admiration. His simple yet powerful words—*And this nation, for all its hopes and all its boasts, will not be fully free until* all *its citizens are free*—filled me with hope and they echoed often through my head. But with his murder, I had felt, as so many of us did at that time, an adult's sense of hopelessness, confusion, and despair. Meanwhile, my parents, to all appearances, were unmoved by it. While they didn't cheer at the news and launch into a raucous rendition of "Dixie," as some of the customers outside Petty's had done, they didn't mourn him either, at least not openly. In the days that followed the assassination, my father sat at breakfast with his coffee, a cloud of cigarette smoke enveloping him, and the *Jackson Daily News* spread across the table. In between sips of coffee, he muttered that President Kennedy probably had it coming.

"The man was a nigger lover," he said. "Shoulda known better."

Only Virgie seemed to feel the loss as I had. For days, her broad cheeks had been damp from tears that she wiped away before Mama or Daddy saw them. Her expression was grave while she sat bent over a pile of peas, shucking them into a bowl, or knelt scrubbing the tub. We never discussed it—she never uttered a word to me about it as long as she lived—but in those days after his killing, her dark eyes held an aching sorrow. I did what I could to comfort her, sitting extra close to her when she sat at the counter to make some sweet tea, and letting my hand linger in hers when we walked back from the mailbox together. But there were no words I could say. I just registered the suffering that flowed from her like a silent song, a low, constant humming of sadness.

At first I assumed Virgie and I were alone in our heartache. But I was wrong. On the day of Kennedy's funeral, I had gone to the kitchen for breakfast and found my mother and Virgie standing close together. They didn't notice me lingering in the corridor. I stood very still. Mama put her hand on Virgie's shoulder. The two of them leaned against the sink with their shoulders nearly touching, their heads bowed together, Mama speaking so low that I couldn't make out the words but their cadence felt like a prayer. As I watched from the doorway, I understood for the first time that my mother had a secret side, a part of her she would never let my father or my sisters or even me see, and that somehow Virgie was privy to it.

I had felt a fierce pride for my mother then, even though I understood that her sympathies were ones she would never be able to acknowledge out loud. Not in Waynesboro. My mother was unorthodox in many ways, but when it came to relations between blacks and whites, she accepted that things were what they were. Sure, she might invite Virgie to sit at the kitchen table to eat lunch when it was just the three of us, but if Daddy was in the house, Virgie ate in the laundry room on a stool pulled up to the washer. And sure, Mama had served sweet tea out the back door to the black field hands who worked on our property, but she never once invited any of them to come inside out of the heat or the cold. I never even saw Virgie use our indoor toilet. Not a single time. To this day, sadly and shamefully, I don't know where Virgie relieved herself when she was working at our house. It's possible she held her bladder until she was back home in Hiwannee, twelve miles away. I hope she wasn't reduced to squatting in the fields or behind the big magnolia tree in the backyard. Maybe she used the bathroom in the pool house. But I simply don't know.

Mama and Virgie's moment by the sink lasted less than a minute, but it seemed to ease Virgie's sorrow a bit. She lifted her shoulders and nodded, then got back to work scouring a pan in the sink.

And here we were again, four and a half years later, mourning not one, but two great men who had promised hope and change and equality. Once again, I grieved, but for Southern blacks, and the rural Southern blacks in my life, the dual assassinations of King and then Senator Robert Kennedy six weeks later left them devastated, but also frightened for their own safety. Over the past fifteen years, they had lived through the deaths of nearly two dozen civil rights workers—and those were just the ones who made the news, so while losing Dr. King was tragic, it was as if they half expected it. But Robert Kennedy's death was different. First of all, he was the brother of the former president of the United States, and while he had been a spearhead of racial change and spoken so eloquently on the night of King's death to a black crowd in Indianapolis, his powerful status in white America supposedly protected him from violence. So, the fact that a gunman walked up to him in a crowded Los Angeles hotel kitchen and shot him dead sent a clear sign that anybody who spoke up, spoke out, and demanded change could and perhaps *would* be murdered anywhere, anytime. And while it's true that on many levels Virgie and Beulah Mae and all the black people in my life had known that awful truth their entire lives, to have two of their heroes, international heroes at that, assassinated within weeks of each other was new. And it was terrifying.

The message was powerful: No one was safe from the violent and often murderous forces that fought against social change. I too felt that something was irreparably broken in the world. *Is this what happens if you go out and fight and try to do the right thing?* But again, I mourned quietly and only with Virgie and Beulah Mae, and only then behind the safety of closed doors. There were no protests in Waynesboro like the ones throughout the rest of the country, no marches or demands for civil rights and justice for Reverend King. And if there had been, it's very doubtful if even one black person would have shown up. I never heard of Virgie or Beulah Mae or Mayfield or any black in town registering to vote, or even talking about it. Their lives were about day-to-day survival, not social change.

Chapter Twenty-Five

You'd have thought my disastrous experiment taking Virgie to eat in Petty's would have taught me a lesson about forcing someone else to be part of my civil disobedience, but it didn't. I remained naïve to how slowly social change can come. Several months later, I was driving my brand-new car—a Monte Carlo—through downtown Waynesboro and saw a small group of people going from car to car passing out pamphlets and taking donations in little buckets at the four-way stop in front of the First Baptist Church. They were all wearing white robes and white pointed hoods.

I knew the Klan existed, of course, but I rarely saw it up close. Under those white hoods and robes I could see *real* people. For all I knew, they were my very own teachers and preachers and doctors and store clerks. All full of hate and rage, hiding under their shameful robes. I knew what the Klan had done and what they were capable of doing still. I had heard about fourteen-year-old Emmett Till of Money, Mississippi, a few hours north of Waynesboro, beaten beyond recognition and killed for speaking to a white woman. I knew that the civil rights activist Medgar Evers had been shot dead in his driveway in Jackson. I had been to the Shubuta Bridge, just a few miles up the Chickasawhay River from our farm, where four blacks, including a pregnant woman, were lynched in 1918. Someone had pointed to a large dent in one of the bridge's iron struts and told me, "That's where they hanged the pregnant one."

But mostly people around Waynesboro just shushed up talk of the Klan, like they did most ugly and awful things.

"That was a long time ago" was their glossing over of the murder and rape and carnage of our shared history.

"Let it be," they'd say, to which I would mutter, "Like hell I will."

Outraged by having the brazen barbarians right in front of me on the main street of Waynesboro, I made a quick U-turn, and headed to the dry cleaners where I knew Virgie's daughter Cindy was working.

Cindy looked up from the back where she was pressing sheets as I rushed in.

"Hey, Mr. Graham," I said, talking to Cindy's boss behind the counter. "Can I talk to Cindy outside real quick?"

"Sure thing, Miss Tena. How's your daddy been? Haven't seen him in a while."

"Oh, he's just fine," I said over my shoulder as I pulled Cindy out the door.

"Listen!" I said, the minute we were outside my words coming out in a jumble of nerves and anger. "The Klan is passing the collection plate on Azalea Drive! I need you to go with me and take a stand, tell those rednecks they're evil and to get out of town!"

"Naw!" Cindy said. "I ain't doin' that!"

"Come on, Cindy," I pleaded. "Just go tell Mr. Graham that my mama is sick and I need you, but you'll be right back."

I knew, like Virgie before her, she wouldn't be able to say no to me. In the same way I'd forced Virgie to eat in Petty's, I didn't stop to think that I was pulling Cindy into what could have been a very dangerous, even deadly, situation. All I was thinking about was showing those horrible people that not everybody goose-stepped to their hate.

Cindy followed me out to the car. Like her mother, she instinctively reached for the back door, but I insisted she sit up front with me. Without a word, but with her eyes asking me if I knew what the hell I was doing, she got in and we drove to the intersection.

As my car stopped, all eyes, those behind white sheets as well as every other pair in nearby cars and on the sidewalk, turned to me and the black girl in the front seat next to me.

"Oh Lord, Tena, what they gonna do t' us?" Cindy was bouncing up and down on the seat, like a kid who has to go to the bathroom, but I knew it was her nerves. She and Virgie both had a nervous habit of bouncing their legs and feet up and down. They also both had an anxious laugh, but she wasn't laughing now.

I looked over at Cindy and saw something I had never seen on her open, wide face: terror. I too felt a fluttering of fear tickle deep in my belly, but with it I also felt indignation and, yes, excitement. Like I had at Petty's, I thought I had the best insurance policy around: Lamar Clark. I also felt that something had to give. Enough was enough. They might get mad, but I trusted they wouldn't hurt me, or her. Cindy, wiser than

I, knew she had no such guarantee of safety with these illit-
erate rednecks and quickly turned around so that she could
jump in the backseat.

I put out my hand and held her arm.

"No, don't you jump in the backseat. This is nineteen sev-
enty, you have every right to sit up here with me. These creeps
aren't going to stop you, not with me driving."

I still didn't get it.

"Please, Tena, just drive on through. Please. No need to get
'em all riled up. They seen me in the front seat. That's enough.
Keep drivin'. *Please.*"

"No. You sit tight."

I rolled down my window and looked at the eyes under the
white hood nearest us. I could see the hate and outrage burning through the little holes cut into the cheap, white muslin.
The man nearest us leaned down, looking across me at Cindy,
then back at me, his eyes behind the white mask moving like
a doll's.

"Ya'r goin' straight t' hell havin' that nigger in your front
seat. God's 'shamed of you. God hates niggers and He hates
nigger lovers worse!"

The muslin covering his face moved in little puffs as he
spoke, and his voice was high-pitched and whiny. I could
tell, just by the thick, backwoods drawl, that these men and
women—and yes, there were women, judging by their hands
poking out of the sleeves—were the poorest of the rural Mississippi poor and about as ignorant and hostile as they come.

Rage took over. I opened my door and jumped up on the
running board of the car.

"No," I screamed, my finger pointed to the closest white sheet's face. "YOU'RE the ones goin' to hell. God is ashamed of YOU, the way you act and talk!" My words were coming out in a frenzied rush, and I started pointing at the other white robes gathered around the car. "You and you and YOU are going to hell! Why don't you take off those hoods? If you're so damn sure you got God on your side, why don't you take off those hoods?"

"You gonna git yo'self in a whole lotta trouble, 'less you git back in tha' car, little girl," the man closest to me said. "We all know who yo' daddy is. Maybe we's give him a call. Whaddya say t' that?"

"I say call him! Cowards! Call him!"

Behind me I heard Cindy's pleading voice, sobbing now, "Please, Tena, let's *go*. Git back in the car. *Please!*"

I looked in the car and saw Cindy curled up in a ball, shaking, but I wasn't quite finished.

"I bet y'all don't have a full set a teeth between you! *NO ONE* is going to tell me who I can and can't have in my front seat!" I yelled at the holes in the sheets.

"Y'all gonna git yo'self in a whole lotta trouble," a voice growled near me.

"Cowards!" I gave them a wave of my arms. "Y'all a bunch of country-ass, redneck cowards! God is ashamed of YOU!"

It was then that I saw a familiar car come careening around the corner. Daddy jumped out before it came to a complete stop and ran over to my car. As he got closer, I saw something in his face I never had before: real fear. Oh, he was also pissed as hell all right, but he knew the Devil with whom he was dealing better than I, and that those folks around him in white hoods made up their own rules.

"Tena, git in the car, *now*," he said, calm to the point of conversational. It was one of the rare times when he didn't stutter.

"Yo' little girl's been sayin' some ugly things, Mister Lamar, some downright ugly things," one of the white hoods said.

Almost imperceptibly, I saw Daddy register relief: *They know who I am. It'll be okay.*

"And she'll be hearin' some ugly things from *me* when I get her on home, you can be GODdamn sure of that," Daddy told the man.

I stumbled off the running board. My fight was gone. In fact, as my adrenaline rush faded I realized I was exhausted to the point of nearly falling over. I got in the car and with trembling fingers turned the ignition.

"I'll see you at home, young lady," Daddy said, but I could see the fight had gone out of him too. He just wanted to get all of us the hell out of there before anyone decided my little confrontation should end differently.

From the rearview mirror, I saw Daddy get in his car. The hoods watched as we drove down the street.

When I got to Mama's after dropping Cindy back at the dry cleaners, she was pacing nervously, waiting for me. Her phone had been ringing off the hook.

"Oh my Lord, what in the hell are you thinking? You're gonna get us all killed. Is that what you want? You, me, your sisters, Cindy, Virgie—they could come after *all* of us. They could burn a cross on our lawn!"

"We have to do something, Mama, we have to take a stand!"

"No we don't, because it ain't gonna do any good. You and I both know it ain't right, and those folks hidin' under their sheets are pure evil, but they don't care what a little rich white girl and her mama think about their lynching and their burnin' crosses. They're *crazy*, Tena, and so are you for thinking your shouting from your car is going to change them any!"

"I'm so sorry, Mama, but I had to do something. I just had to."

"I know, honey. But next time don't drag poor Cindy into it. Bless her heart. She must have been scared half to death."

And I knew she was.

I wasn't looking forward to seeing Daddy, but turns out it was Elizabeth who was loaded for bear. Like Mama, she had already heard the story and came flying through the door a short time later.

"You need to be careful, Tena, or else people around town are gonna start talkin', maybe thinkin' you're a . . ."

Her words trailed off, but I knew what she was about to say. I stared at her, shocked. Elizabeth had always had my back. Sure, as an older sister she often gave that back a mighty pinch or shove, but I knew she loved me and would do anything for me. But now, fear and anger had gotten the best of her. I knew she loved Viola and Virgie. But that day in Mama's living room, she wasn't thinking about them. She was only thinking that the whole damn town would be talking about her *nigger-loving* sister.

I didn't answer her. I didn't know what I could say. So I just walked away.

Chapter Twenty-Six

By the summer of 1970, after sixteen years of delays and token desegregation, the U.S. Supreme Court ordered Mississippi to dismantle the state's ninety-five-year-old "separate but equal" education system. Knowing that that included Waynesboro Central High School, Daddy took action. One afternoon a few weeks before the start of my senior year, he called me at Mama's house.

"Hey, Tena Rix! I got excitin' news! You're g-g-gonna go to a p-p-private school in Meridian!"

I just stared in shock at the wall phone in Mama's kitchen.

"And," he continued with his best salesman's voice, "I g-g-got you and ya mama a nice apartment up there so y'all can live t-t-together while you finish out high school." He sounded extremely pleased with himself.

"Daddy, what are you talkin' about? I am not leaving my senior year to finish up with a bunch of strangers in Meridian."

"Listen to me, Tena," he said, getting to the point of it all. "No d-d-daughter of mine is goin' to go to school with n-n-niggers. That's for d-d-damn sure."

"Well, none of my friends are leaving, so I'm not leaving

either!" I said. "*I'm* not the one who has a problem going to school with black kids!"

"The only ones who ain't leaving Waynesboro d-d-don't have the money to go, but I do, and you're g-g-goin'!"

"No I'm not!"

"Now d-d-don't you go thinkin' like a girl, Tena Rix," he said, his voice all smooth and oily again. "All I ask is that you drive up there with your m-m-mama and t-t-take a look, that's all."

After a few more rounds of "You're goin'!" followed by "No I'm not!" I realized I had to at least drive up to take a look. The next day Mama and I drove up to Meridian.

The "private school" turned out to be nothing more than three broken-down trailers that looked like they had been thrown together overnight with a handmade sign tacked to one of the doors. I could just picture it: a few good ole boys sitting around one night, swilling their bourbons and coming up with this sorry excuse for a school—anything so that their precious little darlin' girls didn't have to share the same class-rooms with *them niggers.*

As we turned into an empty field and drove up the dirt path to the trailers, Mama looked over at me, nervous.

"Now, honey, don't you be judgin' a book by its cover. Come on, let's go in and take a look."

After the school's "administrator" took us on a tour, which took all of ten minutes, I turned to Mama and said, "Okay, I've seen it. Let's go."

On the ride back to Waynesboro, I repeated over and over, "No. Way. I am *not* going."

"Well, your daddy is set on you going there. I think it's pretty much a done deal, and I don't see how there's anything you can do."

I looked over at her, wishing I could say that those words sounded downright strange coming out of her mouth. She was, after all, the only person in the entire state of Mississippi, as far as I could tell, who had told Daddy to go straight to hell. But this time, she wasn't thinking about herself. She was thinking about me and what my battle against him would be like.

"Don't worry, Mama, this is my fight with Daddy and I will fight it. If I have to, I will run back to Waynesboro every time I get dragged up there. I'll just run home and back to school with my friends."

Which is exactly what I told Daddy when we got home.

"You'll get used to it," he said. "It's all s-s-set. I paid for you to go, I g-g-got you and your mama a nice apartment c-c-close by. That's it. You're *going*." He stood with his hands on his hips, a cigarette bouncing in his lips as he spoke.

In the end, I didn't go. Eventually even Daddy knew he'd lost the battle and I stayed put in Waynesboro. But that doesn't mean my senior year was much fun, and it certainly wasn't what I expected it would or should be. The tension was thick the entire year. The white kids stuck with the whites, and the blacks stuck very much with the blacks. Try as I might to make the black students feel welcome and comfortable, I largely failed. I had a few black girlfriends, mostly those kids whose mamas I knew, like Cindy, but there were many more who kept their distance.

One day I was at my locker and was suddenly surrounded by a group of about four or five black girls. Tough girls. They had already made themselves known at Waynesboro Central High.

"We heard you called one of us a nigger," the biggest girl sneered as she pushed me into the steel lockers behind me.

Alarmed, but also just plain shocked, I responded, "I would never use that word! Not ever."

"Don't you lie to me," the girl said, her face only inches from mine and her index finger pressing hard against my chest.

"Listen, y'all got the wrong girl. I've tried to *welcome* y'all here," I said. "I'm on *your* side!"

"They ain't no *sides*, white girl."

Suddenly, three other black girls I had befriended appeared and they pushed their way through to me.

"Y'all best move on," one of my friends told the girl in my face. "Tena ain't said anything 'bout ch'all."

Finally, the tough girls moved on, but not without a lot of sneers and even some spit on the floor.

Things didn't get much better from there. Just as I had been wrong about Virgie wanting to eat inside Petty's, I was also wrong about assuming every black boy and girl was dying to attend the previously whites-only Waynesboro Central High. Those kids were leaving the comfort and familiarity of their school, the only one they'd ever known, and entering hostile territory. Very hostile. Never again in their years in Mississippi public schools would they see a black student elected president of their class. It would come, but not in their time. Never again would one of them be voted King or Queen or "Most

Likely to Succeed" or "Most Congenial" or "Best-Looking." Never again would their best football player receive the MVP award and be carried around the field on the shoulders of his teammates. Instead, they would be shunned, harassed, spit on, jeered at, bullied, beat up, and worse. School would become yet another battleground in their struggles to survive in our white-dominated world.

The white kids and their parents were mad, and the black kids and their parents were mad *and* frightened. We became a school with an invisible dividing line down the middle. Most of the white parents had no interest in seeing their kids share desks and bathrooms and hallways and football teams. When it came time for our prom, it remained stubbornly segregated. We white kids had our prom, and the black kids had theirs, a shameful two-prom tradition that would last well into, and in some towns through, the 1990s and 2000s.

As far as I remember, integration didn't spark violence in white Waynesboro. No one had a cross burned on their lawn, no one got strung up on Shubuta's "hanging" bridge or run off the road. That said, my cousin Rita Faye will tell you she drove by burning crosses as late as 1973 on her way from Waynesboro to Alabama, and she remembers kids at our football game yelling "Kill the nigger!" when a black player on the other team scored a touchdown or caught a Hail Mary pass. For whatever reason, I didn't or couldn't see it. Maybe I was too wrapped up in my music or focused on my last year in high school and getting the hell out of Waynesboro. Or maybe, I just didn't want to see it, along with the Confederate flags flying over the bank and post office and gas station and general store.

One thing that was integrated in name, but not in fact, were the various Mississippi beauty pageants. I know because I competed in the Miss Wayne County Junior Miss Pageant in 1971 and I didn't have a single black competitor.

As incongruous as it now feels, I competed in pageants my whole life, as had each of my sisters. Our family home movies, most of them dutifully shot by our proud mama, are chock-full of images of us headed to our pageants and proms, dressed to the nines and looking like Scarlett O'Hara headed to the Wilkes' barbeque. Elizabeth insisted I be part of something she considered important and traditional and part of the life of any girl who was raised in the South. Southern belle, and all that. For over ten years, I dutifully played the part she wanted me to play. But when I graduated from high school, I knew I was also leaving pageants behind. The 1971 Mississippi Junior Miss Pageant was my last. For the talent portion I played the drums.

From that first moment when I put drumsticks to drum at the music store in Laurel, I had been obsessed with the drums and dreamed of one day playing professionally. I wanted to play like I had heard Mahalia Jackson sing or Martin Luther King Jr., speak—with power, with grace, with joy, and with a language all my own. In seventh grade, I had gone to the school's band director and asked him for an audition.

"Miss Tena," he said, sizing me up, "we are a *marching* band and, what are you? Five feet if you're an inch? You are way too small to carry a snare drum back and forth across the field."

But if I could . . . ? And so I convinced the band director to let me try out, and at the next football game I marched with the band and played "The Pink Panther Theme Song" for the length and breadth of the field and back. The song was frivolous and the snare drum's sound a monotonous staccato, but as I marched and whaled away on the head with the drumsticks, I felt a surge of joy, deliverance even. The harder I beat the drum, the better the sound. The better the sound, the louder the crowd roared. It felt like a shot of adrenaline was flowing from my hands and arms and right through my hip where the drum rested, like an unwieldy messenger bag. It was nothing short of redemption, from what I'll never be sure, but I beat those sticks so hard my teeth vibrated and my hands blistered and sweat poured into my eyes.

I made the band and had been playing the drums ever since. I was pretty good. Actually, I was damn good. My friends knew I could play the hell out of them, and they even compared me to the best of our day: Karen Carpenter, Keith Moon, and even Ringo Starr. But the Junior Miss Pageant audience sitting in the Waynesboro Central High School gym had no idea I could beat the tar out of a set of drums. So I decided to have a little fun.

When it was my turn to perform, I walked out in a little girl's pinafore with a white apron, a white bonnet, tap shoes with white anklet socks, and a demure "aw-shucks" expression, looking around in mock surprise at finding myself in an auditorium full of people. I tapped my way over to the drums, still looking around, wide-eyed, as if to say, *Why, Lord have mercy, what're these?*

I picked up the drumsticks and, putting a finger to my cheek, iced the cake by asking, "Well, I might as well give it a try? Wha' ch'all say?"

By that time, my friends were cheering and whooping; they knew what was coming, while the rest of the audience was trying to figure out why a seventeen-year-old girl was wearing a skirt short enough to shock the church ladies in the audience.

I sat down at the drums, mumbling, "Well, by gosh and by golly, I'll see if'n I can figure these here things out." After a few timid taps of the drums and a clang or two of the cymbals, I let loose in a no-holds-barred rendition of the drum solo in "Wipe Out." Soon the bonnet went flying, my stiff bouffant was in my eyes, my pinafore had ridden up to my hips as my legs spread wide to pound the foot keys (I had thought ahead and worn little shortie shorts), and my hands were a blur.

I won. My closest competition, Mary Lou Smith, had sung a decent enough rendition of "New York, New York," but once I had the audience on its feet, even she knew she was cooked.

Chapter Twenty-Seven

Ever since the day I had cast my innocent eyes on my sister's friend in the majorette outfit, I knew my attraction to that beautiful girl was about more than just her sparkling green leotard and tasseled white boots. For years I didn't know what it was called and in my head I thought I was the only one who had these feelings. I have to assume I was Waynesboro's lone white radical, and I was evidently also one of its only lesbians, except of course for the two women who ran the drugstore, my friend's aunt Wendy, and possibly "Mrs. Robinson."

When my own cousin Bubba told me in confidence that he was gay, I stood there in shock, my mouth hanging open so long I could have caught flies. But it wasn't the surprise of his being gay—I had known for years that he had no interest in girls. My shock was that he would say the word out loud, in Waynesboro no less. And I also feared he would then ask me straight up, "Well, you are too, right?"

Yes, I had feelings for girls, but I didn't want anyone else to know. Not here. I figured if I could ignore those feelings, then no one else would have to know either, and I could quietly escape and figure it out later, far, far from Waynesboro.

I put up a decent façade. I was still considered a tomboy in many respects—I loved sports, hated dressing up, played the drums—but I was never without a boyfriend, and I could play the part of prude. Thankfully, things were different for junior high and high school girls in the 1960s and 1970s South. Sure, there were those girls who did fool around, even slept around, but by far the majority of us were "good girls" who easily maintained our virginity without a lot of pressure from our boyfriends. *It was just the way it was.* All through high school I dated a sweet boy, David, and in fact loved him as deeply as I would ever love a man, as much as I was capable of loving any man, but only as a treasured friend, not as a romantic partner. In fact, the thought of having sex with him, or with any man, was foreign and wrong. I just couldn't even imagine it. And I didn't want to.

After high school, most of my girlfriends were heading off to early marriages—typical of that time in the South— and I realized someday I too would have to marry, even if it meant suffering a miserable marriage and maybe even taking my own life in the end. I knew that if I tried to live out my life as a heterosexual, the lie would eventually destroy me. I had watched the television shows and movies, read the books and magazines, and listened to my mother and sisters and girl-friends talk about marriage and sex and babies. But it all felt and sounded like a fantasy world, totally unrelated to me and to what I wanted for my life.

All through high school, I thought that if I had to marry a man, it would be David. He loved me unconditionally, and I knew he would understand and maybe even accept that our marriage wouldn't be a traditional or physically passionate one. But in the end, I couldn't do that to him, so I ended it. He deserved better. So after David and I broke up, I figured I'd have to find some other man, get married, have the standard 2.3 children, settle into my faux-Colonial house in the suburbs, and at least make my family happy.

In the fall of 1971, I headed off to the University of Southern Mississippi in Hattiesburg, because of the three colleges available to me—Ole Miss, Mississippi State, and USM—USM had the best music program. Once settled, I soon found a series of boyfriends, all from good families who put fraternity pin after fraternity pin on my collar and never once questioned why I didn't want to progress beyond our chaste kisses. No questions were asked, and I didn't volunteer the truth: Far from enjoying those boys' kisses, I could barely stomach them.

I loved college but only tolerated my studies, knowing I might need my education to fall back on if my music didn't pan out, but it was Mama who ended up having the time of her life. She visited me often and would party like *she* was the sorority sister. As much as I loved my mama, her visits were every college student's nightmare. Rather than get a hotel room, she stayed with her best friend, Midge, who was the nearby Pi Kappa Alpha fraternity's house mother. That's right. My mother would stay at USM's Pike House, as it was called; *the* party frat on campus. During most of her visits, she was boozed up as she made the party rounds to fraternity houses and the local bars. Everywhere she went, she was surrounded by an entourage of my friends, who all adored her. She was the life of every party as a college drunk, so different from the way she was when I was younger and she drank largely by herself, alone in her living room. Often I would come back to my room after classes and find a gaggle of my girlfriends, and sometimes a few boyfriends, at Mama's feet while she held court, telling stories about getting married at fifteen and being hunted down Highway 84 by her Big Papa and chasing Daddy through town with a loaded .38, her audience laughing until the tears rolled down their cheeks.

Those visits were both embarrassing and endearing. I cringed at the sight of my mother stumbling drunk at a Pike party, or dancing too close with some random frat boy. But she and I also had some of our best talks during that time, sitting at opposite ends of the couch, our legs stretched out under a quilt, our toes touching. She told me of her childhood, and her mean mother and spiteful sisters. She told me about her marriage to Daddy, and just how painful it had been. She told me that she'd had a lot of manfriends after Daddy, probably too many, but that her one chance at remarrying fizzled when I had refused to move with her to Meridian, where the man's business was based.

She also admitted that she had fallen in love with another man close to the end of her marriage to Daddy, a sweet man from town named Curley. And I remembered that Daddy used to just talk about Curley all the time, obsessively. She told me that she had loved Curley "because he was nice to me and he liked my music and he thought I was funny. And, he thought I was really beautiful."

"And so what happened, Mama?" I asked her.

"Well, I wasn't ready to leave your daddy."

"Do you wish you had?"

She thought about it for a minute, then shook her head slowly.

"No, because I needed to be on my own for a while. To see if I could find Vivian. I had lost Vivian a long time ago."

I looked at her, my surprise showing. "Mama, I've never heard you talk this way."

She smiled her sly little smile and nodded. "I know, baby, but even your old mama can do some real thinkin' every now and again."

On one visit, she stayed sober until well into the afternoon, reading in my rocking chair at my apartment and waiting for me to come in from classes.

"Come here, honey, and sit down. I got somethin' to say," she said, patting the couch near where she sat on the rocker.

Instantly worried that she was sick, or had some other awful news, I sat down.

"Honey, I feel like you're keepin' somethin' from me, and it hurts. It feels like there's a wedge between us, and I don't like it. We've always told each other everything, but now . . ."

I looked into her sweet, beautiful eyes the color of black coffee, and tried not to break down sobbing. I knew it was time. It was finally time. A few weeks before, one of my friends in a nearby fraternity had been "outed," although we didn't call it that at the time. He had gone home to tell his parents that he was gay, and afterward, had gone to the guesthouse behind their garage and shot himself in the head. When they found him, he had the gun in one hand and the Bible in the other. I too had fought against the truth of who I was for so long. Now, facing my mother's pleading eyes, I was almost relieved to be done with the lie.

"It's big, Mama," I said, my words barely a whisper. "It's really big."

"Oh Lord, Tena," she said and grabbed my shoulder. "Are you pregnant?"

I almost laughed, but thankfully didn't.

"No, Mama. It's not that."

"Oh my Lord. You havin' an affair with a married man?"

"No, Mama, I'm not. It's not that either," I said, a chuckle finally escaping me.

"Well, those are the two worst things I can think of. What else is it, then?"

She sat back in the chair and rocked, waiting.

Well, I thought, *if those are the two worst things she can think of, maybe I'm in pretty good shape here.* I took a deep breath.

"I'm gay, Mama."

She never blinked, but looked at me with the saddest eyes I'd seen since she left the farm so many years before. Her eyes filled, and a huge tear rolled slowly down her cheek.

"Are you sure, baby?"

"Yes, Mama. I've always been gay, I just didn't know what it was." Then my tears started. "I'm so sorry, Mama."

She shook her head slowly from side to side, opening her arms.

"Come here, baby, and sit in my lap."

Like a child, I crawled into her lap on the rocker and she held me as tightly as she ever had. We rocked in silence, and she stroked my hair and wiped the tears from my cheeks. Then she spoke.

"I'm not cryin' because I'm ashamed of you, or wish you were any different. I love you with all of my heart and always will." She began to sob. "I'm cryin' because it's gonna be so hard for you, baby, so hard. I wish I could protect you from the world of pain and hurt coming your way, but I can't. *That's* why I'm crying."

I felt her arms tense to hold me tighter as she took a huge breath, letting it slowly escape her lips. I pressed my head against her as we rocked. I couldn't speak.

We rocked until the room was dark.

Chapter Twenty-Eight

Even though I had shared my secret with Mama, I was far from being "out." While I understood, intellectually, that I was gay, I was still stuck in the middle ground between embracing it as a concept and living my life authentically. All I felt was frustration and confusion. And as loving as Mama had been when I told her I was gay, she was conflicted morally: I knew she would soon be quoting me chapter and verse on the evils of homosexuality, just as she had those many years ago when I asked her what Daddy meant by "spinster." Then one afternoon, a notice was put up in my sorority house about an upcoming talk by two representatives from something called the Campus Crusade for Christ. Sounded like one of those hippie cults from California we had been hearing about. I audibly groaned when I read the notice because attendance was mandatory—or else face getting a demerit. So that evening, dragging my heels and slumping my shoulders, I went in and sat down.

Sure enough, Ron and Nancy Kaiser were an attractive twentysomething couple from California. They were positively perky. *Typical!* I thought, and sat in the audience mentally chanting, *Don't listen, don't listen, don't listen—it's all a bunch of culty crap.* Then I heard: "God isn't about what your neighbor is doing, or even what your priest or preacher is doing; God is about you and your relationship with Christ. And no matter what that relationship is, He loves you, and loves you unconditionally."

I sat straight up in my chair, a chill running the length of my spine as the words settled. Who *were* these people? Young and hip, how could they also be Christians? I didn't know you could be all those things at once.

All my life I had seethed at the hypocrisy of the so-called faithful who drank and swore and sinned on Saturday night and then stood up in the choir as if they had halos floating above their heads; at the hypocrisy of the message "God loves all of his children," but evidently not his black children; at Mama's hypocrisy as she held the Bible in one hand and a tumbler of Jack Daniel's in the other. It had never made any sense to me how someone could behave terribly one day and then sit in church with an angelic little smile on his face as if his slate had just been wiped clean of all and any sins. And here was an answer: This couple's simple message was that others' hypocrisy doesn't matter. It was only *my* relationship with God that did.

I felt something in me shift, and as I left the lecture I realized that what I felt was free. Free from the hypocrisy, free from the heavy cloak of righteousness, free from the burden of witnessing others' sins and worrying that I needed to do something about it. A few weeks later, I received a letter from the Kaisers urging me to think about joining their next Bible study workshop in California. I turned the letter over in my hands, then folded it carefully and tucked it in a drawer.

On my next trip home after coming out to Mama, Elizabeth suggested we go for a ride. In my family, "Let's go for a ride" was always code for "We gotta talk some shit." Once Elizabeth and I had bought some Cokes and were parked out at the old farm, her lips started to quiver and she turned to me with tears in her eyes.

"Tena, I just gotta ask you. Are you a *homosexual?*" the word coming out of her a pinched, painful squeak.

I couldn't stop myself. I laughed and said, "Yes, I guess I am a *homosexual*, if that's what you want to call it."

She immediately began crying, wailing actually, and her words came out in a great tumble of tears and gasps of breath.

"No! You're not! You're just confused because you've never been with a man. But I have a plan. We're gonna go to the Ramada Inn, we'll each get a room, then we'll go to the bar and drink and dance, and I want you to pick out a guy, any guy, and once you take him up to your room, you'll see you are NOT a homosexual!"

Amused as well as horrified, I knew I could parlay her crazy idea into leverage.

I jumped up in my seat, full of righteous indignation. "I'm going to tell Daddy what you said!"

Her eyes got big as saucers.

"Tena! Listen to me, it'll work! Daddy doesn't have to

know a thing! And then you'll be cured! You won't be a *ho-mosexual* anymore!"

"Oh my God, take me to Mama's now!"

We drove back into town without speaking and she dropped me at Mama's. I slammed the car door and went into the house.

"Hey, baby, how was your drive with Elizabeth?" Mama asked.

"Mama, did you tell Elizabeth I was gay?" I demanded.

She suddenly got very interested in her puzzle, avoiding looking at me.

"Why, heavens no," she said, but without a lot of conviction.

"Mama?" I persisted.

She threw the puzzle on the table. "Well, all your sisters have been askin' me what's going on with you, why you're not datin' any college boys anymore, and Elizabeth just wouldn't let up. I couldn't keep it from her any longer!"

"And Georgia, did you tell Georgia?"

"No, I did not!" she said, outraged at the mere suggestion.

"All right, then. I gotta go and tell her," I said and headed to my car.

I walked into Georgia's kitchen and started right in.

"You better sit down, I have something to tell you," I said.

Georgia sat down obediently and looked at me as she always had: the sister-mother always there to pick up any of my scattered, shattered pieces. Her dark brown eyes were the same color as mine. Had I never noticed before that none of us Clark girls got Daddy's steel-blue eyes? We all got Mama's Indian princess dark brown. The realization made me happy.

"I'm gay."

Her eyes got a littler bigger, but that was her only reaction. Without a word, she got up and came around the kitchen counter to sit next to me. She put her arm around me and pulled me close.

"I don't quite know what that means, but you're my sister and I love you, and that's all that matters. I love you."

Like with Mama before her, we sat holding each other for a long, long time.

Last among the siblings to hear my news, Penny instantly turned it into a social occasion.

"Listen, I want you to come to the football game at USM next week. There are two men who go to every game who we tailgate with and they're *friends*, if you get my drift. Not just *friends*, but *together* together. And they're so cute and so nice, bless their hearts, and I told them that I have a sister that's like them and—"

"You already told them, before you heard it from me?"

"Well, Lord knows how long it was going to take you to tell me! Besides, they're so nice and sweet and I know you'll just love 'em!"

Of all my sisters, Penny was not only the bravest one when it came to facing down Daddy, she was also the most progressive in her politics. For her, my being gay was merely an excuse to raise a beer at the football game with their gay friends. Being nearly fifteen years older than me, she was closer in age to my mother, and our relationship was filtered through that age difference. But the times we were together remain vivid and dear, particularly plum-picking season when she'd drive over to the farm and yell down the hall to me in my room, "Come on, Tena! Grab your pail! The plums are ripe and we're goin' plum pickin'!"

"Just you and me goin'?" I'd ask.

"Yes, just you and *I* are goin'," she'd say, correcting my grammar, like Mama always would. Being from the South, especially Mississippi, we have our own language, using words I'm not even sure exist in the dictionary. But Penny knew the difference and she'd let me know it too. I hated the lessons then, but I try to remember them now, because now I miss them.

We'd spend the afternoon picking red plums and, when they were in season, the gumball-size yellow plums, and eat through just about our entire pails before we got back to the house.

While Penny was arranging a night out for me with her gay friends, Elizabeth had been busy telling Daddy. As Georgia and I sat around a few days later sipping sweet tea, he pulled up to the house, honked twice, and waited for me to come outside.

"Get in. Let's go t-t-take a drive," he said, waving toward the passenger door with a lit cigarette in his hand.

I got in as commanded, my stomach knotting up. We cleared the downtown streets of Waynesboro, crossed the railroad tracks on the west side of town, and headed to the farm where I'd spent most of my childhood. Daddy had long since sold the house, but we still owned the land around it. When we got there, he pulled into the pasture and turned off the engine. His face held its usual scowl, betraying nothing.

He lit a cigarette, looked straight out the windshield, and made his statement, pronouncing the word as if for the first time in his life.

"Well, Tena Rix, your s-s-sister tells me you're a HO-MO-sexual. Is that true?"

While fearing I might throw up if I opened my mouth too fast, I nonetheless had to smile. I waited until my nerves were calmed a bit before speaking.

"Well, Daddy, that's not a word I use, but now that you bring it up. Yes. Yes, I am."

He shook his head, taking a long drag on his cigarette and letting the smoke out in a slow exhale.

"I j-j-just don't git it," he said, his thick Mississippi accent sounding thicker than usual. "Can you p-p-please explain that to me?"

And in a flash I knew just what to say.

"Well, Daddy, you know how you really love women, a lot of women?"

He looked at me confused. "Well, ah, ah, ah, yeah . . ." he sputtered, actually confessing his infidelity to me for the first time.

I waited a few beats for effect. "Well, so do I."

I wish I had taken a photograph of his face. For perhaps the first and only time in his life, he was speechless. Then he cranked the truck and we headed back out onto the main road as if we'd just talked about the cows in the pasture. That was it. He never spoke of it again.

Whenever I came home from college, along with making the rounds to my mama's, daddy's, and sisters' houses, I would visit our family chiropractor, Dr. William Jones. Billy, as we all called him, had worked on the entire family for years, from Daddy on down. My father may have hated doctors, but he swore by chiropractors ever since his log truck accident years before.

In addition to being a chiropractor, Dr. Jones was a fire-breathing Christian fundamentalist and a Holy Roller preacher. Even with all of the Bible-thumping, the whole family trusted, even loved him, and he loved us right back, me included, albeit with some serious reservations after I came out as gay.

On one particular visit, I went to him for my regular adjustment and he locked the door behind me. *Uh-oh*, I thought. *This can't be good.*

"Now, Tena, I'm gonna pray over you cuz you have the demon in you and that demon is HOMO-sexuality!" His eyes were flashing and his hands were already coming toward me.

Oh my God, I thought, *how in hell am I gonna get out of this one?*

"I gonna beat that demon right out of you, but you gotta trust me! I've done it before! I've seen that demon runnin' away! AMEN! IN THE NAME OF JEHOVAH! I've seen it happen. HALLELUJAH JESUS!"

While his eyes were closed and his hands clasped toward heaven, I made my move and busted out of the room before he could say another "AMEN!!"

I drove home so fast I barely closed the car door. When I got to Mama's house, I ran into the living room, panting.

"What in the hell . . . ?" she asked, looking up from her crossword puzzle.

"EXACTLY!" I shouted. "Billy just tried to *beat the demon of homosexuality out of me!*"

"WHAT? Why, I'm gonna kill that sonofabitch!" Mama may have found Jesus Christ as her Savior and Redeemer, tithing her 10 percent faithfully every month, but she sure as hellfire was not going to have *anyone* tell her what the Good Lord wants and doesn't want for her own baby daughter.

Before I knew what was happening, Mama was out of her chair and in her car, driving back to Billy's office.

When she got home, I asked her what she'd said to him.

"I told him that if I ever hear of him telling you that he's gonna beat the homosexual out of you again, I'll be over THERE beatin' the livin' hell outta HIM!"

Mama, my one-woman crusade. Her conservative Christian beliefs couldn't hold a candle to the ferocious mother-lion in her, determined to never again let harm come to her baby. Even so, when I got back to college after that visit, I found a little piece of paper tucked into my suitcase. It wasn't a love note. It was First Corinthians, chapter 6, verses 9–10: *Or do you not know the wrongdoers will not inherit the Kingdom of God? Do not be deceived: Neither the sexually immoral nor idolaters nor adulterers nor <u>men who have sex with men</u>* (she underlined this part just in case I missed her point), *nor thieves nor the greedy nor drunkards nor slanderers nor swindlers will inherit the Kingdom of God.*

She just couldn't help herself, sending me back with a little hellfire and damnation.

Chapter Twenty-Nine

On a hot and muggy Hattiesburg morning in June of 1976, I stood in the stuffy USM gymnasium awaiting my turn to walk across the stage, shake the dean's hand, take my diploma, and get on the road.

"TENA RIX CLARK."

Unlike many of my classmates around me, I didn't feel any euphoric elation or swelling pride in having graduated college—after Penny, only the second one in my family to do so. All I felt was an itching desire to get out of there and to start my musical life.

As I descended the metal stage, I found Daddy in the milling crowd of new graduates and their families and well-wishers. No one else besides Daddy and Shirley, his latest girl-friend, had come to see me graduate. In fairness, Mama and my sisters had wanted to come, but I told them not to bother, that it meant nothing to me and that I was going to hightail it out of there the minute the ceremony was over—no party, no fancy lunch in some expensive restaurant, nothing. But Daddy had come anyway. With Shirley.

Shirley and I actually went way back—all the way to kindergarten. That's right, she was a year *behind* me in school, right through senior year, although she never made much of an impression on me. That is, not until she hooked up with my father, a man thirty-seven years her senior. Her father owned the town's stockyard, and she worked in the office as soon as she was old enough to help. Not exactly poor, but far from wealthy, hers had been a modest upbringing. Until Daddy.

Soon after they had begun dating, she and I found ourselves alone and she couldn't resist bringing up my recently revealed sexuality.

"I don't understand your choices. I just don't git it," she said, echoing Daddy to the letter.

Taking a deep breath, I tried to answer without spitting the words in her simpering "bless your heart" face.

"Shirley, it's simple," I began. "It's just how I don't understand *your* choice of dating a man almost forty years older than you. I find that kind of disgusting. But I accept that it's your choice. So, I don't judge you, and I ask that you don't judge me."

That shut her up and we never discussed it again.

And here she was, at my graduation.

"This is for you, Daddy," I said as I handed him my diploma. I hadn't even looked at it.

He might have said "Congratulations," but he didn't. I might have said "Thank you," but I didn't. It would be the last major thing he would buy me in my life. My life of independence from him and his money was finally going to start.

For the next few years, I was on the road with my band, and

we played the South, from Nashville to New Orleans, and although we were a biracial band, we only had one run-in with the dangerous reality of the Deep South.

In order to save every penny we could, we'd all share one motel room, tossing a coin for the available beds and couches, the loser sleeping on the floor in a pile of blankets and pillows. One early morning after a gig in Montgomery, Alabama, we were awakened by a crowd gathering in the parking lot outside our window. Casey, our black pianist, climbed off the sofa and went to the window.

"Holy shit!" he said, pulling the curtain shut so fast a few of the rings came off the end of the rod. "Don't open the curtain!"

The rest of us jumped out of our beds and peered through a crack in the curtain at the object of his terror. The parking lot was full of people in white hoods and robes. We all looked at each other in the early-morning light, our breath coming in rapid pants.

"Do you think they're here because of us?" I asked no one in particular.

"Holy shit, I hope not," said our lead singer.

We looked at Casey, who stood crouched in the darkest, farthest corner of the room. My heart broke for him. Our sad, screwed-up world caused this wonderful man to stand trembling and cowering in the corner of a rat-nasty, fleabag motel in the middle of Alabama, scared for his life. Black as well as gay, he didn't stand a chance if exposed to the goons outside. It turned out the motel parking lot was just the crowd's gathering place before a march, and they never knew we were there.

If they found us, the rest of us might get roughed up for being with Casey, even beaten up for sleeping in the same room with him, but chances were good we wouldn't be lynched. Nothing gave him the same assurance.

After a couple of years in the club scene, playing from 9 P.M. to 3 A.M. in a fog of cigarette smoke, drinking one too many free beers from the audience, and being asked to play Boz Scaggs's "Lowdown" for the zillionth time, I was exhausted and looking for "what's next." It came in the form of a letter from the Campus Crusade for Christ folks in California, once again urging that I join them for an intensive, three-month Bible study in the hills above San Bernardino, followed by a possible world tour with their band. With a shrug of my shoulders, I thought, *What the hell. Might as well play my drums for the Lord for a few months. Besides, won't Mama be thrilled?*

She was, and so was I, at least until I was asked in a final interview before hitting the road with the CCC band if I'd ever had "any homosexual tendencies." Refusing to lie, and heartbroken that these good Christian folks were demanding that I do so in order to stay in their band, I left California and headed back to Mississippi.

When I got there, I had a whole new world of worry. Once again, it was Mama.

Thirty years of consuming upward of two to three fifths of bourbon a day, Mama's laundry list of complaints became real illnesses, and my sisters and I found ourselves huddled around her as she lay in yet another hospital bed. She had a tumor the size of a cantaloupe in her abdominal cavity, most likely too large and entwined with veins and arteries to simply remove, but they had to at least try. Chances of her surviving the surgery were fifty-fifty, at best.

As my sisters and I paced the waiting room, I looked out the window and saw snow filtering down through the magnolia trees. Snow. While not unheard of in Mississippi, it was rare enough to be special, and special enough to give me just a measure of happiness on that awful day. We stood mesmerized, watching the almost magical flurries, and then another miracle occurred: the arrival of a dozen red roses.

"Get Well Soon, Lamar," the card read.

Holy shit.

Hell was freezing over outside *and* in.

Turned out the tumor was benign, but the doctor's warning was not.

"Vivian, enough is enough. If you drink so much as one more drop of alcohol, it will kill you. I mean that. It will kill you. The drinking ends. *Today.* Do you understand me?"

She did. And bless her iron-will heart, she quit cold turkey. After decades of hard drinking, it was as if she simply turned off the spigot. She not only quit, but she formed Waynesboro's first Alcoholics Anonymous, which gathered in the basement of her Methodist Church. It was composed entirely of white men, because white women would sooner die than go "public" with their drinking and black folks kept pretty much to themselves, especially where their addictions and abuses were concerned.

The last thing a black person needed to add to his already heavy burden of oppression was being known as a drunk.

For about a year, everything was great with her. And then, once again, it wasn't. My sisters and I started noticing she was slurring her words and seemed loopy, groggy, but we knew it wasn't booze because you can smell booze from across the room. It was something else, and when we went looking for it, we found it: Percodan. Lots of it. Bottle after bottle, from a variety of pharmacies and doctors. Granted, the pain from her pancreatitis was no mild headache, but she was an addict nonetheless, and Percodan was just another form of substance abuse. Major league.

"Mama, you can't be doing this shit," we told her as we flushed the pills down the toilet. She promised she'd quit.

As addictive as alcohol is, for Mama Percodan was worse. She tried and failed to quit for months, and time after time we'd see the droopy eyelids and slack mouth, search around, and find more bottles hidden in her linen closet or bra drawer or hatboxes. It didn't stop until we had gone to each of the three pharmacists in town and begged, then threatened, them not to give her any more pills. They finally stopped, and she was once and for all clean of addiction.

It had only taken thirty years.

Feeling like Mama was finally safe, I refocused on my music and my life. My musical *career* soon developed into a musical *business*, and I found myself in Nashville, the world's unofficial music-writing capital. Soon, I was not only writing, but writing *and* producing for other artists. Things were going great, but personally, I was still pillar to post, as I had been since I was a teenager when I shuttled between Mama's, Daddy's, and my sisters' houses.

One day Daddy called. He was uncharacteristically anxious.

"T-T-Tena Rix, I n-n-need to talk to you. I'm having M-M-Mayfield drive me up to Nashville this m-m-mornin'."

So I cleared my afternoon calendar and headed over to his hotel after he arrived. When I saw him, he was pacing the lobby and huffing and puffing on his cigarette, sounding as if he were stoking a fire with bellows.

"Come on," he said, taking my arm, "let's g-g-go up to my room so we can t-t-talk in private."

"Daddy, what's wrong with you? You're a wreck," I said, genuinely concerned at the state of this daddy I had never seen before. Even when Mama was packing her car and leaving him for good, he wasn't this distraught.

When we got to his room, he started in.

"It's Shirley, she's left me," he said, reaching for a cigarette with hands that actually shook. I stared as he struggled to steady the flame enough to light the cigarette. "Won't even t-t-t-take my c-c-c-calls."

Daddy and Shirley had been living together for most of the several years since I had graduated from college, and she had been, much to my sisters' and my revulsion, a near-constant, and I gotta say, somewhat smug presence on Daddy's arm.

"Well, why'd she leave?" I asked, thrilled that she had, but also alarmed at the anxiety her leaving had caused Daddy.

"Said as a good Christian woman, she couldn't go on livin' together in sin, that I'd have to marry her. I tried to tell her I was done with g-g-g-gettin' married but that I'd be sure to take care of her, and that's when she s-s-s-stormed out. And now, she won't even t-t-take my calls." He looked at me, embarrassed that he'd repeated himself. "I need you to c-c-c-call her for me. Will ya do that, T-T-Tena Rix?"

Now it was my turn to pace the floor. I was torn between elation that Shirley might finally be out of our lives and the grim reality that perhaps he needed her, and worse, even loved her. Like Mama, he too was afraid of living alone. Watching his utter despair as he sank deeper into the chair, I realized that as much as I would never warm to Shirley, he had.

I picked up the phone and dialed the number he gave me.

"Shirley, it's Tena. Daddy's here and he's a wreck. He asks if you'll just please give him another chance, he's sure y'all can work it out. He doesn't want to lose you."

Of course, she agreed to talk to him. She'd won. I handed the phone to Daddy and left the room. When I came back they were engaged, and within weeks they flew to Vegas and got married.

That girl wasted no time. Besides, she knew the truth about Daddy and that his so-called aversion to marriage was pure talk. And she was right. Daddy had gone through two marriages since Mama, both of which ended in divorce. Then came wife number three, Carolyn. She was a piece of work, but a beautiful one, almost a cross between Connie Francis and Elizabeth Taylor. But she could also be batshit crazy, and after one too many wild rampages, the last involving waving a gun around the Waynesboro Country Club where Daddy was entertaining, he decided enough was enough. When Carolyn learned he was filing divorce papers, she stole his office key, got some of her brawny brothers, a furniture dolly, and a pickup truck and drove to Daddy's office in the dead of night. Once in, she stole file cabinets full of his oil and gas leases, millions of dollars' worth. She could be crazy but, damn, she was smart. She called Daddy in the morning, a few minutes after she knew he would have arrived at his office.

"Well good morning, Lamar. I hear you're missing something?"

After he screamed and yelled and cursed, she continued, dead calm.

"You write me a check for one hundred thousand dollars and I'll bring them back. Otherwise, I have a cigarette lighter right here. Your choice. One hundred grand, or I torch them. All."

Because this was in the mid-1970s, before the days of digital files and computer storage, those paper leases were his only proof of ownership. Without them, he had nothing.

He paid the $100,000, which in those days was real money (about $700,000 in today's dollars).

Shirley, having heard all the stories, knew Daddy would cave. And he did, and settled into his fourth and final marriage.

Meanwhile, I remained decidedly single. Oh, sure, I dated a lot of women and even fell in love with a few of them, but I always moved on before they could. As usual, I made sure I was the one who decided when "it was over."

And then just as I hit my thirties in 1983, I met Dell, the woman I would marry. She was smart and sassy and we made each other laugh. And, she was from Mississippi. Within just a few months of dating I asked her to marry me, and she accepted.

Telling Mama was another story. Dell and I drove to Waynesboro, and I wasn't as nervous as I would have been back in her drinking days. At least now I didn't have to fear that she'd pull a loaded .38 out of her purse. Still, I knew it wouldn't be easy for her to hear.

"Well, bless your hearts," Mama said, looking stunned from where she sat in her recliner. She reached out and gave Dell's knee a little *pat pat pat*. "Congratulations, of course," she added. She was eerily calm.

"Thanks, Mama, for being so supportive," I said, unsure of what to make of her reaction.

She smiled and refilled Dell's glass with sweet tea from a pitcher on the coffee table. A horn honked outside. Daddy had come by to take me for one of his rides.

"Okay, then. Dell, do you mind sittin' with Mama while I take a little ride with Daddy?"

I knew Dell wanted a chance to get to know my mother a bit, so she readily agreed and off I went, elated. At least one roadblock had been passed, actually cleared with flying colors. But when I walked back into the house an hour later, Dell looked pale and shaken.

When Dell and I were alone in the car driving to Georgia's for dinner, I asked her what the hell had happened.

"Your mother told me to run."

"She said what?" I asked, pulling the car to the side of the road so I wouldn't drive us into a ditch.

"She pretty much talked nonstop from the minute you walked out the door until you returned. She told me that you were just like your daddy. I believe the words she used were 'the spittin' image of Lamar Clark, and she's gonna screw around on you the way her daddy done to me.'"

"You gotta be shittin' me," I muttered. "My own mama?"

"Oh, I'm not done," Dell said.

Uh-oh. I kept my eyes straight ahead, my hands clutching the steering wheel. Dell continued.

"She said, and I quote, 'You'd be better off taking that ring off right now and runnin' in the opposite direction.'"

I confronted my mother the next day. But if I had thought I'd get an apology out of her, I was wrong.

"Baby, I was just tellin' that poor woman the truth," she said, sitting in her recliner, her feet crossed at the ankles, her poodle Bubba perched between her shins, and her eyes on her crossword puzzle.

"Mama! How can you say such a thing?"

She looked up at me then, her eyebrows arched ever so slightly above her glasses.

"You *are* just like your daddy. You change girlfriends like you do your drawers."

"Mama!"

"Listen, baby, I really, really like your Dell, she seems sweet. I don't want to see her hurt," she said matter-of-factly, filling in a word on the puzzle.

"That's a terrible thing to say! I've never been married. How do you know I'm not ready to settle down?"

She looked at me with her sly smile, all too wise for my liking, and said, "Yeah, well, we'll see." Then she went back to her puzzle.

"My Lord, Mama. Someday I'm going to have to write a

book about all this insanity. But I don't think anyone will believe that my own mama told my fiancée to hightail it down the road she came in on!"

She looked up at me, dead serious.

"That's fine, you write that book, but just wait until I'm dead. You promise?"

I promised. Then we both laughed and hugged goodbye. "I'm gonna prove you wrong, Mama," I said.

"Aloha, baby," she said.

Next up was introducing Dell to my sisters, all of whom gave her hugs and little pats on the back and "Bless your heart"s, while shocked that I'd actually put a ring on someone's finger, never mind another woman's. Finally, I took her to meet Virgie.

"She's my second mama" was all I really needed to tell Dell.

Virgie gave her one of her wraparound hugs and rare smiles.

"Now, yo take care of my baby girl, ya hear?" she said to Dell, who promised she would.

"You'll come out to visit us in California, won't you, Virgie?" I asked, hoping I'd be able to show her the Pacific Ocean when Dell and I moved to the West Coast in the coming weeks.

Virgie just laughed.

"Uh-uh, no I's ain't! I's ain't going out there where that ground's gonna open up and suck me in. I's gonna stay right here where my feets be on the ground!"

And that's exactly what she did, never once getting onto an airplane in her entire life, and never going much farther from Waynesboro than her trips with me to Mobile. The one exception she made to her overall travel ban was driving with Mama to my new apartments during my nomadic early years in order to help "set me up." Mama, true to form back then, would pull up to the curb in front of my building in a squeal of tires, often jumping the curb before fully stopping the car. And as she had on so many mornings driving to work with Beulah Mae, Virgie would stumble out, scared to death, having once again been forced to ride shotgun with a drunk.

While Virgie had continued to work for Mama that one day a week, Daddy had fired Virgie a couple of years earlier, soon after he married Shirley. From the day they had married, Shirley tried to wipe everything from Daddy's life that even suggested a connection to the *first* Mrs. Lamar Clark. Starting with Virgie.

When I had learned of it I was horrified.

"Well, Shirley s-s-says she stole some j-j-j-jewelry," Daddy said.

My body went cold as rage flooded through me. I couldn't be sure whether Shirley had somehow convinced herself that Virgie would steal, but I was furious that Daddy had.

"Shirley's wanted to get rid of Virgie since the day you married, you know that! Daddy, you look at me and tell me you believe Virgie could steal something."

He couldn't. Fumbling to light a cigarette as he avoided my eyes, he said, "Well, now, you know you can't t-t-trust anybody. I been t-t-telling you that your whole life."

"You know Virgie wouldn't steal the peel off an orange!"

"Well, people change" was all he would say.

"Shame on you, Daddy. To accuse Virgie of something like

this, as long as she's been with us, and taken care of me, and *you*? Shame on you!"

But he wouldn't budge. While he assured me he wouldn't let Virgie starve, he nonetheless wouldn't keep her on. Shirley was in charge, and Virgie never worked for him again. It's a sin I never quite forgave Shirley for.

Soon after we returned from our "tell the family" trip to Waynesboro, Dell and I were married in the Methodist Church by perhaps Nashville's only progressive minister. Although gay marriage was still not legal in the eyes of the government, it was just fine in the eyes of the Methodist Church, at least this one in Nashville.

We then packed up our house in Nashville and drove two thousand miles to Los Angeles, taking our time and treating ourselves to a little vacation.

Along with knowing I wanted to marry Dell, I also knew I wanted to have a child with her. But it was 1984 and artificial insemination, for a gay couple no less, was unheard of. In fact, we were told by a list of specialists and attorneys that it wasn't possible, physically or legally. Once again, not willing to take anyone else's "No, it can't be done" for an answer, I persisted. It took two years to find our donor, and Dell's and my daughter, Cody, was born in 1986, on our first try.

It would not be an exaggeration to say Cody is the purest gift of my life, but then again, perhaps every mother has that reaction to her child. Every mother should. While my mama was the bravest person I'd ever known, and Virgie was the kindest, and Georgia was the steadiest, Cody was the purest. She came without any conditions, complications, or strings. When she was handed to me in the delivery room, wrapped tight in the blue-and-pink-striped blanket, I realized finally and forever that God did exist, because how else was I able to feel such immediate, unconditional love? It was unearthly and yet solid and real. It was—and is—as eternal as the wind and the stars and the sun.

I thrived as a mother, but not so much as a partner. While Mama was wrong about my not being able to be faithful to Dell while I was with her, when the relationship eventually soured and we parted, I already had my eyes on somebody else. *Just like my daddy*, I thought.

Chapter Thirty

While my personal life struggled to find its moorings, my professional life soared. I was never without writing and production work, and over the years I collaborated with a dream list of artists, from writer Maya Angelou to recording stars Aretha Franklin, Patti LaBelle, Gladys Knight, Natalie Cole, Chaka Khan, and Dionne Warwick, with whom I had my first hit, *Reservations for Two.*

Through the years and my successes and failures in work and love, I constantly checked in on my family back in Waynesboro, and flew home as often as possible—to eat hush puppies and fried chicken and coleslaw with my sisters, ride shotgun with Daddy, who still loved to take me on his errands around town, help Mama with her crossword puzzles, and sip sweet tea on Virgie's front porch. And I took Cody on just about every trip with me. I wanted her to know this essential part of who I was and, by extension, who she was.

When Cody was about a year old, I flew home and took her over to meet Virgie. As she always had with babies, any baby, Virgie took my daughter and cradled her close to her bosom, as if absorbing her soul through the layers of clothes and skin. She sat down on the porch swing and hummed one of her soft hymns while Cody looked up at her with alert, wondering eyes.

"Virgie, aren't you going to ask me how I got Cody?" I asked.

Virgie smiled down at her, taking a wisp of Cody's fine, curly hair and twisting it loosely around her arthritic finger.

"Nope. Don't matter to me how you gots yo' baby. Only thing that matters is she yo's."

And that was all she ever said about it.

Several months later, when I once again flew home and drove over to see Virgie, my heart almost stopped in my chest. Mama had warned me that Virgie wasn't feeling well, but I wasn't prepared when I saw the shrunken version of the woman I loved so much, bent in half and oddly pale underneath her dark skin. She told me she had "the cancer" in one of her breasts, but that the doctors said there was nothing to be done. And besides, even if there was, they couldn't afford it.

"Ain't no reason to pay for all that," she said, "just let it be. The Lord must be ready for me, and I's just fine."

After tucking Cody under a blanket on the couch for a nap, I followed Cindy to the front porch.

"Tumor's the size of a grapefruit, pokes right out of her breast like a stalk of cauliflower," Cindy said, her hand rising to her own breast. "Doctors say even if they took it out, there's no cure. And even with Medicare, the treatments would cost well into the thousands." She shook her head miserably. "We just don't got it."

"Well, I do," I said.

For years I had tried to buy Virgie the most basic of modern comforts—a full-size refrigerator, an air conditioner, indoor plumbing—and she had always refused. "I's just fine," she'd always say. "Don't be needin' nothin'." But this time, finally, she agreed to let me pay for something. We all hoped that something would be her life.

Cindy believed that it was the years Virgie spent bent over buckets of chemicals and poisons keeping white people's houses clean that had filled her body with toxins. She said there was one time Virgie had been so determined to clean a fireplace chimney, she mixed bleach and ammonia, and had had to run for her life out of the house, gasping and choking for air.

Within a few days of my making the arrangements, Virgie had a radical mastectomy, removing the entire breast, several lymph nodes, and a huge swath of surrounding skin and tissue in her armpit and upper arm.

As was her nature, as soon as her chest drains were pulled and the deepest of the incisions were healed, she went straight back to work. As much as I pleaded with her to slow down, not to worry for a second about the money because I would never accept a penny even if she tried, she wouldn't listen. Besides her family, work was the only thing she felt she had any control over, the only thing that had ever given her a measure of security and purpose. She wasn't about to let it go now. So back to work she went, only to relapse within a few short months. Because she'd so recently gone through chemotherapy after the mastectomy, the only treatment option was radiation, and it took what was left of her lifeblood, burning her from the inside out.

As if all of that were not enough to kill her, she lost her beloved Jack. She was still weak from the radiation when he went in for surgery on his leg, and he died on the operating table. The doctors said that once they cut into him, they realized they had opened a Pandora's box of various undetected and undiagnosed infections and tumors harbored in poor old Jack's body. Cindy says as bad as the cancer was, losing Jack was what finally took Virgie's will to live.

In September of 1989, I returned to Waynesboro to spend what time I could with Virgie. When I got to her house, she was wearing a new wig, a crown of little white curls. Even her children, Cindy in particular, ribbed her about it.

"Mama, you's look just like a little ole white woman in that thang!"

Virgie's answer was typical: "It be juss fine fo' me. Y'all leaves me alone, now, heah?"

When I joined the chorus, she finally gave in and let Mama and me drive her to Laurel to buy a proper wig. The three of us spent the day laughing and gossiping; we even persuaded Virgie to let us take her to lunch. After our disastrous experience at Petty's, which seemed like a lifetime ago, I rarely suggested going out for lunch together. But the incident at Petty's was over twenty years earlier, and even Virgie could see that the world was changing, *even* in Mississippi.

When we dropped her back in Hiwannee, Cindy came out to the car to help her mother into the house.

"Well there now, you's be lookin' like my mama again," she said, giving Virgie a big hug, "not some ole white lady from Jackson!"

I thought I saw a little smile on Virgie's face as she shuffled through the front door. "Y'all leave me alone, now."

Before I returned to Los Angeles, I went over to Virgie's house and found her watching TV on the couch, its ripped black Naugahyde held together with duct tape, tinfoil wrapped around the rabbit ears on the black-and-white TV, and a noisy fan clanking in the window. I took her hand, the hand that had made me feel safe and comforted through all those years, and asked if there was anything she needed, anything I could get her. She said, no, she was "Juss fine."

"Surely you can think of something you want. Something that will make you feel better, Virgie. Please tell me. I'll get you anything at all. Anything in the world."

It took her a while, but she finally thought of something she had always wanted.

"Well, I's never had chocolate, scrawberry, and 'nilla ice cream, all at the same time."

"Do you mean, like Neapolitan?" I asked.

"I don't know anything about that. All I knows is it be chocolate, scrawberry, and 'nilla, all in the same bowl."

I raced to the store and bought two gallons of each flavor, six in all, and raced back to her house. Grabbing a big spoon for each of us from the kitchen drawer, I put a gallon of each on the table, and opened all the lids. We sat there, laughing and talking and eating spoonful after spoonful, Virgie as content as I'd seen her since our afternoons walking back from Ramey's Rolling Store at the end of our driveway.

At the end of her life, the biggest extravagance she could think of was a bowl of Neapolitan ice cream. I was flooded with shame. After all she had done for my family, for me, there was nothing besides ice cream that I could give her. She had been, for over thirty years, my one steady source of acceptance, of unconditional love. Had I ever truly appreciated it? Had I thanked her enough for all she'd taught me, for all she'd done for me? Did she even know that she would forever occupy a permanent place in my soul? Did she even know how much I loved her? Yet here I was, only able to thank her with ice cream.

We sat and talked and laughed and ate ice cream until I could see exhaustion weight her eyes and sag her shoulders, and I knew it was time to leave.

"Goodbye, Virgie. I love you more than you'll ever know, and I'm going to see you real soon. You take care of yourself until I come back. I love you, Virgie."

"I loves you too, baby. I shaw do."

I turned back from the doorway and watched her carefully lick the spoon clean.

It was the last time I saw her.

Virgie was buried next to Jack in the pig pasture behind the Hiwannee Baptist Church. In her obituary in the *Jackson Daily News*, I was listed among her many children.

Chapter Thirty-One

After Virgie died, I threw myself into work, hoping to avoid the pain. But the void she left had a terrible finality, unlike other deaths I'd had in my life. Even after I left Waynesboro, I knew she was always there when I needed her, even hundreds and thousands of miles away, ready to offer peace and security. With her absence, I felt an uneasy current run through me whenever I thought of her, rather than the tender warmth that being near her had always provided. And with a sinking heart, I knew, with losing Virgie, I had lost that tender warmth forever.

Soon, I forced myself to stop thinking about it entirely because I was in a total panic trying to start a new company, not just writing and producing music, but using music to brand companies and corporations. It was a bold idea, and I was petrified of losing everything in the process. But my gut told me to do it. After some fits and starts, I got the business up and running enough to justify an order of letterhead and business cards. It wasn't much, but it was a beginning.

One day, when I was still struggling with the company's growing pains, Daddy called to ask if I would meet him in Nashville because he needed to talk to me.

"We'll go to dinner when you get in. I want you and me to sit and talk."

This was not the father I knew. This person on the phone was a man requesting something, with almost hat-in-hand timidity, kind of like when Shirley had walked out on him. This time, I was the nervous wreck, imagining what could be wrong, what he would tell me. A few days later, I met him at the Opryland Hotel. By the time we were sitting together in the hotel's indoor faux garden, a fountain splashing lazily behind plastic palm trees, my stomach was in knots.

"I ain't been f-f-feeling well," he began, his voice soft, if not a bit tremulous. Again, my heart sank, fearing the worst. "I want you to come b-b-back home," he continued, "and take over my b-b-b-businesses."

I didn't say a word. I couldn't. I was, for one of the only times in my life, truly speechless. He continued in the silence.

"I want to t-t-teach it to you while I still can, to r-r-run it. What you got g-g-going out there in Los Angeles? You got a mortgage? Credit card b-b-b-bills?"

"Well, sure I do," I said, finally able to answer a simple question.

"Whatever you owe in California, I'll p-p-p-pay it all off, everything. You come here debt f-f-f-free, and you'll run my company. I'll help you. I can't rest in p-p-p-peace knowing you're still out there"—he gestured wildly—"in G-G-G-GODdamn California."

And then, as a final salvo, he delivered his coup de grâce, one my sisters and I had heard countless times through the years, depending on which of us was in favor at the time.

"I'm g-g-going to leave everything to you. My entire estate. It will all b-b-be yours. If you come home." He finally stopped, satisfied he'd made a solid pitch, that he had convinced me to pack my bags, sell my house, fold up my company, and move back to Waynesboro.

I certainly ain't Jesus and my daddy ain't Satan, but in that moment I felt as if we were in the biblical scene where the Devil took Jesus up on the mountain, waved his great red arm at the vast lands below, and said, "If you follow me, all of this will be yours."

But I had to admit I was also flattered by Daddy's offer. I didn't know why he saw me as his potential heir, but I loved that he did. As I pondered the offer and reveled in self-congratulations, he spoke, destroying the fantasy he had almost created.

"I need you to do this, *fast*," he said, back to hard-nosed business. Lamar Clark was eager to seal the deal.

"Daddy, I'm speechless," I said. "I'm so flattered and humbled you want to hand me your company. The very fact that you're trusting me with what you've spent a lifetime building means the world to me and I am so grateful."

He nodded and lit a cigarette. I continued.

"Does it sound awesome? To have my debt erased and to come back home and make tons of money? Yes, but"—I took a deep breath and continued—"I would die if I gave up everything I've created to move back to that tiny town. I'm successful. I make a good living in the music business. It's all I've ever known or wanted."

He started to fidget and frown, and I rushed on.

"And as far as your estate, I would never leave my sisters out of it. Ever. No matter what happens, it's an even split between each of us."

I shook my head, suddenly exhausted with this conversation and with my overbearing father, trying to test his daughters like some good-ole-boy version of King Lear.

"Daddy, it makes me feel like you don't really know me, if you think . . ."

"Bullshit," he said, the word coming out like a bullet. His face was bloodred and he was madder than a bull. He got up to leave, brushing the pleat on his pant leg. He was done.

"Oh come on, Daddy. Please don't walk off mad," I begged, reaching up for his sleeve. "Please listen. What you've offered me is an incredible opportunity, but you have to respect what's important to me. I would wither and die on the vine in Waynesboro. You *know* that."

He shrugged off my hand.

"I gotta g-g-get upstairs, I'm leavin' soon," he said, looking toward the lobby.

"But, I thought we were having dinner."

"Nah, I gotta g-g-get back to work. I got a lot to do," he said, lighting another cigarette and putting his hat on his head.

"You told me you're not feeling well, tell me what's going on."

"Hell, I'm fine. I'm fine. Well, then, just call me sometime."

"That's it?" I asked, incredulous.

"That's it," he said. "Gotta go."

And he walked away. I watched his back retreating through the fake ficus trees and bougainvillea bushes and thought I could see steam rising from his shoulders.

I knew that something shifted between us that day, the same way that something had shifted the day I told him I was gay. There were now three strikes against me, his youngest daughter. I was gay. I chose a career in music. And then, the ultimate insult: I refused his offer to take over his business. The three things that defined who I was. And he all but despised me for each of them.

Even with the hurt he kept inflicting, I still returned to Waynesboro, and on each trip would always make sure to see Daddy. I'd either swing by his office or house, or sometimes meet him for breakfast or lunch at his Best Western motel on Azalea Drive.

On one of my visits in the early 1990s, my sisters joined us for breakfast at the motel. I got there first and saw Mayfield, Daddy's long-suffering right-hand man who had driven me home from school years before, bent over a cleaning pole, vacuuming the pool. I went up behind him, wrapped my arms around his thin back, and told him how much I missed him. Mayfield shrank under my embrace and gently moved away.

"What's the matter, Mayfield? You don't want to give me a hug?" I asked, genuinely surprised and a little hurt.

"Now, Miss Tena, you knows if Mister Lamar sees you huggin' on me, he'll kilt me."

I stepped back, shocked and ashamed. We were still in a place where a white woman couldn't hug the hired black help. But worse, I had genuinely put the fear of God, and of Daddy, in this sweet man's heart.

"I'm so sorry, Mayfield. I-I forgot. It's not like that in California. I just wanted to say I love and miss you something fierce."

"I knows you do, Miss Tena, and I sho do 'preciate it," he said, his head down, his hands still on the pole.

As I turned to walk into the motel, I saw Daddy standing in the dining room, smoking a cigarette and watching us through the window. He turned and walked away, disappearing into the dark folds of the room.

After my sisters arrived, we all sat in the dining room and watched as our daddy's face darkened. We turned to follow his gaze out the window and saw a black family—a mother, father, and two little kids—happily splashing in the pool. No one dared speak, but we all knew Daddy's face meant trouble.

"GODdamn n-n-n-niggers," he mumbled, crushing out his cigarette. "They are not going to swim in my pool!"

It took me a minute to register what he'd said.

"Daddy, come on, seriously," I said.

But without another word, he stormed out.

I turned to Elizabeth and Georgia. "That's ridiculous. How can he still be thinking that way?"

"Daddy's never going to change, Tena. It's just the way it is," Georgia said.

"It's almost the twenty-first century! My Lord, they can swim wherever they want to swim!" I said.

"Just drop it, get over it," Elizabeth said, reaching for a roll and butter, apparently bored with the conversation.

Several days later, Cody and I were back to have lunch at the motel with Daddy and, as were digging into our food, I noted the pool had been drained. It was just a hollow cement rectangle.

"Is there a leak, Daddy?" He ignored my question.

Just then a cement truck backed up to the pool and began filling it. Daddy looked out the window at the truck, his eyes narrowing as he took a long drag on his cigarette.

"Daddy, what's wrong with the pool?" I asked.

"I'm fillin' the sonofabitch up. Buildin' a g-g-g-gazebo."

"What?!" I said, my eyes going back and forth between him and the slowly filling pool.

"I told you I'm not gonna have G-G-G-GODdamn niggers swimmin' in my pool and runnin' everybody else off."

"Daddy, that's *horrible*," I said.

"My g-g-g-guests are not going to swim in the same pool with n-n-n-niggers. No way, not at my motel." And that was the end of it. I looked over at Cody. Not quite four years old, her eyes were nonetheless wide with shock.

Through the window, I saw Mayfield standing by the pool, his head down, watching the cement fill the empty hole.

Chapter Thirty-Two

"Mama's real sick, Tena."

Once again, it was Georgia calling to deliver the bad news.

"Doctors want to do some tests to make sure, but it sure looks like cancer, what with all her smoking and drinking all those years."

As awful as the news was, I wasn't terribly worried. Mama was a hypochondriac with more than her share of ailments, but she was, at her core, one tough old broad. All of the Atkinson sisters were. Something in the genetic pool, I hoped. A few years earlier, when she was about eighty, my aunt Ivy had been out picking butter beans in her garden when she suffered a stroke. She lay between the rows all day, staring up at the sky watching the clouds roll by, until someone finally found her. The only side effect of the stroke was a bad sunburn.

Mama was equally tough, but still, Georgia's news unsettled me. I thought Mama'd turned a corner. She'd finally gotten sober from alcohol *and* pills, found religion, and, a few years earlier, she had at last realized a lifelong dream of becoming a professional songwriter.

I had been working as a music supervisor on *Police Acad-*

emy 3. We needed a 1940s-era song for the diner scene, and I took one of Mama's 78s to Paul Maslansky, the producer, and said, "Listen to this."

A year later, I sat with Mama and watched her name come up on the big screen in Meridian's biggest movie theater. Not only had she finally become a bona fide songwriter, she received the first paycheck of her life to prove it. She was sixty-five years old. When I asked her if she wanted to move to a nicer house in a better neighborhood, she shook her head, insisting she was just fine where she was. But when the first royalty check came later that year, she allowed that she had always wanted a carport and did I think that was too extravagant?

"Mama! It's your money," I told her. "As Elizabeth would say, 'You can stick it up a gopher's ass if you want to! It's yours.'"

Pretty soon she had a little tin roof put on the front of her cinder block one-bedroom bungalow. A few days after that she called me again.

"Do you suppose people would think I was silly if I got a *Police Academy 3* license plate for my car?"

Again, I didn't. She ordered it, and THNK U PA-3 adorned her bumpers for the rest of her life.

Mama was a beloved figure around Waynesboro, which was kind of amazing given her years as its most infamous and visible alcoholic. It was the way she carried herself: confident, like royalty. She would enter a restaurant, store, or church, and every head would turn and every face would light up in greeting. And then there was her reputation for being trigger-happy—over the years, the story of her shooting out Daddy's windshield had become legendary, and she still reached for a gun from time to time. For example, rather than buy a squirrel trap, she would stand on her back porch in her pink velvet housecoat and matching slippers and shoot "the little bastards" with her BB gun when they climbed up the clothesline pole.

But as adored as she was, I think she was also deeply lonely. Virgie's grandsons who owned an auto repair shop in town once told me that she would bring her car in two or three times a week to have it cleaned and washed, whether it needed it or not, which it most often did not. While she waited, she would hold court in the garage office, telling her stories to the mechanics who gathered around her like children listening to a bedtime story. Her deep voice and side-splitting delivery would mesmerize even those who had heard the same stories time and again. One she loved telling, because it always got a huge guffaw, involved her stopping at a gas station in Laurel and asking the elderly attendant if he had a restroom she could use.

"No, ma'am, I don't," said the man, tipping his hat, "but if you'll back it up, I'll see if I can blow it out with an air hose."

"You sonofabitch!" Mama yelled, slamming her foot on the gas and hightailing it out of the station, leaving the attendant scratching his head in a cloud of dust.

Only in retelling the story later did she realize the man thought she asked if he had a *whisk broom* not a *restroom*.

And now, Waynesboro's most celebrated and cherished Miss Vivian was very sick with cancer.

Once again, I was on the next plane to Waynesboro. I barely had time to wash my face after arriving at Georgia's house before my sisters and I loaded Mama into the car and we all drove to Hattiesburg for her test results. Eerily, the five of us crammed into one car on a road trip reminded me of our drive to Whitfield nearly twenty-five years earlier. Again, I felt the guilt of that thirteen-year-old girl, unable to save Mama and yet still feeling as if I should have. I reached over and took Mama's hand. She gave it a squeeze and we both watched the road ahead.

We drove the familiar highway south, through small towns without a traffic light and past countless barbeque and fried food joints. The smell of sweet barbeque pork, smoked ribs, and fried chicken livers and shrimp wafted through the car.

In Hattiesburg we got two rooms at the Holiday Inn near the hospital. The five of us sat up most of the night, spread between the two beds in Mama's and my room, and tried to talk each other out of despair. And we told stories, laughing until we cried, our tears of laughter mingling with and disguising those of sorrow.

The next morning we traipsed into the doctor's office, looking like a casting call for *Steel Magnolias*—five women of the South, as different as we could be and yet born of the same soil and blood, all thinking and praying in one silent voice: *Please, God, not cancer.*

"I'm sorry to have to tell y'all this, but it's cancer. And it's in both lungs," the doctor said. He stood with his chart held tightly in his hands, a sympathetic look on his face.

"I'm sorry," the doctor continued, "but there's more. There's a large tumor in the right lung, and an even larger one in the left. Surgery is out of the question. Even if we were to re-

move one of the tumors, inflicting that much trauma would
be catastrophic, given your mother's age, and almost certainly
deadly."

Her only option was intensive chemotherapy. And even
with the toxic doses of chemo, her life expectancy was only
two to six months. Two to six months. I barely comprehended
the words.

We drove back to Waynesboro mute with shock, each of us
trying not to audibly sob. Meanwhile, Mama was calm.

"It's gonna be all right. If it's my time to go, it's my time."

Mama was at peace.

"Girls, I'm ready, if the Good Lord will have me." She
sounded like Virgie.

She sat back in the seat, her purse on her lap, looking out
the window at the passing fields and farmhouses.

Two days later, I returned to California for Cody's fourth
birthday, eager to distract my mind from the idea of losing
Mama. When I saw Cody running toward me in LAX, her
little legs pumping as hard as they could, I once again lost
it, and I buried my face in her hair, hoping it would absorb
my tears. Cody adored her memaw, and she'd only had four
years with her. Four short years, not enough time for her to
remember Mama for who she was—her grace and strength
and humor and beauty.

On the day of Cody's birthday party, I excused myself from
the preparations and went to a nearby park that I visited often
because it was lovely and quiet and almost always deserted.

There, I sank onto a picnic table bench and then onto my knees, clasping my hands in front of my face, pressing them against my mouth.

"Please, God, I can't do this. Not now," I said, the words muffled against my clasped hands. "Please give me and Cody ten more years with her. I want her to know Cody and Cody to know her memaw. Ten more years. I want to be able to let Mama go gracefully, Lord, and I can't. Not now. But in ten years, I'll be able to do it. I promise. But I need ten more years."

I begged with every ounce of my being, the tears running down my face. Then I stood up, collected myself, and went back to my daughter's birthday party.

For the next six months, Mama underwent the kind of chemo and radiation you wouldn't wish on your archenemy, suffering grueling indignities of body and soul. After her last treatment, we four sisters once again gathered and drove Mama down to Hattiesburg for the results and her prognosis.

The doctor walked in and beamed at Mama. Like every single person she'd ever encountered, he had gotten a little sweet on my mother.

"Vivian, I don't know how or why, but your tumors are gone. Both of them. I've never seen anything like this, and I don't know how to explain it."

But I did. I'll always believe He heard my prayer.

Chapter Thirty-Three

With Mama in remission and growing stronger every day, I focused on raising Cody, running my company, and getting my first musical written, produced, and performed.

It was my interpretation of a black Oliver Twist, and told the story of a boy in Prohibition-era New Orleans. It was a bear to stage, but I did it and was thrilled when its premiere was scheduled in Philadelphia's historic Walnut Street Theatre.

The previews went really well, and I invited Mama, Georgia, Penny, and Elizabeth to come see it before it opened. Mama and Georgia came and loved it. In a show of great faith, Elizabeth and Penny said they'd wait and see it on Broadway, thank you very much. As Mama and Georgia left to head back to Waynesboro, I asked them if they thought Daddy might come to the opening.

"He's never seen me perform professionally or heard anything I've ever written," I said, my voice flirting with a whine.

They looked at each other nervously and then at me like I was crazy.

"Well, honey, don't count on that," Mama said, fussing with her purse so that she didn't have to look me in the eye.

"All we can do is ask, Tena," Georgia said, one foot already in the cab that would take them back to the airport.

The next week, I was shocked to the core when Georgia called to tell me Daddy was in fact coming to the opening, that following Wednesday.

"He's coming with Shirley, just so you know."

I didn't care if he was coming with the Grim Reaper. He was coming.

A few days later, I went to meet Daddy and Shirley at their hotel and found them waiting for me on the front sidewalk. Daddy was pacing and as soon as he spotted me, he stubbed his cigarette on the pavement and announced, "Okay, then, let's get going."

So much for hugs and kisses and "Congratulations, I'm so proud of you!"

Ah well, baby steps. At least he had come.

It wasn't until he was seated next to me, front row center, that I realized my mistake in wanting him there, particularly at the opening. On what should have been one of the highlights of my professional life, I felt like I was about to have a heart attack right there in the seat. I was more nervous about him being there than I was about the critics.

Daddy'd always been fidgety, but he was downright spastic in his chair next to me, his legs bouncing like a puppet's on a string and his cigarette-less fingers typing on invisible keyboards. When the curtain rose, things only got worse as I focused on the stage and began to see the play through Daddy's eyes.

Holy shit, I thought, *what the fuck was I thinking? I begged*

Daddy to come to a musical in which a black and white couple kiss in the first TWO minutes?

I couldn't look at him as the actors lingered in their liplock, but out of the corner of my eye I caught him wince. I barely remembered that this was my opening night, my musical, my songs, my heart on the stage. All that registered was Daddy. Once again, it was all about him.

Finally, intermission came and I jumped up, glad to be able to shake my anxious nerves out of my legs and shoulders.

"You want a drink, Daddy?" I asked, wishing I could disappear into the crowd so I could buy myself about four shots of the strongest booze and down one after the other, slamming the shot glasses on the bar.

He said no, but that he'd follow me out to the lobby to stretch his legs and have a cigarette.

As we stood under the theater's chandelier, people came up to me and swooned the way people swoon when they meet the artist, songwriter, or composer who wrote the show. We get swoons whether we deserve it or not. But in the presence of my scowling father, the praise and congratulatory remarks slid off me like melting butter off a stack of hot pancakes.

I tried my damnedest not to suffer through the second half, but when the curtain finally fell and the play was over, I felt a huge wave of relief, so strong it took me a moment or two to realize the audience around me was on its feet. As I rose and clapped for the cast and the orchestra, I looked down at Daddy: He was still in his chair, putting his hands together with limp enthusiasm.

The cast motioned for me to come onstage, so I scooted out of the row and clambered up to join them. As the ovations con-

tinued and a bouquet of fifty roses was put in my arms, I finally
allowed myself to breathe, and smile, and receive the applause.

When things calmed down, and the audience started filing
out of the theater, I made my way back to where Daddy and
Shirley sat waiting for me.

Daddy rose from his seat and leaned toward me, and I
waited for his words of praise.

"Where can ah-ah-ah-I get a t-t-taxi?"

The shock must have shown on my face because Shirley
shot him a look, and I registered a flicker of respect that she
dared do even that.

I looked at him, swallowing the words that were screaming
in my head: *You sonofabitch! I have worked my ass off on this,
and all you can fucking say is 'Where can I get a taxi?' You can't
give me an ounce of approval?*

Instead, I quietly chuckled, shaking my head and letting a
huge sigh release itself from my tight chest.

"Out front, Daddy. You can get a taxi out front."

After he and Shirley were gone, I found myself alone. I sat
down in the empty theater, willing myself not to shed even
one damn tear because of him. Why I thought this time would
be different, I don't know. I had so wanted him to see my
work, maybe even appreciate that I had made the right choice
in sticking with music, that I had talent and worth to share
with the world. But I had gotten so much less than zero from
him that rather than bask in the praise of my peers, the press,
and the audience, I was consumed with what I didn't have—
Daddy's praise—and angry at myself for still craving it.

The next morning my phone rang early.

"M-m-m-mornin'," Daddy said, sounding uncharacteristically nervous, even for him. "Ah-ah-ah-I wanted to come t-t-talk to you. Maybe we c-c-c-can have a little breakfast b-b-before Shirley and me head to the airport?"

Oh shit, I thought, *he's going to tell me he was right all along, and this is why he didn't want me to dedicate my life to music: because I would fail. Shit, shit, shit.* Dread flooded through me as I quickly dressed and ran downstairs to meet him in the hotel café.

He was already there, smoking a cigarette and drinking a cup of coffee.

"Ah-ah-ah-ah-I didn't say the right thing last night," he began. "I've never b-b-b-been to one of those things," he continued, "and I d-d-don't know about these things. I just didn't know how to act. I guess it was g-g-g-good, right? I mean, people seemed to like it? And, ah-ah-ah-I liked it too."

I stared at my father. I was almost forty years old and he seventy-six, still dapper in his fedora, tailored suit, and Italian leather shoes, a cigarette held firmly between two fingers. I had waited a lifetime to hear these words from him, and I doubted he had ever in all of his years uttered anything like them before, and probably never would again. And yet he wasn't finished.

"I j-j-just want you to know, I'm p-p-proud of you."

And there it was. Finally. It wasn't "I love you," another sentence I'd never heard him say to anyone, but I'd take it.

Without a word, because I couldn't speak, I got up and walked around to where he sat on the other side of the table and bent down to hug him. He was never a hugger, but I felt his hand come up and pat me a few times on the back.

Chapter Thirty-Four

I wish I had been able to leave it there. But a few months later, and struggling to raise capital for my music and media company, I gathered every ounce of nerve I had to ask Daddy for a loan. It had been a few years since I turned him down on returning to Waynesboro and running his business, and I figured because he had seen my musical, and maybe even appreciated what I did, he would support my next venture. As always, Georgia acted as my go-between, telling me if he was having a good day or a bad day, and whether he'd had his nap. I finally called him one morning after she had given me the green light.

"He's in a good mood," she assured me.

"HAY-L NO!" his voice roared through the phone after I had explained the company and why I needed the money.

"No? Just no?" I stammered. "Can you tell me why not?"

"Why not? I'll t-t-tell you why not. You have never done a G-G-G-GODdamn thing I ever wanted you to do. You have done *n-n-n-nuthin'* but disappoint me. You've b-b-been *nuthin'* but a disappointment."

I felt the blood drain out of my veins. I had truly thought he was going to be happy that I'd finally asked him for money, finally bowed to his great dictum that "everybody has a price," that I too could be controlled through his pocketbook. I also had a little girl's belief that after all the drama, after all the divisiveness he wrought between Mama and me and my sisters, that he really, truly loved me and, what's more, loved me the *best*.

Staggering, I tried to rally my defense.

"But, Daddy, I'm not asking for you to give me the money. I'm asking for a loan. I'll pay it back."

"Nope, no way," he said, his voice tight and mean.

"Seriously?" I said.

"I told you to g-g-git your head out of your ass about this music s-s-s-stuff, that you'd never make a d-d-damn dime. Wouldn't have t-t-t-two nickels to r-r-rub together. But you're just like your m-m-mama, thinkin' like a girl. I wouldn't give you a G-G-G-GODdamn dime because you can't make ch-ch-ch-chicken salad out of chicken *shit*," he spat.

I felt my blood start to boil as it never had in an argument with Daddy. I was, after all, a forty-year-old executive, music producer, award-winning songwriter. I had *already* made it, on my own and without his sorry help. But here he was, that sonofabitch, who had tricked me into believing he loved me and respected my work and only wanted the best for me.

"Daddy, how have I disappointed you?"

"You've never done a G-G-G-GODdamn thing I wanted you to do."

"What are you talking about? I don't drink, I don't smoke, I've never done a drug in my life, I graduated from college, I make a great living, I'm a workaholic, just like you! I'm a good mother to Cody. What else could I possibly do?"

"I never wanted you to go out to G-G-G-GODdamn California with a bunch of crazies, but you did. I wanted you to come back and run my b-b-b-business, but you didn't. And you show up down here with no m-m-m-makeup and your hair cut short . . ."

Whoa, I thought, *here it comes.* I bent at the waist taking his assault like blows.

". . . you have been *nuthin'* but a d-d-disappointment and a f-f-f-failure to me."

When I could speak, I said, "Daddy, I've spent my entire life trying to please you and hold on to who I am at the same time. . I've done that my whole life." As I spoke, my voice rose until I was yelling into the phone. He yelled right back.

"You have failed m-m-m-miserably. Because you have never p-p-pleased me one GODdamn day of your life."

"Okay, then I guess you don't have to worry about me bothering you again. I'm glad you got everything out, Daddy. Sounds like you been holdin' on to this shit for quite some time. I'm glad to finally know how you really feel." I paused a minute to collect my ragged voice. "Daddy, this time it's too much."

"I agree." And bam, he hung up.

I promised myself I would never again let my father hurt me. I was done. I. Was. Done.

My resolve lasted only a matter of weeks.

"Tena, I got bad news."

It was Georgia. Before she said the words, I knew.

"It's Daddy. He's sick, and it's bad."

I gotta be honest. My absolute first thought was, *That sonof-abitch. He won.*

When he had refused to even consider giving me the loan, I had finally said what I'd been wanting to say my whole life: that I was through with his control and conceit and meanness. But how in hell could I write him off now? You can't write off a dying father, right?

Like Mama a few years earlier, his lifelong habit of chain-smoking unfiltered cigarettes had finally caught up with him and cancer was eating away what was left of his lungs. Suspicious of doctors until the end, he had waited way too long for even chemotherapy to be of any use. His lungs were in terrible shape. The oncologist said the only people with lungs in worse shape than Daddy's were lifelong coal miners. There was almost nothing left to save. As soon as he understood his diagnosis was terminal and that he had less than a month to live, he refused to go to the hospital and instead hired live-in nurses to tend to his medications and bedpans.

His room stank of thick, sour rot and putrid tobacco that oozed from his skin. My sisters and I took turns sitting with him because none of us could spend a lot of time at his bed-side, the stench was so overpowering. Daddy lay in the middle of it, his small body now emaciated from the cancer. It was almost impossible to reconcile the man who had struck fear into the hearts of many with the tiny shell in the bed.

As his final days approached, I begged Mama to go visit him and say goodbye. I think I needed the closure more than she did. Mama agreed, and when she entered the room she was calm, even serene, and grand. She warmly greeted the nurse and Daddy's wife, Shirley. My sisters and I all left the room, and then we stood peeking around the threshold.

"Lamar, it's me," Mama said as she leaned over him, ignoring the stench, and touched his hand where it rested on the bedsheet. She cleared her throat. "It's Vivian."

Without opening his eyes or speaking a word, he yanked his hand away, turned onto his side to put his back to her, and pulled the covers over his head.

I was tempted to run in, pull back the sheet, and shout in his face, *THAT'S MY MAMA AND SHE'S COME TO SAY GOODBYE AND YOU'RE GONNA BE NICE!*

I guess I'd romanticized their reunion and had hoped that when he saw her, he'd see the fifteen-year-old girl he'd married sixty years before. That maybe something would soften in him, that his young love for her would flame, and that they'd be able to have some sort of moment, or at least an acknowledgment of all that had passed between them. It was the fantasy of a child of divorce.

I could barely look at Mama, the sting of his cruelty was so sharp. But Vivian Clark stood firm. Her face held no expression. She nodded once, reached out to touch his arm, and said softly, "I love you, Lamar."

She paused, and leaned in to him, as if giving him one more chance to make it right, but he remained on his side, the sheet over his head.

"Okay, then, I'll be going now. You take care of yourself, Lamar." Then she turned and left the room.

I followed her out and onto the front porch.

"I'm so sorry, Mama. I never would have brought you here if I'd known he was going to act like that."

She reached out and put her arm around me, giving me the comfort I had tried to give her.

"Don't you worry, baby. I didn't come here for him. I came here for me. Do you understand? I came here for *me*."

I nodded, squeezing her hand.

I watched her walk down the steps to her car, her purse slung over her arm and held against her waist, her head held higher than I'd ever remembered seeing it. As she walked away, I could have sworn I heard her humming.

She was free.

I wasn't so lucky.

A week later it was my turn to say goodbye. I approached the foot of Daddy's bed. The cancer had all but swallowed him whole. He was skeletal, just flesh over brittle bones. My sisters were all sitting around the bed.

"Daddy, it's me. Tena."

He slowly opened his eyes. Then, in a scene worthy of a horror movie, he rose from the sheets and tried to sit up. His expression stopped my heart. It was crazed and mean and wild, and I felt myself bracing against him.

"Tena?" he said, his voice a hoarse whisper.

"Yes, Daddy?"

"You know what I have that *you'll* n-n-never have?" he asked me, the air escaping his ruined lungs in a soft, foul hiss.

My sisters all exchanged nervous glances, each of them worried about what was coming.

"What's that, Daddy?" I asked.

"A *dick*. You'll never have a *dick*." He closed his eyes and fell back onto the bed.

It took me a minute before I trusted my voice enough to speak. The last thing in the world I wanted was to crack or cry in front of that man, my father, at that moment.

"Well, Daddy, I've never needed one."

Then I ran. I ran as fast as I could. I didn't know where I was going, but I knew I had to get out of there. Out of the room, out the back door, and down the red dirt road. When Daddy had married Shirley, he'd built them a new house right next to our old farm out on the Chickasawhay River, so the road was familiar under my feet. I ran like I was possessed, toward a memory and a time when things were simpler, and Daddy wasn't dying, and Mama was still my happy mama, fishing in the pond with me and Penny and Aunt Clifford on a summer afternoon.

Behind me, I heard my sisters yelling for me to stop. They were huffing and puffing in a half walk/half trot, struggling to catch up to me. I stopped and turned around, and when they reached me they all started making excuses at once.

"Daddy didn't mean it."

"The drugs have made him crazy in the head."

"You know he loves you, Tena, he does!"

Georgia was wiping at my tears and Elizabeth and Penny were all but patting me to death. They tried to reassure me, but I was inconsolable.

"I am *done*," I said. "I am gettin' the hell out of here."

And I did. I was on the next flight out of Mobile.

A couple of days later I was at my desk in LA and the phone rang.

"Hi, T-T-Tena Rix. It's me." Daddy sounded forty years old again, and happy, as if his last words to me had been *Talk to ya soon, Tena Rix.*

I was so shocked to hear his voice that it took me a few seconds to respond. My hand clutched the phone so hard my fingers hurt.

"Hi, Daddy, how're you doin' today?" I stammered, perplexed. *Had a miracle happened? Was he actually going to be okay?*

I heard him push aside his oxygen mask to take a long drag off his cigarette. In the last few weeks he had been coughing up thick black knots of mucus from his lungs, so I guess he figured, *What the hell. No use quittin' now.*

"Doin' just fine. Just f-f-fine. Tell you what, though. I can m-m-make more money flat on my back in bed than most men can m-m-make in a lifetime. Just signed a new three-hundred-fifty-thousand-dollar oil d-d-deal!"

I silently shook my head. It was just so sad. Money and women had been the only things that ever really mattered to Daddy, and here, even on his deathbed, they still were.

He chuckled, happy with himself, which triggered a violent coughing jag. When he finally caught his breath, he continued.

"Listen, Tena, there's something I n-n-need to t-t-t-tell you." He stopped, and for a moment I thought maybe the cough had killed him before he could speak.

An image floated through my mind. I saw myself as a little girl. Daddy and I were seated at the kitchen counter at the farm, and he was feeding me an apple, scraping the pulp spoonful by spoonful, until it was just an empty peel in his hand. The memory of that gentle father, a father I knew only in rare pieces, was painful.

"Well, ah-ah-ah-I just called to tell ya you've always been my b-b-baby. And, ah-ah-ah . . . I loves you."

It wasn't the more straightforward "I love you" I'd been waiting for my whole life, but it was close. Damn close.

I closed my eyes, and said, "I loves you too, Daddy."

And just like he had a million times before, he hung up without another word. Conversation over. Lamar Clark was still in charge.

Chapter Thirty-Five

Daddy died on a Friday in June of 1996. His funeral, less than a week later, was overrun with politicians, businessmen, and every living governor of Mississippi. Senator Trent Lott and Daddy's bookie both sent wreaths large enough to adorn a Triple Crown winner. But, to my shock and bewilderment, those who actually filled the church that sweltering afternoon were members of the poor and black communities. Every size and shape, age and agility, walked, shuffled, and wheeled in to pay their respects to a man who had left his lifelong church rather than see pictures of "colored" children in its Sunday school pages. The man who had never allowed Virgie to sit in the front seat of his car or at the family dinner table. The man who had filled in his motel swimming pool with cement so that he'd never have to see another black family swim in it. But here they were, saying goodbye.

None of Daddy's daughters were asked to speak at the funeral, which allowed the Holy Roller Pentecostal preacher who performed the service to go on and on about Daddy's Christlike qualities, praising him as "a religious man who never took the Good Lord's name in vain," and "a pious man who valued family and religion highest among the virtues," and "a loyal husband who honored the sanctity of marriage." When I heard that one I nearly choked.

While the rest of the congregation politely nodded, all I could think was: *Obviously, this moron never knew my daddy.* To this day I regret that I didn't stand up, storm the podium, and give Daddy the eulogy he deserved.

Outside the funeral home, I felt a tap on my shoulder and turned.

"Miss Tena, I'm so sorry for yo' loss. Yo' daddy was a great man."

It was a parishioner from a black church outside Waynesboro.

"Yo' daddy told me not to speak of this while he was alive, but he not only built our church, he *gave* it to us. Handed us the key and walked away. Never asked for one dime in return."

Suddenly, I remembered this person from the line of faces that had stood outside my father's office that morning many years before.

Then an elderly black woman approached me. She was so small and frail she looked like a ten-year-old girl.

"When my husband was in the hospital and we couldn't pay the rent, yo' daddy took care of it. He the only reason we got a roof over our head today."

"When I got my back broken and lost my job at the mill, Lamar Clark was the only man in town who would give me a loan to keep the payments up on the house," said an old man, so badly hunched over he was nearly bent to the waist. "The only one," he said, removing his glasses to wipe a tear.

"When my wife got the cancer, I went and asked for a loan and he paid for her medicine. Never asked for a dime back. Jus' gave me the money right out. She's alive because of yo' daddy," said another man.

"Yo' daddy did somethin' fo' me and my family no other man, white or colored, ever did. I asked him for help . . ."

And on and on it continued, as people of every age and color approached me, tears in their eyes and glistening on their cheeks, to pay respects and give thanks.

"I'll always be grateful to Mister Lamar . . ."

"I tell you what, Miss Tena, I don't know where I'd be today if it hadn't been for yo' daddy."

"He told me never to speak of it, but . . ."

As I received their blessings, their prayers, for the memory of a man I never knew existed, but who had raised me, protected me, and yes, loved me the only way he knew how, I struggled to make sense of it all. A man who had proudly paraded around the state of Mississippi as a God-fearing racist, and yet always made sure Virgie arrived home safely. A man who counted among his friends Strom Thurmond and a long list of segregationist governors, senators, and congressmen, but a man who also had paid a fair wage, employed half the town of Waynesboro, built churches, helped with medical bills, and saved strangers' lives. I couldn't reconcile these two very different men. They seemed to occupy two very different worlds.

But then I remembered what Mama always said. "Your

daddy is a complicated man." Her words never made more sense than they did the day we lowered Daddy into his grave.

That night, my sisters and I gathered on Georgia's bed, Daddy's Last Will and Testament spread before us on the chenille spread. We sat cross-legged, Indian-style, our arms around each other, like girls at a pallet party. We all agreed that no matter who may have been out of favor when he wrote the damn thing, we would split the estate evenly, four ways, no arguments, no regrets. Each of us, at one time or another, had heard his threat of "I'm not leavin' you one GODdamn dime!" So we really didn't know what to expect. As we all knew, Daddy was unpredictable.

In the end, he did the right thing. No one was left out.

Chapter Thirty-Six

You reach a certain age when you dread the ringing of the telephone.

"Tena, Mama's cancer's back. You better come on home as soon as you can."

Once again, it was Georgia calling with the news.

It had been ten years, those ten years I had prayed for, since the lung cancer had almost killed her, but we all knew it was just a matter of time until Mama's "something" would get her. We all have a *something* that is going to take away the people we love, and we all knew cancer was probably Mama's. I will admit that there was an odd comfort in knowing what Mama's something was, and yet it would never be the right time. I still wasn't ready to let her go, and I never would be.

This time the cancer attacked her esophagus, which was not only a devastating diagnosis, but a very painful one. Not that lung or breast or bone cancers aren't horrific, but esophageal takes your ability to fully swallow anything, including your own mucus.

It seemed God had granted me my ten years with Mama, but at what cost?

*   *   *

Mama's treatment this time consisted of intense levels of radiation and, like Virgie before her, it burned her from the inside out. After a few rounds, she was unable to live on her own, so my sisters and I moved her into Waynesboro's Southern Living Specialty Care nursing facility, where she would have 24/7 care and monitoring. She didn't like leaving her little white cinder block house with the carport she was so proud of, but she knew it had to be. Always the pragmatist, she packed her bags quietly and with dignity, and boarded her beloved poodle, Bubba, in a kennel. Moving her out of her house and into her drab room at the nursing home reminded me of her leaving the farm back on my tenth birthday, only this time there were no armloads of mink coats and negligees in the backseat. There were only a couple of suitcases holding her housecoats and slippers and her cosmetics bag. Her life had become very simple.

Once settled in her ground-floor room in the nursing home, she spent most days sitting by her window watching for a visit from one of my sisters, usually Georgia, who lived closest and went to sit with our mother every day. When she wasn't watching for Georgia, she sat and looked at her white Lincoln parked out front. She loved that car, with its THNK U PA-3 vanity plates, and dreamed that one day she would be well enough to drive it to the kennel, pick up Bubba, take him to the groomer to have his toenails painted blue and ribbons tied into his hair just like she liked it, and then head on home for supper.

On one of my visits in early November, I took her for a ride out to Hiwannee, past her parents' old shotgun house where she had pirouetted through its narrow rooms, singing her songs. It was a perfect fall day and we drove through the countryside, its summer green faded to an autumn russet.

"Honey, tell me what I can get you for your birthday," she said.

It was a common refrain between the two of us. Every year she saved her few extra dollars and always gave me something special but inexpensive—a pair of Sears and Roebuck's earrings or a family picture in a frame or moccasin slippers she claimed to have bought straight from an Indian reservation—but time and again felt she had failed because "your daddy can always buy you anything you want."

Through the years I had tried to convince her that her little trinkets and mementoes meant more to me than Daddy's latest diamond necklace or fur coat or gold bracelet, but she never quite believed me.

As in so many previous years, I couldn't think of a single thing I wanted, or wanted her to spend money on.

"I want to buy you something *big* this year," she said. "I want to give you something special, something that will make you think of me every time you use it."

"Mama, no," I said. "I don't want you spending a lot of money."

"Honey, what am I going to do with the money?" she asked, her voice breaking a bit.

I suddenly understood. It wasn't about outdoing Daddy. It was about her rewriting my tenth birthday, vanquishing the ghosts of 1963 that had haunted every birthday since and replacing them with something that would only speak of happiness and a mother's love. A mother who probably wouldn't live to see many more birthdays, hers or mine. I kept my eyes on the road.

"Well, Mama, I sure do love watching those old Super 8 movies you shot of the family parties and reunions. It would be fun to start filming again so Cody can watch them when—" I felt my throat close up on the words.

In the end, she bought the latest and the best video camera, insisting on getting the most expensive one in the store, and when she gave it to me, she was smiling the biggest smile I had seen on her face since she began the radiation treatments. And she was right. Long after its analog technology became outdated and its worn-out parts impossible to replace or repair, that camera sits on my shelf like a talisman, and every time I look at it, I am filled with my mother's love and kindness all over again.

Day by day the radiation burned what was left of Mama's insides, taking with it any remaining strength she had. Finally, we realized it was no use. She was only getting worse. There were days when she was too weak to even use the toilet by herself, so one of us would go in to help her, an indignity she suffered with tremendous grace. Then she started vomiting everything she ate or drank, and the doctors realized the radiation had burned a hole through her esophagus. They inserted a feeding tube and she never swallowed another mouthful of food or drink. We held crushed ice to her mouth and it was the closest she got to anything passing her lips. She longed for a good cup of coffee, but we could only dab a few drops of it on her lips.

As her last months became her last weeks, I traveled back and forth between LA and Waynesboro like a very-long-distance commuter, running my business over the phone and taking Cody with me for long weekends whenever I could for "just one more" time with her memaw. But by the end of March I knew the end was near, so Cody and I went back for the dura-tion. I needed her to be part of Mama's last days. Death is one of the only things we Southerners don't sugarcoat.

For nearly two weeks, my sisters, Cody, and I stayed by Ma-ma's bedside, taking turns to go home and shower and change our clothes. She had an attendant with her a lot of the time, a lovely black woman who treated her just like Virgie would have and tenderly wiped her mouth and rubbed lotion onto her swollen feet while Mama read from the Bible.

I too massaged Mama's feet, but it just about killed me every time I did. She'd lie back, eyes closed, a little smile on her lips, as calm, relaxed, and happy as perhaps I'd ever seen her. Looking down at my sweet mama, I realized I had never, in my entire life, given her any kind of massage, until now. Why? Why had I waited until she was almost gone to give her this simple gift? She had always been the best back scratcher—all of us girls loved the feeling of her long, hard nails going up and down our backs, giving just the right amount of pressure. As I sat on her bed, guilt and sorrow flooded through me, and I rubbed her feet until my hands were numb.

"Baby, can you ever forgive me?" Mama asked one after-noon as I sat in an easy chair nearby, calling out crossword clues and then filling in the answers for her. She was too weak to hold the paper and pen.

"Mama, please don't start that again. Please," I said, looking at her over my reading glasses. She lay on the bed, her eyes closed, her hands folded on her chest above the covers. She looked disturbingly still, like she was already at rest in the casket. I shook my head to clear the image.

"Fictional wood-carver. Seven letters," I prompted.

"Alibaba," she said, not opening her eyes.

"How do you know this shit?" I asked, laughing, and filled in the answer.

"Language," she said, her eyes still closed. Then, "Answer me, Tena, please. Can you ever forgive me?"

I looked up from the puzzle and saw she had opened her eyes and was looking at me, unblinking and earnest. I clenched my jaw against the tears and nodded.

"Of course I do, Mama. I did a very long time ago. You're the bravest woman I know, and I know that you had to leave. But you always came back."

We looked at each other, and I reached out and took her hand. She nodded and closed her eyes. Once again peaceful.

Lying there in her last bed, her breath in shallow little gasps from the esophageal cancer, she still hoped to find and to feel redemption. And try as I did to give it to her, I fear she took the guilt to her grave.

As weak as Mama was in her last days, she clung on. I didn't know what was keeping her alive, but Georgia did.

"Tena, Mama is not going to let go until you and Cody leave," Georgia said one morning in the hall outside Mama's room.

"What are you talking about?" I asked.

"She doesn't want to leave you. Again. I know that's what's keepin' her back. She just can't do it. The first time nearly killed her," Georgia said. Even my strong and steady sister was fighting back tears.

Suddenly, there it was, the vision of Mama taking the broken music box from my hands as she told me, "I'm so sorry. I have to go," and me standing with Virgie watching the Cadillac disappear down the driveway.

She doesn't want to leave you. Again.

I folded myself into Georgia's arms and wept. I felt her hand patting my back and smoothing my hair. How many times had she comforted me just like this, just like a mama, through the countless traumas? I wondered if Georgia herself had ever had a proper childhood. I never asked, but somehow I doubted it. She was just too busy taking care of everyone around her. So strong and solid, this sister of mine.

"I can't leave, I just can't," I said. "I can't leave until . . ."

"I know, honey, I know. But you have to. She'll hang on forever if you don't, and it's her time to go. You know that. You don't want to see her suffer anymore."

"I *can't*." I moaned. "How can I not be here? How can I miss holding her hand, being there when she goes?" My voice cracked and broke on the last word, remembering my promise to God that I would in fact let her go gracefully if He gave me ten more years with her. And He had. Damn. He had.

"Okay now, listen to me. This is what you're going to do," Georgia said, her voice firm and gentle. "You're going to tell Mama you have important business in New York, but that you'll be back the next day. Just a one-day trip. Please, Tena. It's time."

I raised my head. I knew she was right, but I didn't have her mettle in facing it head-on. I looked into Georgia's eyes, and nodded.

The next day Cody and I went to Mama's room at 6 A.M. Our flight out of Mobile was at nine, giving us only a few minutes with her before we had to drive south to the airport.

"Hey, Mama, how you feelin' this mornin'?" I asked.

She tried to sit up but could only smile, her chapped lips cracking with the effort.

"I'm okay, baby," she said, looking at me and reaching out for Cody's hand. Cody immediately went to the side of the bed and took her memaw's hand, gently stroking the dry, bony fingers.

"We're headed to the airport," I said, praying my voice wouldn't betray my mission, "but we'll be back early tomorrow morning, okay?"

She nodded.

"Be safe, baby. See y'all tomorrow." Her voice was calm, but her eyes flickered with agitation.

"What is it, Mama? Is there anything you need?"

She thought about it, then her teeniest shy smile touched the corners of her mouth.

"You know what I want?" she asked, her voice mischievous, like a kid playing Truth or Dare. "I want a Popsicle. A *purple* Popsicle. Do you think you could get me one?"

I knew the nurses kept boxes of Popsicles on hand for patients, but Mama was under strict instructions not to eat or drink anything.

"But, Mama," I protested, "you know it's doctor's orders. You'll choke, possibly get an infection . . ." My words trailed off when I realized how utterly ridiculous it was to deny this woman anything, ever again. It didn't matter if she choked, or got an infection, or even if she stopped breathing right then and there.

"Of course, Mama. I'll get your Popsicle."

She rested back into her pillows, smiling a smile that was pure, young, and full of simple happiness.

"I'll be right back," I said, and ran out of the room and down to the nurses' station.

"My mama wants a Popsicle, a *purple* Popsicle," I blurted, out of breath and already frenzied with the urgency of getting her that damn Popsicle. The possibility that she could die before I got back with it was unthinkable. It was the same panic I had felt in making sure Virgie tasted Neapolitan ice cream for the first, and last, time in her life.

"Why, Tena," the nurse said apologetically. "You know she can't have anything to eat. She might aspirate."

"Are you serious? She's dying, she might even die today, and if my mother wants a purple Popsicle before she goes, by God, she's going to have one. Now. Please. *Please* can you do that for her?" I begged.

The nurse looked at me for a few seconds in silence, then nodded, got up, and went to the little kitchen behind the reception area. I could see her dig through the freezer, and then she came back with a Popsicle. Purple.

I raced back to the room.

"Mama!" I said, out of breath from my sprint back to her room. "I got it! Look! A purple Popsicle!"

She struggled to sit up, and she watched like a little girl on Christmas morning as I pulled the paper off and handed it to her. I too felt like a girl on Christmas morning, pleased and proud that I was handing my mother the one cherished gift she had been waiting for all year. She put the Popsicle to her dry and cracked lips and fell back against the pillows, eyes closed, with a sigh of pure bliss at just having the sugary syrup against her lips. She then slowly savored the flavor and the cool, wet sweetness, tentatively swallowing the melted syrup, the first thing to have gone down her ruined throat in weeks.

"Is it good?" I asked, relieved that it hadn't made her choke.

"Mmmm, mmmm, mmmm," she sighed, and we both laughed.

A drop of the purple syrup trickled down her chin. I reached out and caught it with my finger, and she smiled.

Swallowing a lump in my throat that felt like it was the size of a Key lime, I breathed deeply and prayed I'd hold it together at least until I got out of the room.

"Okay, Mama. Cody and I better be headin' to the airport," I said, bending over the bed to kiss her forehead. "We'll see you tomorrow morning, and I'll bring you an entire box of purple Popsicles!" My voice held a false gaiety that hung in the air.

Cody hugged Mama so tightly that I feared she wouldn't be able to let go. "I love you so much, Memaw. We'll see you tomorrow, okay?"

"Yes you will, my sweet little angel," Mama said, giving Cody's face a light brush with her fingers. "Yes you will."

I went to the door, but try as I might, I couldn't make myself open it. I knew, as sure as I knew anything, that I would never see my mama again. I stared at the door, at its wood and its stainless-steel handle.

"You'd better get going," Mama said, and with her words I nodded and finally pulled the door open. I lingered in the doorway, my left hand holding the door open to look at Mama for a few more moments.

"Aloha, Mama. I love you."

"I love you too," she said, pausing and catching her breath. And then she said: "Goodbye, baby."

It was the first time in my life I had heard her actually say the word.

"Mama, I said *aloha*."

She smiled, her eyes gentle and sad, as another drip of purple syrup dropped onto her hospital gown. She too knew this was it. That I had to go and that she wouldn't be there when I got back.

"I love you, baby. Goodbye," she said again, more firmly.

I nodded and finally stepped out of the room. The only reason I didn't sink to my knees on the cold linoleum was that Cody stood outside, anxiously waiting for me. I took a deep breath, reached for her hand, and we walked out of the hospital to my car.

Forty-five minutes later, as we crossed the Alabama line, my phone rang. I didn't have to look at the number to know who was calling and why.

"Tena . . ." Georgia said, and then fell silent. It took her several moments to say the rest. "Mama's gone."

Unable to speak, I nodded, as if she could see me acknowledge the news. Cody reached over and placed her hand on mine where it gripped the steering wheel. She knew. I didn't have to tell her. We sat silently until I could breathe again, enough at least to drive the car. Then, heavy with despair and taking deep breaths through the vise grip that held my throat, I turned around and headed back home to bury my mama.

Mama picked a good time to die. It doesn't get much prettier than April in Mississippi—the days are warm, but not yet hot, and the gentle breeze floats with hints of honeysuckle, jasmine and gardenia, and roses and wisteria, and of course, magnolia. On the day of Mama's funeral, I felt as if God pulled out all His stops, making sure the last air that touched her body would be as soft and succulent as nature could provide.

Daddy's funeral five years earlier had been a command performance of politicians he'd bought and local folks he'd supported. There had been a lot of gratitude at his service, but not a lot of tenderness.

Mama's funeral was one of pure love. It was also one of respect and compassion. She wasn't the only wife of Waynesboro to drown her sorrow in Jack Daniel's, but she had been one of the first to walk out on that misery and start a new life, and people respected her courage. They also just plain loved her for who she was—her humor and grace and dignity.

Waynesboro showed up in the hundreds to say goodbye. Those who couldn't make it sent dozens upon dozens of bouquets and wreaths of pink roses, her favorite flower. It took hours for the mourners to pass by her casket, reaching out to touch her fingers and see her face one more time. Most bent over her and whispered that they'd miss her laugh, her kindness, and her stories. They promised they would never forget her. And I doubt any have. When I stood to deliver the eulogy, I gritted my teeth against the tears in my throat and stinging my eyes. Determined to hold it together, I read some of the lyrics of a song I had written for her at her bedside, two days before she'd passed:

> God, we're gonna miss her
> It feels like more than we can bear,
> But I guess you really need her
> For something special up there.
> We have to believe
> That you always know what's right,
> But, Lord, it's gonna be raining tears
> In Mississippi tonight.

At the reception, Waynesboro's church ladies put out a spread worthy of feeding a hungry platoon: casseroles of every imaginable combination, fried chicken, seven or eight different pasta salads, ham and potato salads, Spanish rice, deviled eggs, pork and beans, pulled pork and brisket, sausage and garlic potatoes, corn bread, ham salad, chicken salad sandwiches, chicken spaghetti and lasagna, meatballs, baked ham, and bowl after bowl of vegetables—collard and turnip greens, fried okra, peas and butter beans, creamed corn and tomatoes—although none of what we called the fancy vegetables, broccoli and asparagus and artichoke hearts and the like. I didn't know those vegetables even existed until I left Waynesboro for college.

I ate as much as my stomach and sadness would allow, not

wanting any of the ladies to feel insulted that I hadn't tried *their* dish. With the excuse of "needing to get some air after all this food!" I escaped out the side door and found myself walking the short distance back to the graveyard.

Her grave was impossible to miss. It sat among hundreds, perhaps thousands of flowers—wreaths, bouquets, vases, and single stems wrapped with ribbon. The ocean of flowers reminded me of the scene outside Buckingham Palace after Lady Diana's death. And in a way, Mama *was* Waynesboro's Lady Di; she certainly was loved as much.

I approached the fresh mound over her grave slowly and then knelt on the ground next to it, my fingers digging gently into the cool dirt.

"I'm so sorry, Mama," I whispered. "I'm so sorry I wasn't able to save you this time."

And suddenly it all came pouring out, and with my fingers spread wide like a sprinter poised for a race and my head bowed over the grave, I sobbed alone among the silent tombstones. I had held it together for so long—for myself, for Cody, for my sisters—but I could hold it no longer. It felt as if grief had split me wide open.

I remembered that day, over forty years earlier, when I sat on my sad mama's lap, careful to avoid the bandages on her wrists, and promised to keep her safe for the rest of her life. I wept over her now because I felt as if I had failed. She was gone. I hadn't been able to prevent her death and keep her here, by my side, safe and sound and doing her crosswords in her chair and quietly singing her songs. I had promised her. But I had failed.

I cried until I could cry no more, my chest aching and my eyes raw, and then crumpled down, lying back on the grass, the last of my tears falling from my eyes.

"I'm sorry, Mama," I said, one last time.

I looked up through the pine trees, a gentle spring breeze moving the branches and carrying their clean, sharp scent through the air. And suddenly I realized: I was done. I didn't need to worry anymore, or feel guilt that I hadn't done a better job of being my mama's mama, or sadness that I hadn't been able to ultimately save her from death. Mama was gone and I was done.

I took a deep breath, feeling the air fill my lungs and expand my rib cage, and then exhaled slowly.

"You're free, Mama," I whispered into the wind, "and so am I."

And with the words came the realization of their truth. She was free, but *so was I*. We were *both* delivered from our burden.

I sat up, and put my hand back on the mound of dirt. On Mama.

"Mom, are you okay?"

It was Cody, who had come to find me and make sure I was all right. I turned and smiled, brushing my hands free of dirt. I patted the ground next to me and she sat down and reached over for my hand.

"Yes, baby, I am now. I just needed to say my own goodbye to Memaw."

We sat for several minutes, saying nothing, just holding hands and looking at the explosion of beautiful flowers surrounding the grave, and us, and Mama.

Finally, I gave Cody's hand a couple of squeezes, just as Virgie had done so many times to mine, and said, "Come on. Take a walk with me."

We rose, brushed off our clothes, left the graveyard, and crossed the street toward downtown Waynesboro. As we walked through the quiet streets, I told her about the town I knew as well as any place on Earth. We walked past the two-room walk-up above the dry cleaners where Mama had lived after she left Daddy for good, past Petty's, where Virgie and I had sipped our sweet tea on the back steps, past Glitter Lane, where Mary sold the best sno-cones in the world, past the café where Daddy had taken me for breakfasts of Coca-Cola and doughnuts, past the intersection where I had confronted the Klan while Cindy, terrorized, cowered in the front seat, and past the football field where I took my anger and frustration and confusion and beat it all into an enormous snare drum.

As we walked and our shadows grew longer and longer in the setting sun, I felt an ease, and a comfort, I had never felt in my thirty years living in Los Angeles. I realized, walking those wide, empty streets the afternoon after Mama's funeral, that while I've always raged against the South's ugly racism and oppression, and always will, it also is home to the people I've loved most in this world: my mother, Virgie, my three sisters, and yes, my wildly flawed and complicated father.

Now, they were all gone: Virgie, Daddy, and that day, Mama. Then, all too soon, we would lose Penny, whose battle with diabetes finally killed her. My sad, sweet sister went to her grave never having achieved the one thing she wanted: our daddy's love. And it would be left to me, Elizabeth, and Georgia to remember the ghosts. And we would. But it wouldn't just be the three of us. Shocking all of us, Cody, who had her choice of colleges from coast to coast and from north to south, decided to attend my alma mater, the University of Southern Mississippi.

My sisters crowed: "You just wait. She's gonna fall in love with the South and never leave."

"That is *never* going to happen," I assured them.

That's exactly what happened. Yes, it's complicated.

Acknowledgments

This book could not have been written without Jennifer Jordan, who guided me through every step of the process with dedication, patience, and an uncanny ability to find the heart of my story. You are amazing. Thank you for going on this journey with me.

I'm so grateful for my daughter, Cody, who gave me the strength and encouragement to write my story. Cody, you changed my life forever for the better the day you were born. You are by far my greatest accomplishment. I love you more than you can imagine, and I always say I want to be just like you when I grow up. Thank you to my Southern son-in-law, Josh Mannino, for being the husband you are to my daughter. I love you.

I am blessed and forever grateful for my partner, Michelle LeClair, and for the beautiful life and family we've created together. Michelle, you have shown me a love that I never knew was possible. You have taught me how to trust. I love you more than you will ever know.

I'm grateful to have been the youngest of three incredible sisters whom I love with all my heart.

To my sister G.: You have been my rock, my buoy through the storms. G., your love and constancy in my life has given me strength and hope. I love you so much, Big Sis.

To my sister S.: You have made me laugh my entire life. Thank you for sharing your sense of adventure and your eye for beauty with me. And thank you for always being there when I needed you. I love you so much.

To my sister T., who died three years ago. I miss you every single day. I loved your candor. I loved your resilience and courage. I loved your authenticity. You were one of a kind and I will always love you.

To my brothers-in-law, J., D., and C.: Thank you for choosing to be a part of this family. I love you.

To my nieces Stephanie, Suzanne, and Jessica, and my nephews Scott, Steve, and Donnie: I am proud of each of you and love you so much.

To Burke, my best friend, and my partner in crime through all those years: Our friendship is still as strong today as it was when we were children. Thank you for the hours of conversation that enriched my memories and helped shape this book.

To Cindy Chapman: Thank you for sharing your beautiful mother with me. She would be so proud of you today, of your courage and kindness. You remind me of her in so many ways. I love you, my dear friend.

To my cousins Rita Faye, Francis, and Bubba, who helped me remember so many stories and colorful details: I am forever grateful for each of you. My dear Bubba passed away after the book was finished, but his spirit can be felt in these pages.

To Debbie Allen, my best friend, who encouraged me for years to share my story: Debbie, you are fierce and brave. You make me laugh harder than anyone I know. I love you.

To Norman Lear, Elaine Rogers, Mark Seelig, Sela Ward, and Maria Shriver: Each of you encouraged me to share my story and to honor my truth. Thank you for your many years of friendship, support, advice, and love.

To Ed Bacon and George Regas, my spiritual compasses and lighthouses of love and hope for more than thirty years: You taught me grace and humility and how to fight for justice for those who do not have a voice. You showed me how to love unconditionally even when it might seem impossible. I will be forever grateful for both of you.

I'm deeply grateful to my extremely talented agent, Brettne Bloom, and her colleagues at the Book Group. Brettne has mentored me through this process and has truly become part of my family. BB, I adore you!

I am so blessed to have landed with the most incredible editor in the world, Trish Todd, a fellow Southerner, and her amazing team, including Kaitlin Olson, Susan Moldow, Meredith Vilarello, Tara Parsons, Brian Belfiglio, Abigail Novak, and Cherlynne Li. Many thanks as well to Jason Richman at UTA for believing in *Southern Discomfort*.

Finally, to the readers of this story, I'd like to say this: I still believe in the goodness of people and that real change is possible. I hope and pray that before my daughter is my age, the lessons of this book will feel antiquated, and that the profound bigotry that I witnessed as a child and that continues to keep America from being a country of true equality is a permanent part of our past. I truly believe that with love and forgiveness, we can all heal and move forward to create a better world.

We are all God's children.

Tena Clark is a Grammy Award–winning songwriter, producer, entrepreneur, and social activist. She has worked with some of the biggest stars in music and the arts, including Aretha Franklin, Patti LaBelle, Chaka Khan, Natalie Cole, Jennifer Holliday, Gladys Knight, CeCe Winans, Dionne Warwick, Patti Austin, Stephanie Mills, Yolanda Adams, Pastor Shirley Caesar, and Maya Angelou. Tena's success spans film, television, records, and theater. She and her partner live outside of Atlanta.

Southern Discomfort

Tena Clark

*T*his reading group guide for Southern Discomfort *includes an*
introduction, discussion questions, ideas for enhancing your book
club, and a Q&A with author Tena Clark. The suggested ques-
tions are intended to help your reading group find new and inter-
esting angles and topics for your discussion. We hope that these
ideas will enrich your conversation and increase your enjoyment
of the book.

Introduction

Tena Clark was born in 1953 in a tiny rural Mississippi town, where the legacy of slavery and racial injustice permeated every aspect of life. On the outside, her childhood resembled a fairy tale. Her father was a successful businessman and her mother was a beauty queen. But behind closed doors, Tena's life was deeply lonely and chaotic. By the time she was three, her parents' marriage had dissolved. Adding to the turmoil, Tena understood from a very young age that she was different from her three older sisters, all of whom had been beauty queens and majorettes. Tena knew she didn't want to be a majorette—she wanted to marry one.

On Tena's tenth birthday, her mother, emboldened by alcoholism and enraged by her husband's incessant cheating, walked out for good, instantly becoming an outcast in society. With her parents distracted and her sisters grown up and out of the house, Tena was left in the care of her black nanny, Virgie, who became Tena's surrogate mother and confidante, and whose acceptance and love gave Tena the strength to be herself and challenge the strict rules of the society in which she was raised.

Southern Discomfort is a moving story of Tena's coming-of-age and the people—and places—that shaped her.

Topics & Questions for Discussion

1. Why do you think Tena chose to title her memoir *Southern Discomfort*? Describe the South in which Tena came of age. What aspects of life in the South does Tena take umbrage with? Why?

2. From an early age, music has a profound influence on Tena's life. When she first plays the drums, she says, "I knew that whatever that sensation was, I wanted more of it." What doors does it open for her personally and professionally? How does music help Tena connect with her mother?

3. Tena writes that "In many ways, [Vivian and Lamar] were meant for each other." Given that *Southern Discomfort* begins with Vivian leaving Lamar, were you surprised by Tena's statement? What did you think of Vivian and Lamar's relationship? Do you think that they were ever well suited for each other? If so, explain how. What are Vivian and Lamar initially attracted to in each other?

4. Lamar Clark is nicknamed "the Dictator of Waynesboro" by some of the town's residents. Did you see any of his

actions as dictatorial? Share some examples of behavior that might have caused Lamar to earn this title. How do you think he was influenced by growing up impoverished? What did you think of Lamar? Did you learn anything about Lamar that you found surprising? Discuss your discoveries with your book club.

5. While Lamar is upset each time Vivian gives birth to a girl, she "adored each new baby, and vowed to be a different kind of mother than the one she'd endured." Describe Vivian's childhood. What was her mother like? Does Vivian succeed in mothering in a different way than her own mother? If so, how? Compare Vivian's style of parenting to her mother's and to Tena's.

6. Describe Tena's reaction when she first sees Virgie. Were you surprised? Why do you think that Tena is so unwelcoming to Virgie? Rather than ignore Tena's tantrum, Virgie kneels down in front of Tena and speaks to her. Why? How does this help her gain Tena's trust?

7. Although Tena wants her father to see her musical, once he is at the opening she "realize[s her] mistake in wanting him there, particularly at the opening." Why does Tena think she has made an error in inviting her father? How does his presence affect the way she experiences the opening? How does Lamar react to the show and to Tena's achievement? Why do you think attaining Lamar's praise and approval is so important to Tena?

8. Tena begs Vivian to visit Lamar when he is on his death-bed. Why is it so important for Tena that Vivian make this visit? Vivian tells Tena, "I came here for me. Do you understand? I came here for *me*." Explain her statement. How does the visit help Vivian achieve closure with regard to her relationship with Lamar?

9. According to Tena, hearing the name "Whitfield" is enough to strike "cold fear in the heart of every Mississippian." Why? Describe Vivian's reaction upon being taken there by Lamar. Tena says that, "for the first time in my life, I realized how much power Daddy had over all of us." Explain her statement. Do you think that Tena and her sisters had any choice in going along with Lamar's plan? Discuss the family dynamics.

10. When Vivian leaves Lamar, she tells Tena, "I have to go. If I don't go now, I never will." What prompts Vivian to leave Lamar? Why do you think Vivian stayed married to Lamar as long as she did? What sorts of obstacles does she face as a divorced woman in the South during the early 1960s? Did you think that Vivian was brave for leaving Lamar? Does Tena? Why or why not?

11. Tena recounts two instances where she attempted to eat with Virgie at Petty's Cafe, one during segregation and one after segregation is illegal. Why does she include both in her memoir? Describe Virgie's reaction to Tena's gesture in each instance. Why is Tena excited to take Virgie to

Petty's after segregation has been outlawed? Why might Virgie have been uncomfortable? How does Tena view her own actions in hindsight?

12. When Vivian meets Tena's fiancée, Dell, she warns Dell about marrying Tena, telling Dell that Tena is "the spittin' image of Lamar Clark, and she's gonna screw around on you the way her daddy done to me." Why does Vivian think this about Tena? How does Tena feel about her mother's statements? Do you think that Tena is like Lamar? If so, in what ways are they similar?

13. How does Tena's family react when she tells them that she is gay? Did you find any of their reactions surprising? If so, which ones and why?

14. Tena says that "With Virgie . . . and all the other black folks in my life, I felt more *me* in my own skin." Discuss her statement. How do Virgie and the others put Tena at ease? Compare Tena's life in her parents' house with that of the families in Hiwannee. Why does Tena secretly wish that she could live in Hiwannee? How is Virgie's presence a stabilizing one for Tena?

15. As Tena gets older, she says her mother "time and again [tells her] she felt she had failed [in gift giving] because 'your daddy can always buy you anything you want.'" Why is giving Tena a big birthday gift so important to Vivian? Does she succeed in getting Tena a meaningful gift? If so, what is it and why does it mean so much to Tena?

A Conversation with Tena Clark

Congratulations on the publication of *Southern Discomfort*! What has been the most rewarding part of publishing your memoir? Were there aspects of publishing that surprised you?
The process of going back in time and looking at the events and people that shaped my early years has been illuminating and difficult. It hasn't always been an easy process. Telling the truth about your own life—the good, the bad, and the ugly, never is—but it's been very healing for me. It's also been wonderful to be in a kind of conversation again with my mother, my father, and Virgie. Writing about them has brought them back to life in a way, affording me the chance to say things to them now that I couldn't say when they were alive.

Publishing this book has also forced me to reckon with all of my complicated feelings about Mississippi and the South. It's a love-hate relationship for sure. It's a beautiful place; it's a tortured place. It's a place trapped in a different time; it's a place where real progress is possible. I'm not sure if I'll ever wrap my head around Mississippi—it's like a puzzle I'm still figuring out.

I've definitely shed a lot of tears as I looked back on my life, but this is a story that I feel needs to be told, and I've been waiting all my life to tell it. So it also feels like a weight has been taken off my shoulders.

You recount how your mother told you, "You write that book, but just wait until I'm dead." When did you begin writing your memoir and why did you choose to publish it now? What do you think your mother would think about your memoir if she could read it?

In 1990, my father said something to me about our family that I knew to be a blatant lie, and in that moment, something inside me just snapped. I was traveling for work at the time and I remember sitting in my hotel room and not being able to sleep. So I turned on my tape recorder and decided I had to tell my story to myself. The truth as I knew it. Eight hours and more than a hundred transcribed pages later, I felt like I had finally started the process toward healing. At the time, I thought of it as something I'd done just for myself, but then I ended up showing the pages to my mother. She read them in one sitting through tears. That's when she said she wanted me to write a book about my life, but she asked me to wait until she died to have it published.

I filed the pages away and didn't turn back to them until several years after my mother passed away. My daughter and several close friends had been after me to write a book about my life. Finally, I sat down and went through the document I'd shared with my mother. It was very rough, but it was the start I needed. The book progressed from there.

My mother was always a big supporter of my creative endeavors. When I was performing as a musician she was always my balcony person, cheering me on. She was, and remains, my number one fan. Even though she's physically gone from this world, I still feel her presence with me all the time. She's still my balcony person. I know she'd be proud to see *Southern Discomfort* in print, and I know she'd be especially thrilled to know if my book inspired even just one reader to live a more authentic life.

Has the rest of the family read it? If so, were you nervous to share it with them? What do they think of it?

As of this writing, my daughter is the only member of my immediate family who has read *Southern Discomfort*, and she is so thrilled and proud. She's an avid reader, so her approval meant the world to me. My two surviving sisters have not read it yet, and I'm not sure if they ever will. I'm sure it's difficult for them to relive those years and to know what I went through. I know they wish I had just "let it be," as they say in the South. "Just let it be" was the refrain from my childhood. Don't rock the boat, don't go diggin' up old bones. I hope and pray that they'll come to understand why I couldn't just bury my story out in the backyard in a box—that there's a redemptive power in telling the truth, and then sharing it with others.

Did you find writing your memoir cathartic? Were there any sections that were particularly hard to write? Can you tell us about them?

Writing the memoir was an extremely cathartic experience for me. It was sacred and holy. That's not to say it was always easy or pleasurable. From start to finish, this has been one of the most difficult journeys I've ever taken. I had to look at the South through a new lens. I had to examine painful moments that happened in my family. I had to look at my own motivations and assumptions, I had to confront my own privilege, and I had to expose the prejudices of the world in which I was raised. There were so many times during the writing process when I had to pick up the phone and call my best friend Burke and ask: "Did this really happen? Was it as crazy as I recall?" And he'd always say: "Yes, Tena. Only it was even crazier!" I'm grateful to have close friends from that time who are still in my life and who have been supportive of me.

Writing this book has also helped me see that my childhood wasn't all doom and gloom. There are many things that were magical about growing up in rural Mississippi. The smell of magnolia in the summer, riding horses bareback through the fields, the sound of Virgie's gentle humming, the look on my mother's face when she was singing . . .

That said, a flood of painful memories also surfaced during this process. I had to relive my mother's alcoholism and confront my father's dichotomies. My dad was the most complicated man I've ever known. Truly. I know he loved me, and I believe he tried to care for me the best way he knew. But he was the ultimate gaslighter. As readers will see, even his racism was extremely complicated, and not in the way you might expect.

I also had to go through the deaths of my parents and Virgie again and again while writing and revising this book. I still cry every time I think about their final days.

You've written and produced Grammy Award–winning music, worked with iconic artists, and written the theme song for NASA. Did your previous creative experiences help you

when it came to writing *Southern Discomfort*? How was writing your memoir different?

Songwriting and memoir writing are similar in that in order to work well they need to be complete narratives with a strong voice and sense of rhythm, and a clear beginning, middle, and end. Other than that, they are two very different worlds and two very different crafts. A song is three to four minutes, and the lyrics usually spill out of me in one day. Writing this book took three years of active work. It took me a good year to find the right voice, one year to focus the narrative, and another year of revision.

You recount scenes from your childhood so vividly. How were you able to do so? Can you tell us about your writing process?

In my experience, Southerners are natural storytellers—and most tend to be longwinded too! We can't just tell you we went to the store to buy a loaf of bread; we have to recount every little thing that happened from the moment we left the house. Make a long story longer, that's our motto.

I do have a vivid memory, especially when it comes to sensorial details and imagery. I can remember how our local cafe smelled for lunch everyday, and the way Virgie's skin felt scratching my back. I can still see the color of the trees outside my fifth grade classroom the day Kennedy was shot. I can remember so much of what happened fifty to sixty years ago. Unfortunately, my short-term memory is shot. I cannot remember where my phone, keys, or glasses are, but I can remember exactly what I was wearing the day my mother left, on my tenth birthday. I wonder sometimes if childhood trauma causes certain painful memories to embed in our brains even more than the beautiful times and moments. I've always remembered with detail colors, smells, expressions, surroundings of moments.

As far as my process goes, I've never been able to just sit down and write on demand. Whether I'm working on a song or an article or a chapter in my book, the words have to come when they come, unbidden. I cannot force them. When they do surface, I find I can disappear into writing for days. I get in my groove and don't come up for air. And then I hit a wall and put the work away for a week, and then go back to it. I know many writers who say they have to write every single day, but that's not how I am. I go in bursts.

You've been an activist from an early age, from standing up to the Ku Klux Klan to insisting that Petty's Cafe uphold laws that made segregation illegal. What did you learn from your early activism? Do you have advice for people who are looking to become activists?

One of my earliest memories was secretly watching, with great awe, President Kennedy's landmark speech on civil rights on June 11, 1963. The whole speech resonated with me, but this part stuck with me in particular:

> One hundred years of delay have passed since President Lincoln freed the slaves, yet their heirs, their grandsons, are not fully free. They are not yet freed from the bonds of injustice. They are not yet freed from social and economic oppression. And this Nation, for all its hopes and all its boasts, will not be fully free until all its citizens are free.

I was ten years old, and I felt like I'd finally met someone who felt the same way about things that I did. I had never understood why Virgie wasn't allowed to ride in the front seat of our car when my father drove her home after work. My parents had little interest in Kennedy, and absolutely no interest in integration or in the civil rights movement that was gaining traction as I came of age. As far as my parents and their friends were concerned, everyone in Mississippi was perfectly happy with the status quo.

Hearing Kennedy's words had a profound impact on me. I looked around at the African Americans I knew and loved—my nanny, Virgie; her best friend, Beulah Mae—and felt in my bones that the legacy of slavery and racism was a poison that still infected our world. I was a little girl and couldn't have articulated any of this at the time, but it's what I felt in a visceral way. We were on the wrong side of history; we were on the wrong side of righteousness and justice. Kennedy's words echoed through me and stayed with me. I was devastated when he was assassinated.

I'd always known deep down that I was different from my peers, and from others in my family. Part of it was circumstantial—I came out as a lesbian when I was twenty-one, but all my life I knew I was different. I didn't have the word to describe what I was, I simply knew from an early age that I was attracted to girls, and I didn't see myself as feminine or womanly in the same way my sisters did. I didn't want to be a majorette like they had been—I wanted to *marry* one! Knowing I was different caused me to feel more compassion for those who live without the dignity they deserve, without rights that every human being deserves, on the fringes, and it laid the groundwork for my early activism.

I was also aware that I was a child of privilege, which gave me the motivation to take a stand on behalf of others who didn't have the same advantages I did. I was white; my father was wealthy and powerful. I felt it was up to people like me to be part of the change, and to stand with my black brothers and sisters and resist the racism and bigotry that poisoned our world. I wanted to break the cycle that had persisted for generations. I still do.

Standing up for what you believe and being authentic is not easy, and it is definitely not always popular, especially in places where outdated prejudices still linger. Your family may turn on you, some acquaintances or friends may turn on you, but doing what is right will set you free.

You grew up in a society where gender roles were clearly defined. How were you able to overcome the pressure to comply? Do you have any advice for others who are in a similar situation?
I look back on myself as a little girl, all dressed up in crinoline, my hair curled, and I wish I could hug her and say: "Don't worry! This won't last. You're going to have a great life. Stay strong." It was hard growing up a tomboy in a world full of petticoats. I remember seeing Idgie Threadgoode in *Fried Green Tomatoes* and thinking "That was me!" It was the first time I felt like I saw myself represented in a Hollywood film. In my town every girl dreamed of marriage, motherhood, the white picket fence. I knew I would not survive if I had to live that life.

For me, music was my savior. I fell in love with the drums when I was ten and then it just went on from there. Making music was an outlet for my aggression and frustration, my sadness and my fear. It was a safe place for me to be myself. And it was through music that I finally found the courage to embrace who I was. So my first piece of advice would be to find a creative outlet, whether it's painting or writing or sculpture or music . . . whatever it is. Find a way to channel your feelings into something beautiful and meaningful and personal.

A second piece of advice is to surround yourself with people who love and accept you for who you are. I found those people in the most surprising places. Virgie was certainly one of the first people who silently and tacitly accepted my differences and adored me even more because of them. My friends in the music world did as well. Friends I've made through my church, through activism. You'll find your tribe, I promise.

Finally, realize that a life lived as a lie will never be a happy life. As difficult as it may be, I urge you to find the courage to be your authentic self. Understand that it might be hard for the people in your life to accept it at first. Understand that there will be some people in your life who will never fully understand—and that that's okay. You will survive, and you will thrive, but first you *must* be true to yourself.

What do you hope readers take away from *Southern Discomfort*?
I hope people reading my book will see that there's redemption in telling the truth. I also hope they'll see the power of love and forgiveness. As dysfunctional as my family was, and still is, and through all the chaos, we have stayed close, and we love each other very, very much.

I hope readers will be inspired by my story to be kinder, braver, more compassionate, and more tolerant. And at the end of the day, that the message will be that love is what sustains us and unites us. Love is what heals; love is what always gets us through the hardest of times—love of family, love of community, love of the downtrodden and less fortunate, and, most of all, love of self. Love and respect. That's what it's all about.

Finally, I hope readers will be inspired to be an agent of positive change, to realize that one person really can take a stand and make a difference.

Are you working on anything now?

I'm busy working on a variety of music projects for film and television, and of course I am as active as ever in social justice reform.